IN the FLESH

IN the FLESH

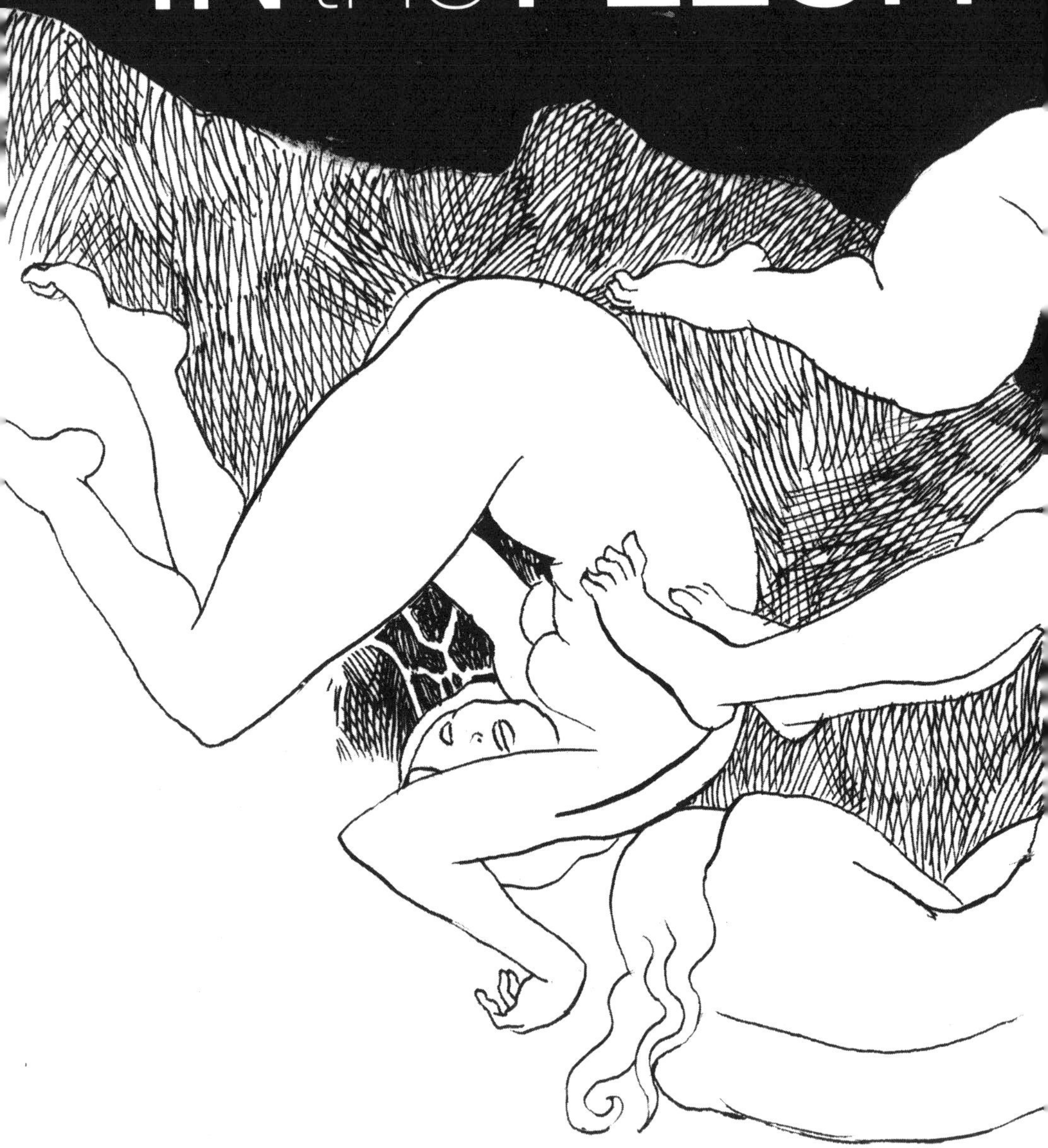

VILLARD Ⓥ NEW YORK

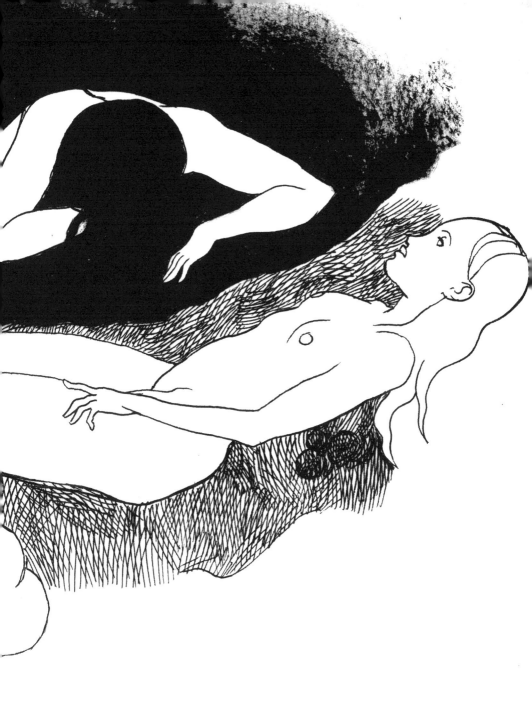

KorenSHADMI

Special thanks to Emily Felger

In the Flesh is a work of fiction. Names, characters, places, and incidents
are the products of the author's imagination or are used fictitiously.
Any resemblance to actual events, locales, or persons,
living or dead, is entirely coincidental.

A Villard Books Trade Paperback Original

Published in the United States by Villard Books,
an imprint of The Random House Publishing Group,
a division of Random House, Inc., New York.

VILLARD BOOKS and VILLARD & "V" CIRCLED DESIGN are registered trademarks
of Random House, Inc.

Portions of this work were published in French in
Dissymétries and *Cours intérieures,* by La Boite d'Aluminum, France.

LIBRARY OF CONGRESS CATALOGING-IN-PUBLICATION DATA
Shadmi, Koren.
    In the flesh / Koren Shadmi.
        p.   cm.
    ISBN 978-0-345-50871-3
1. Graphic novels.   I. Title.
PN6727.S46I5 2009
741.5'95694—dc22   2008044703

Printed in the United States of America

www.villard.com

9 8 7 6 5 4 3 2 1

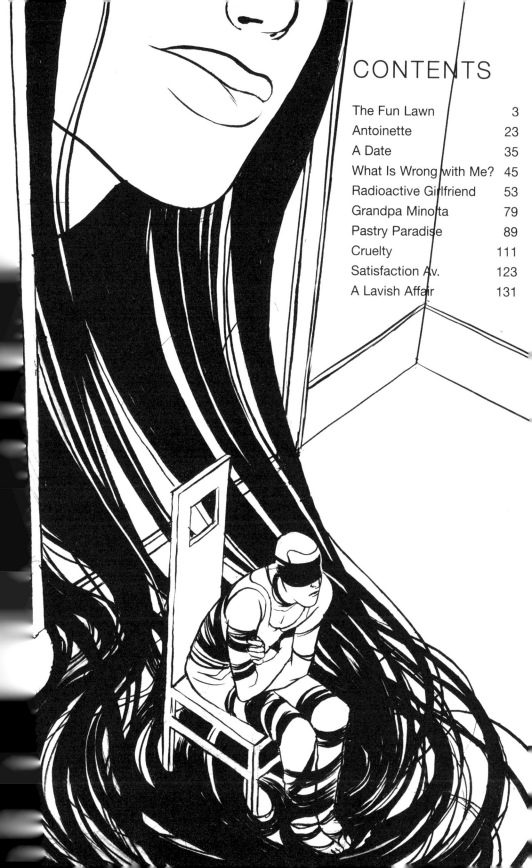

CONTENTS

IN the FLESH

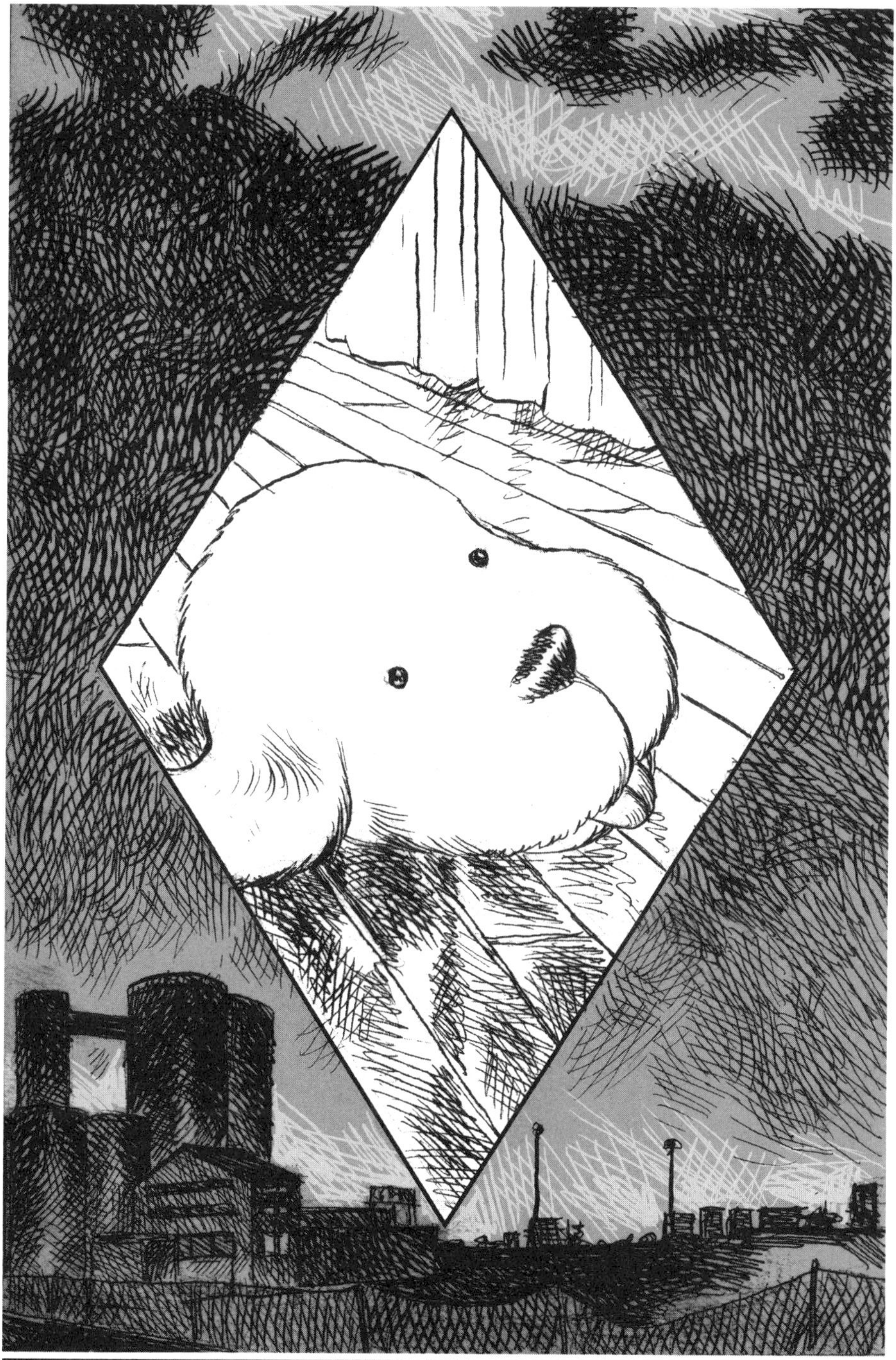

· THE FUN LAWN ·

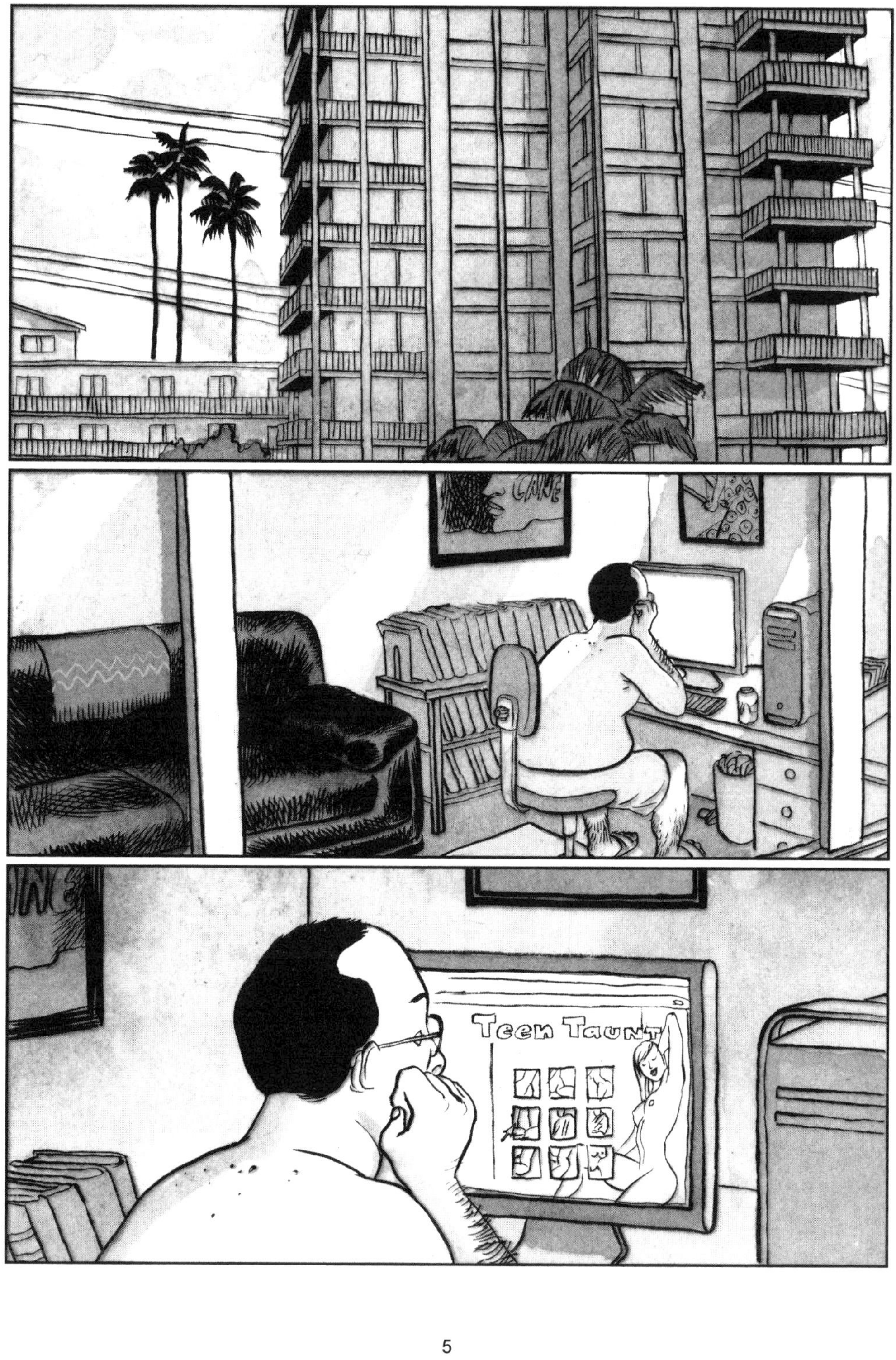
Teen Taunt

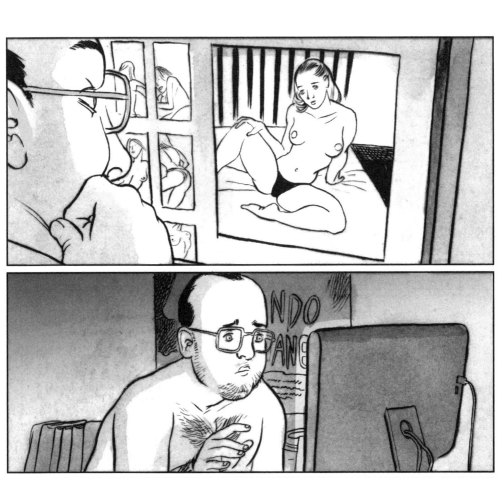

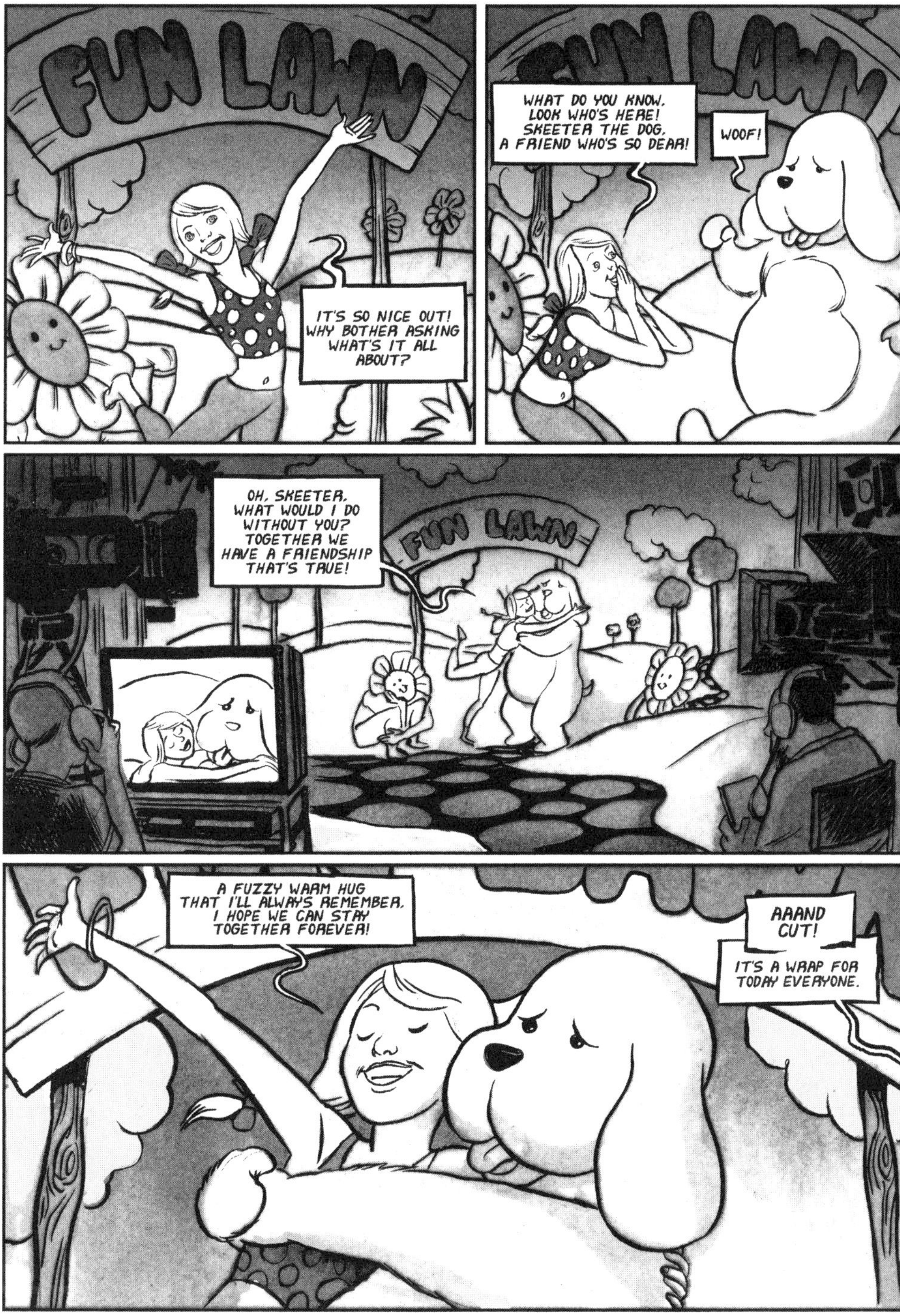
FUN LAWN
IT'S SO NICE OUT! WHY BOTHER ASKING WHAT'S IT ALL ABOUT?
FUN LAWN
WHAT DO YOU KNOW, LOOK WHO'S HERE! SKEETER THE DOG, A FRIEND WHO'S SO DEAR!
WOOF!
OH, SKEETER, WHAT WOULD I DO WITHOUT YOU? TOGETHER WE HAVE A FRIENDSHIP THAT'S TRUE!
FUN LAWN
A FUZZY WARM HUG THAT I'LL ALWAYS REMEMBER, I HOPE WE CAN STAY TOGETHER FOREVER!
AAAND CUT!
IT'S A WRAP FOR TODAY EVERYONE.

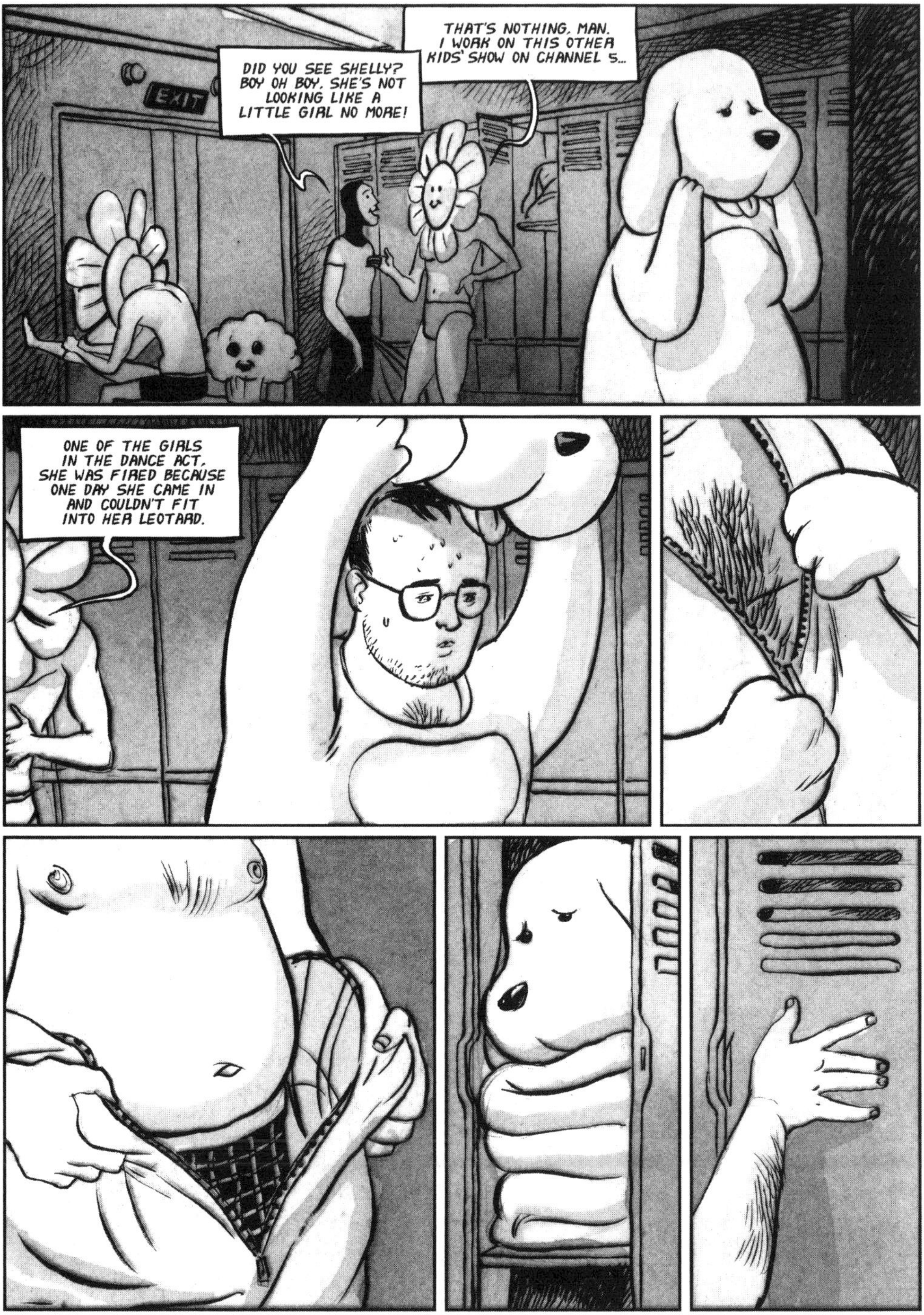
DID YOU SEE SHELLY? BOY OH BOY. SHE'S NOT LOOKING LIKE A LITTLE GIRL NO MORE!
THAT'S NOTHING, MAN. I WORK ON THIS OTHER KIDS' SHOW ON CHANNEL 5...
EXIT
ONE OF THE GIRLS IN THE DANCE ACT, SHE WAS FIRED BECAUSE ONE DAY SHE CAME IN AND COULDN'T FIT INTO HER LEOTARD.

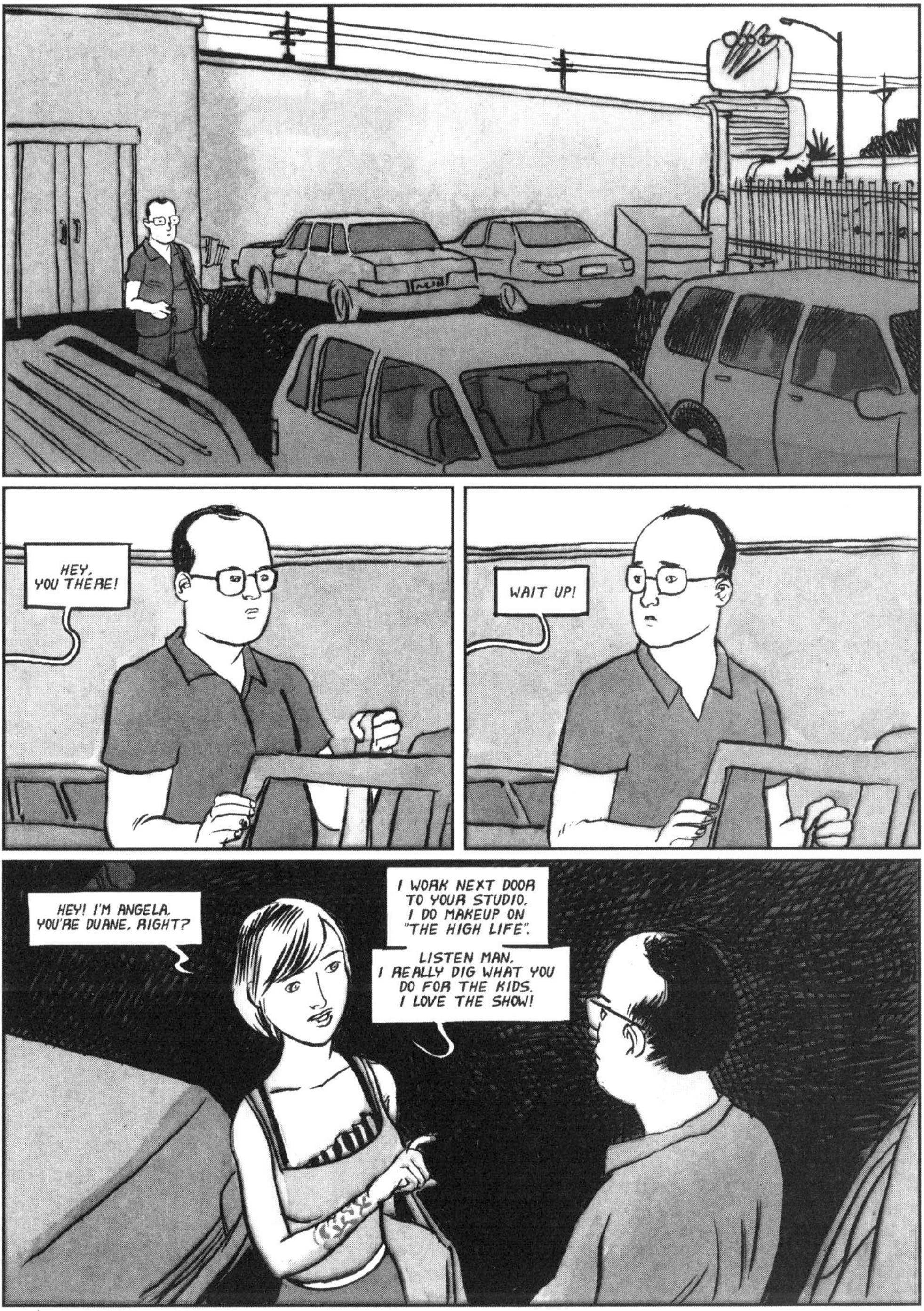
HEY, YOU THERE!
WAIT UP!
HEY! I'M ANGELA. YOU'RE DUANE, RIGHT?
I WORK NEXT DOOR TO YOUR STUDIO. I DO MAKEUP ON "THE HIGH LIFE".
LISTEN MAN. I REALLY DIG WHAT YOU DO FOR THE KIDS. I LOVE THE SHOW!

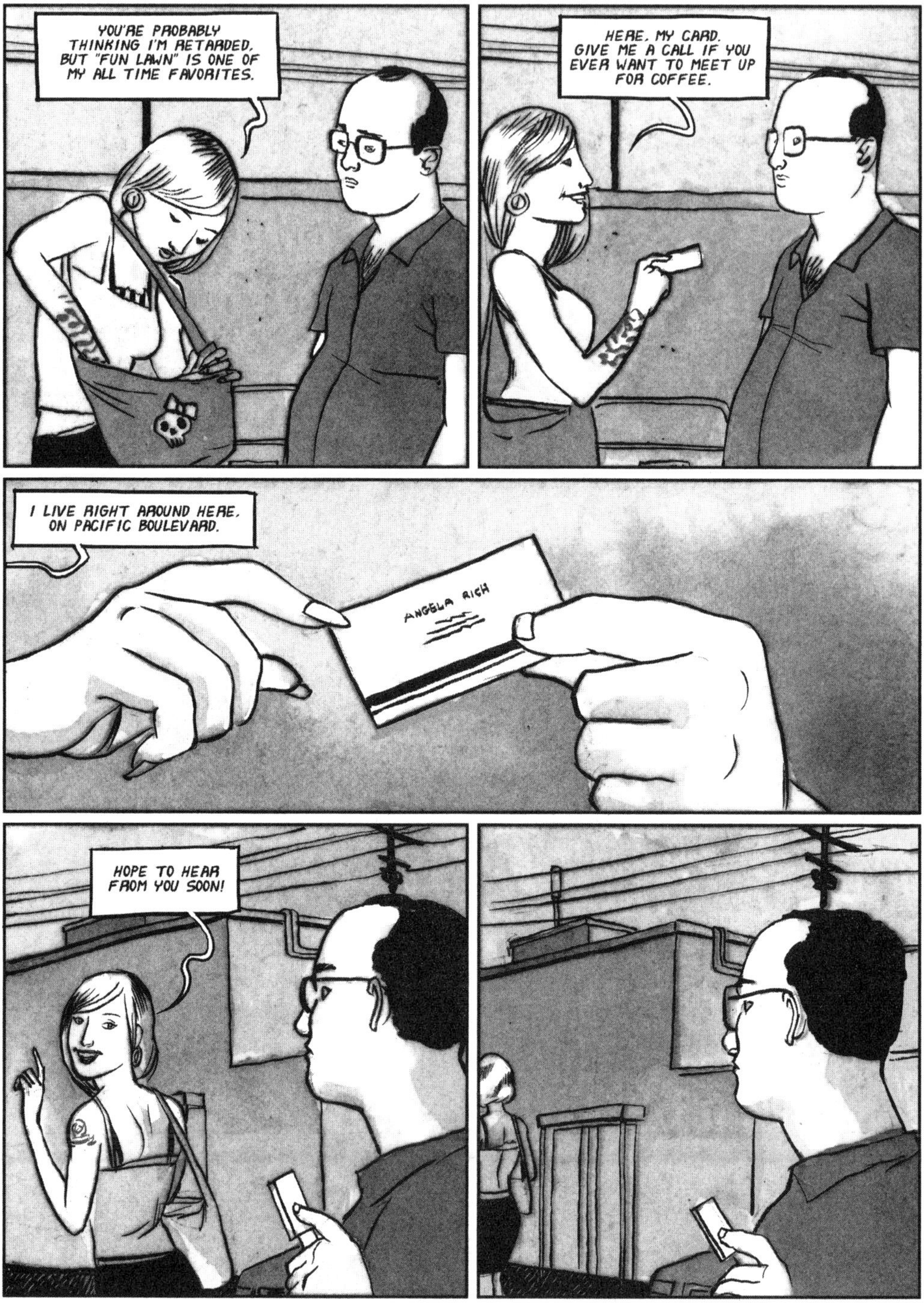
YOU'RE PROBABLY THINKING I'M RETARDED, BUT "FUN LAWN" IS ONE OF MY ALL TIME FAVORITES.
HERE, MY CARD. GIVE ME A CALL IF YOU EVER WANT TO MEET UP FOR COFFEE.
I LIVE RIGHT AROUND HERE, ON PACIFIC BOULEVARD.
ANGELA RICH
HOPE TO HEAR FROM YOU SOON!

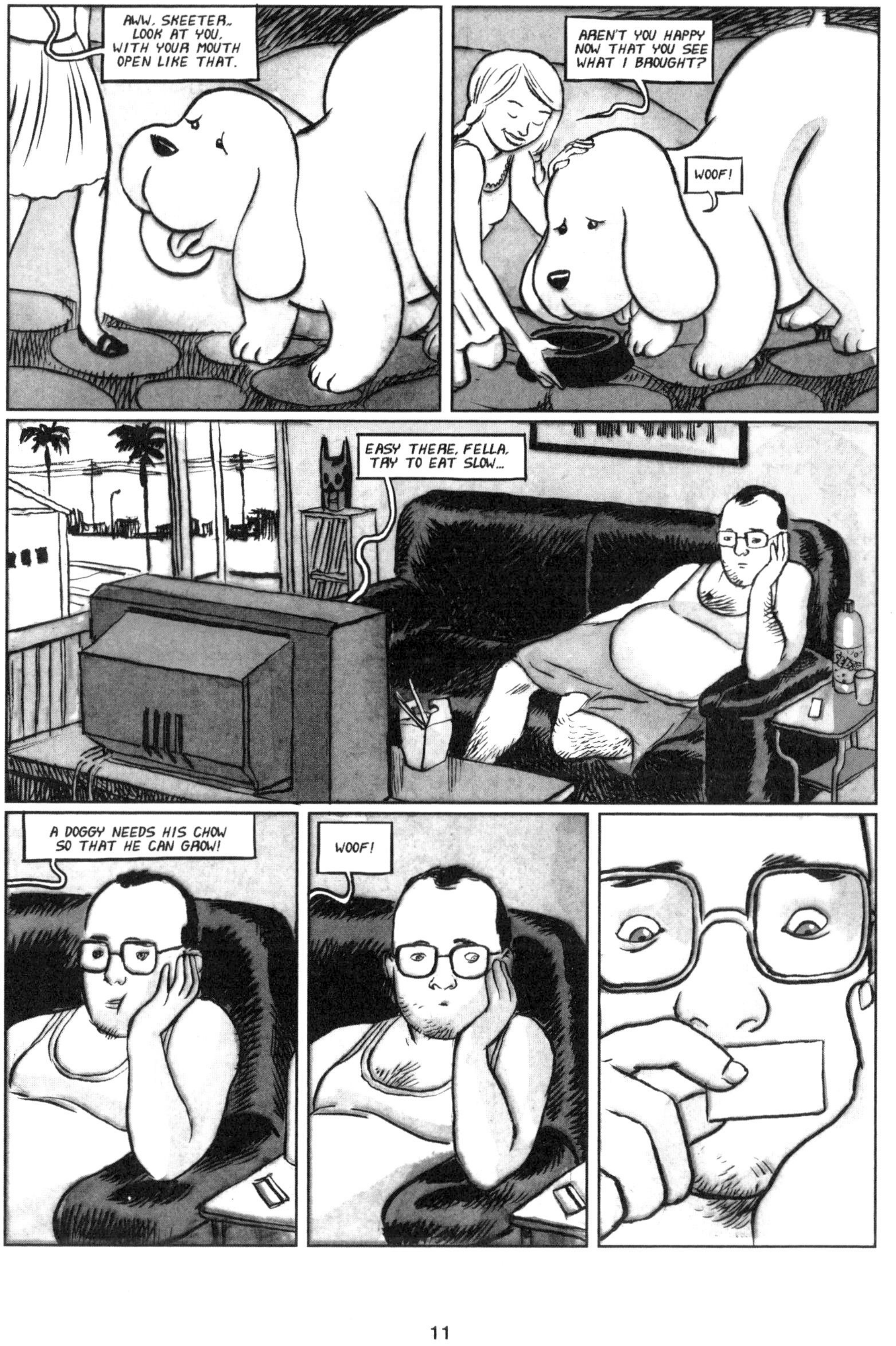
AWW, SKEETER.. LOOK AT YOU, WITH YOUR MOUTH OPEN LIKE THAT.
AREN'T YOU HAPPY NOW THAT YOU SEE WHAT I BROUGHT?
WOOF!
EASY THERE, FELLA, TRY TO EAT SLOW...
A DOGGY NEEDS HIS CHOW SO THAT HE CAN GROW!
WOOF!

MMMMM...
I LOVE THESE
SMOOTHIES!

YOU KNOW,
WE'RE NOT SO FAR APART,
YOU AND I...

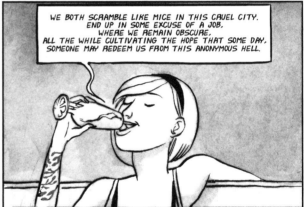

WE BOTH SCRAMBLE LIKE MICE IN THIS CRUEL CITY.
END UP IN SOME EXCUSE OF A JOB,
WHERE WE REMAIN OBSCURE,
ALL THE WHILE CULTIVATING THE HOPE THAT SOME DAY,
SOMEONE MAY REDEEM US FROM THIS ANONYMOUS HELL.

BUT IS THAT EVER
GOING TO HAPPEN?

THAT SMOOTHIE WAS REALLY SOMETHING.
YOU SURE YOU DON'T WANNA TRY ONE?

I TRY VERY HARD TO KEEP AT IT, GOING TO WORK EVERY DAY, PAMPERING THE FACES OF THE STARS.

IT'S NOT EASY. AND I'VE BEEN GETTING RESTLESS.

I'M TWENTY-NINE ALREADY. I NEED SOMETHING TO SPEED THINGS UP. GET ME AT LEAST THOSE DAMN FIFTEEN MINUTES OF FAME TO START WITH. THAT'S NOT A LOT TO ASK.

YOU DON'T SAY MUCH, DO YOU?

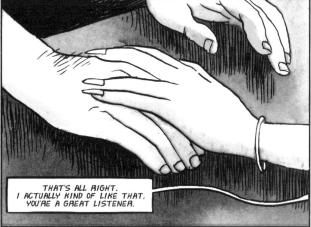

THAT'S ALL RIGHT. I ACTUALLY KIND OF LIKE THAT. YOU'RE A GREAT LISTENER.

BLIP
BLIP

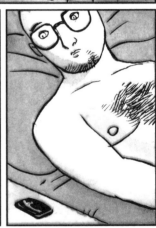

hey, u there?
my roommate will
b out of town this
weekend.
u should come
over for dinner on
saturday.

i just have one
small request.
i want you to
bring one thing
when you come...

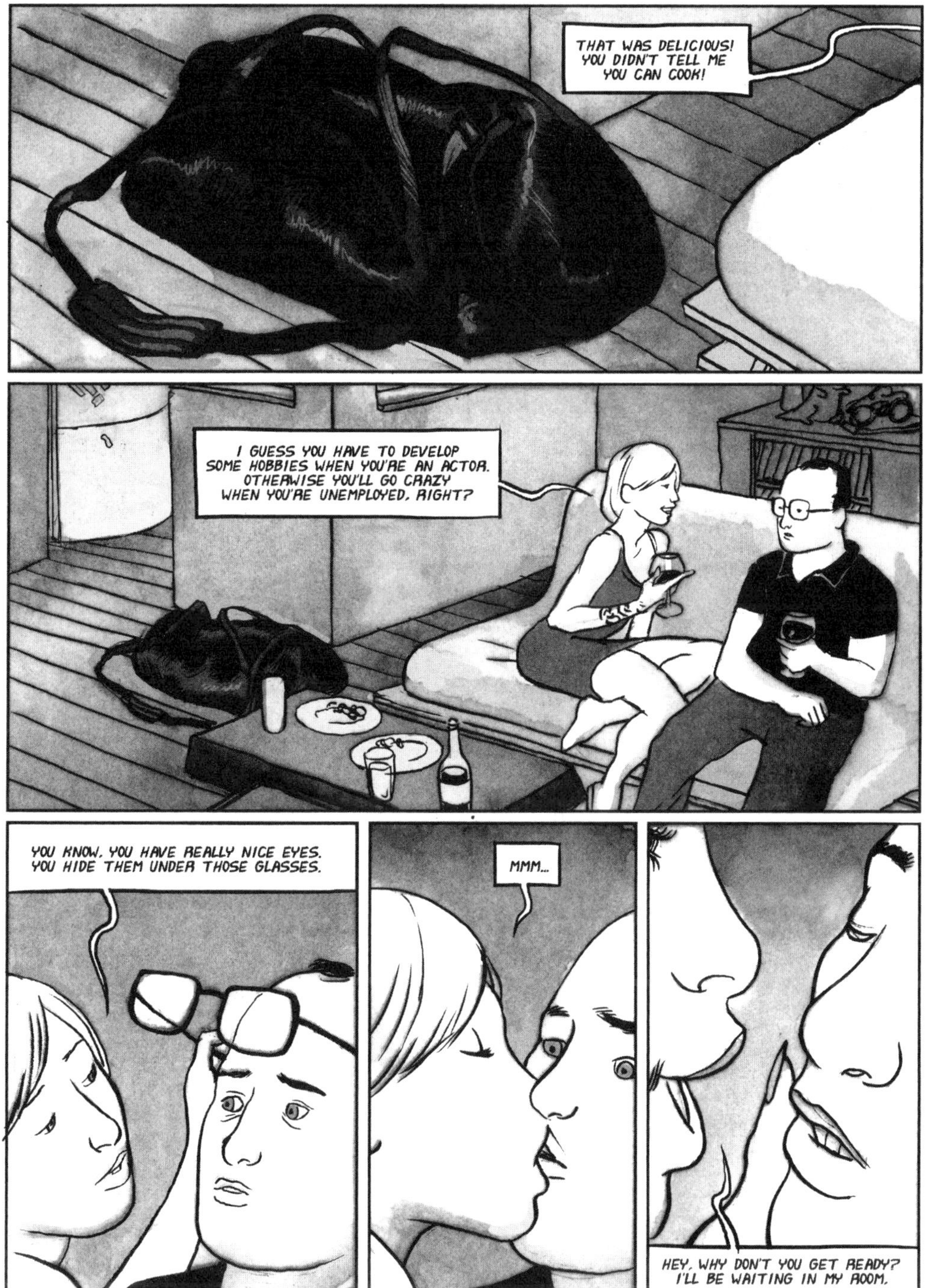
THAT WAS DELICIOUS! YOU DIDN'T TELL ME YOU CAN COOK!
I GUESS YOU HAVE TO DEVELOP SOME HOBBIES WHEN YOU'RE AN ACTOR. OTHERWISE YOU'LL GO CRAZY WHEN YOU'RE UNEMPLOYED, RIGHT?
YOU KNOW, YOU HAVE REALLY NICE EYES. YOU HIDE THEM UNDER THOSE GLASSES.
MMM...
HEY, WHY DON'T YOU GET READY? I'LL BE WAITING IN MY ROOM.

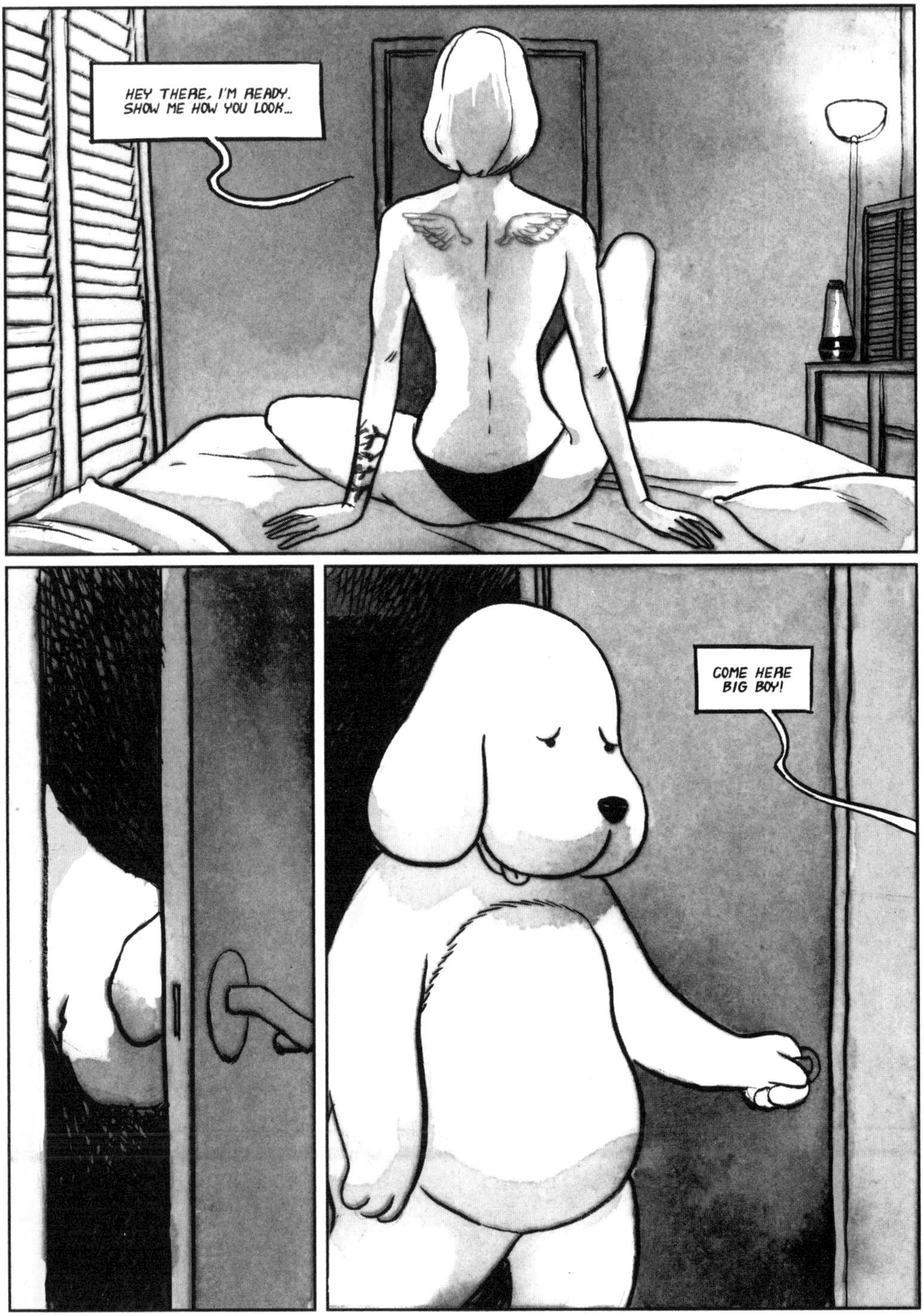
HEY THERE, I'M READY.
SHOW ME HOW YOU LOOK...
COME HERE
BIG BOY!

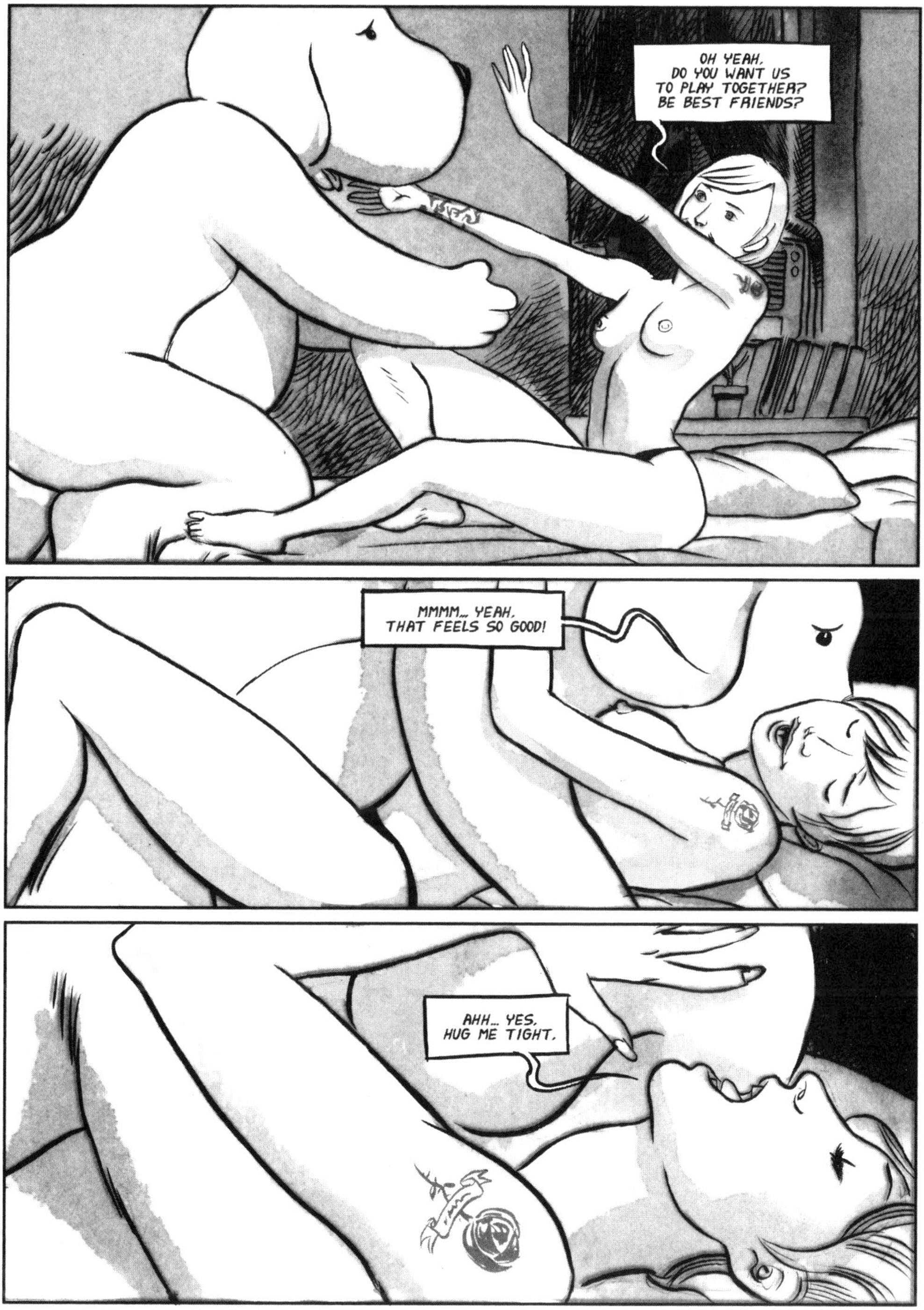
OH YEAH,
DO YOU WANT US
TO PLAY TOGETHER?
BE BEST FRIENDS?
MMMM... YEAH,
THAT FEELS SO GOOD!
AHH... YES,
HUG ME TIGHT.

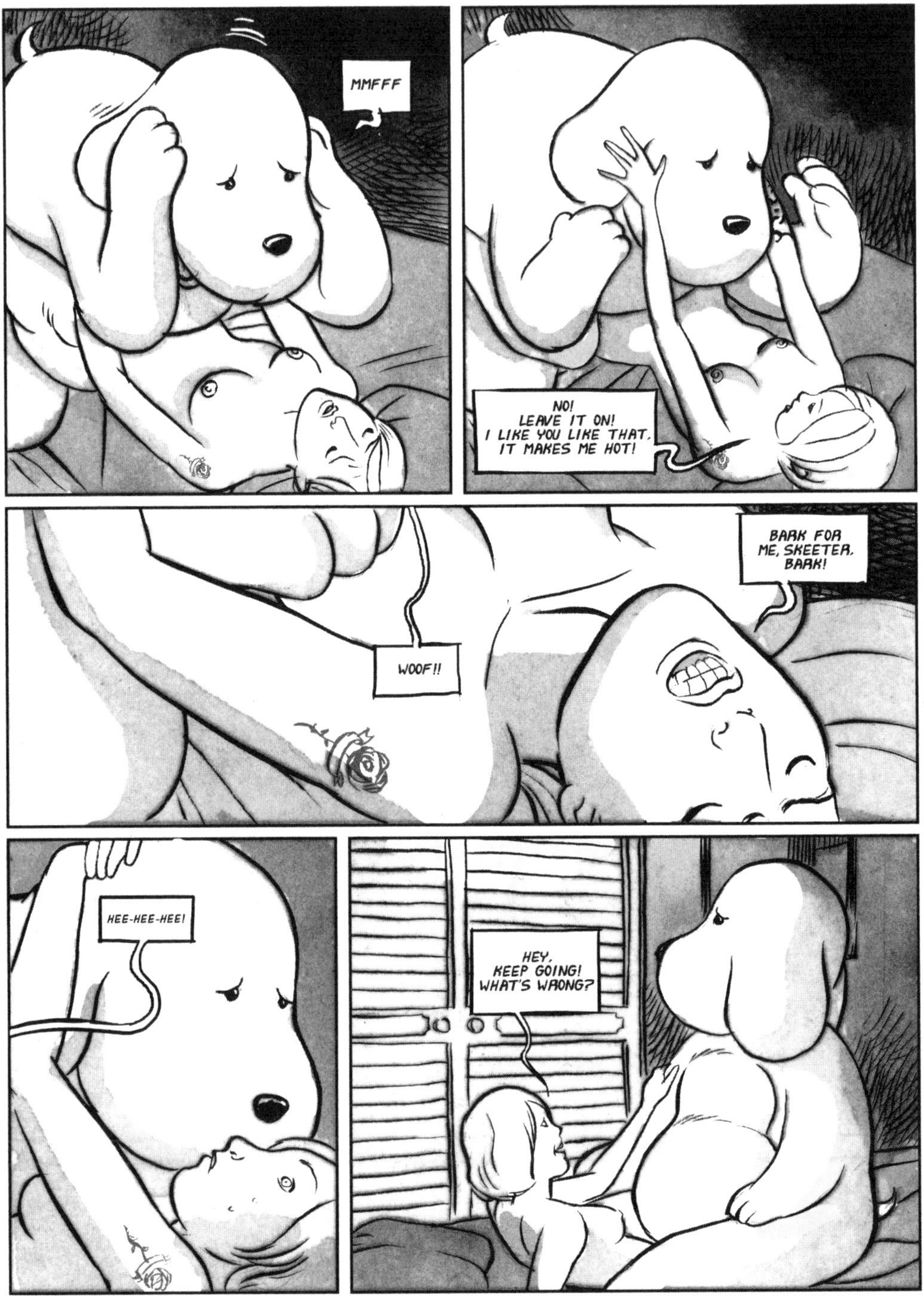
MMFFF
NO! LEAVE IT ON! I LIKE YOU LIKE THAT. IT MAKES ME HOT!
BARK FOR ME, SKEETER, BARK!
WOOF!!
HEE-HEE-HEE!
HEY, KEEP GOING! WHAT'S WRONG?

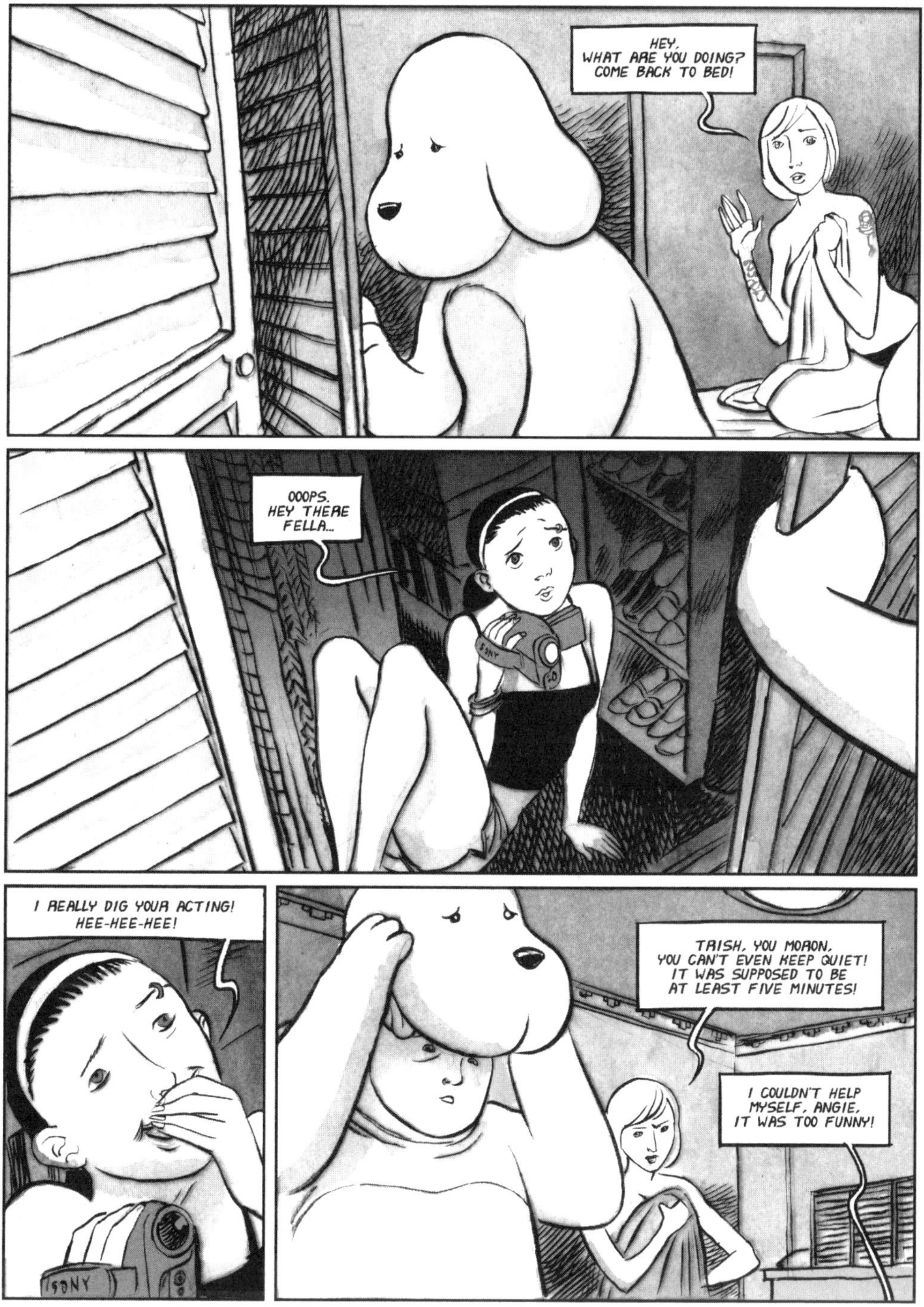
HEY, WHAT ARE YOU DOING? COME BACK TO BED!
OOOPS. HEY THERE FELLA...
SONY
I REALLY DIG YOUR ACTING! HEE-HEE-HEE!
SONY
TRISH, YOU MORON, YOU CAN'T EVEN KEEP QUIET! IT WAS SUPPOSED TO BE AT LEAST FIVE MINUTES!
I COULDN'T HELP MYSELF, ANGIE, IT WAS TOO FUNNY!

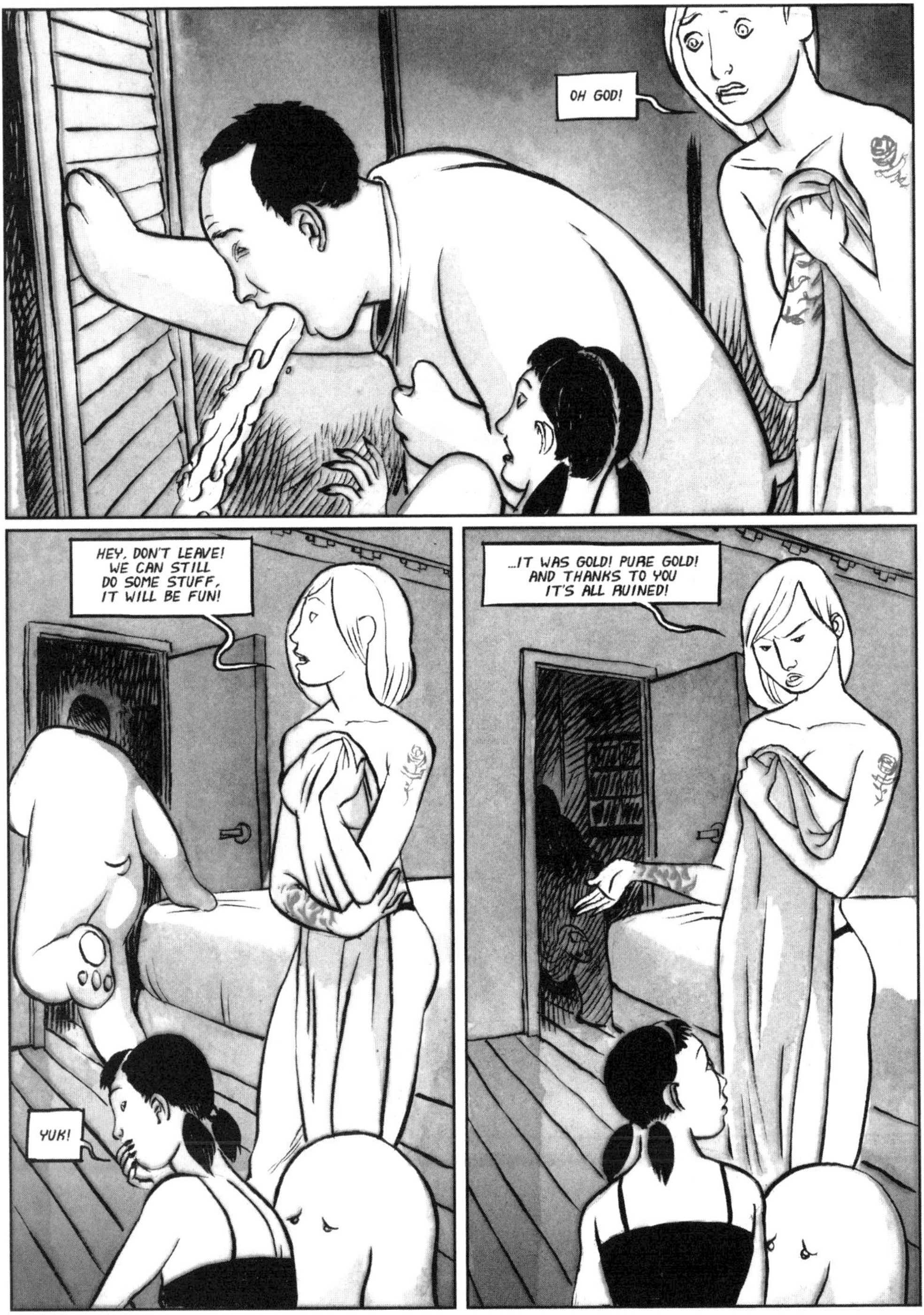
OH GOD!
HEY, DON'T LEAVE! WE CAN STILL DO SOME STUFF, IT WILL BE FUN!
YUK!
...IT WAS GOLD! PURE GOLD! AND THANKS TO YOU IT'S ALL RUINED!

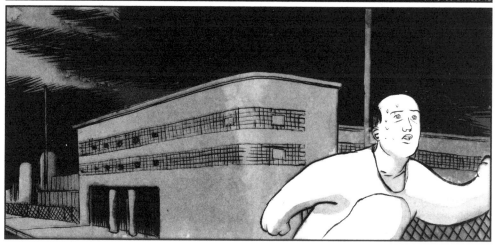

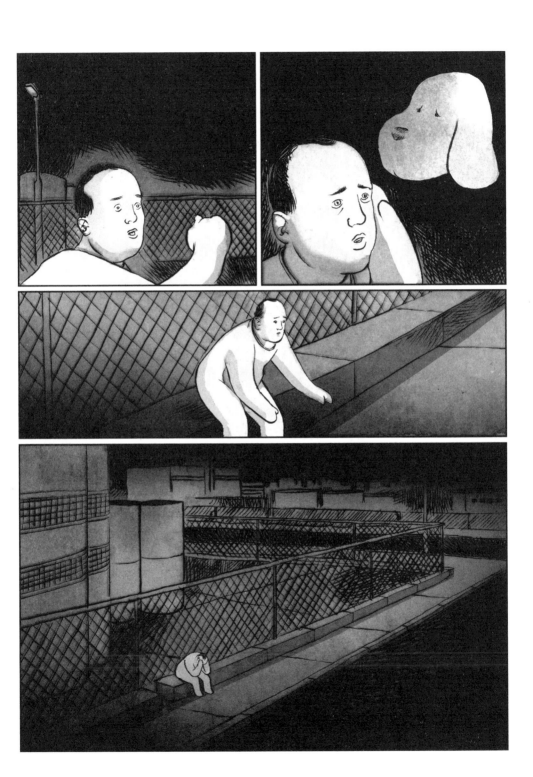

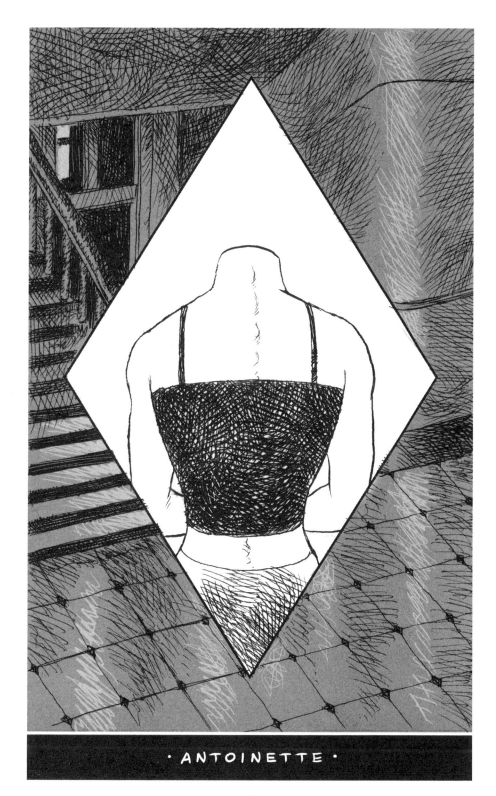

· ANTOINETTE ·

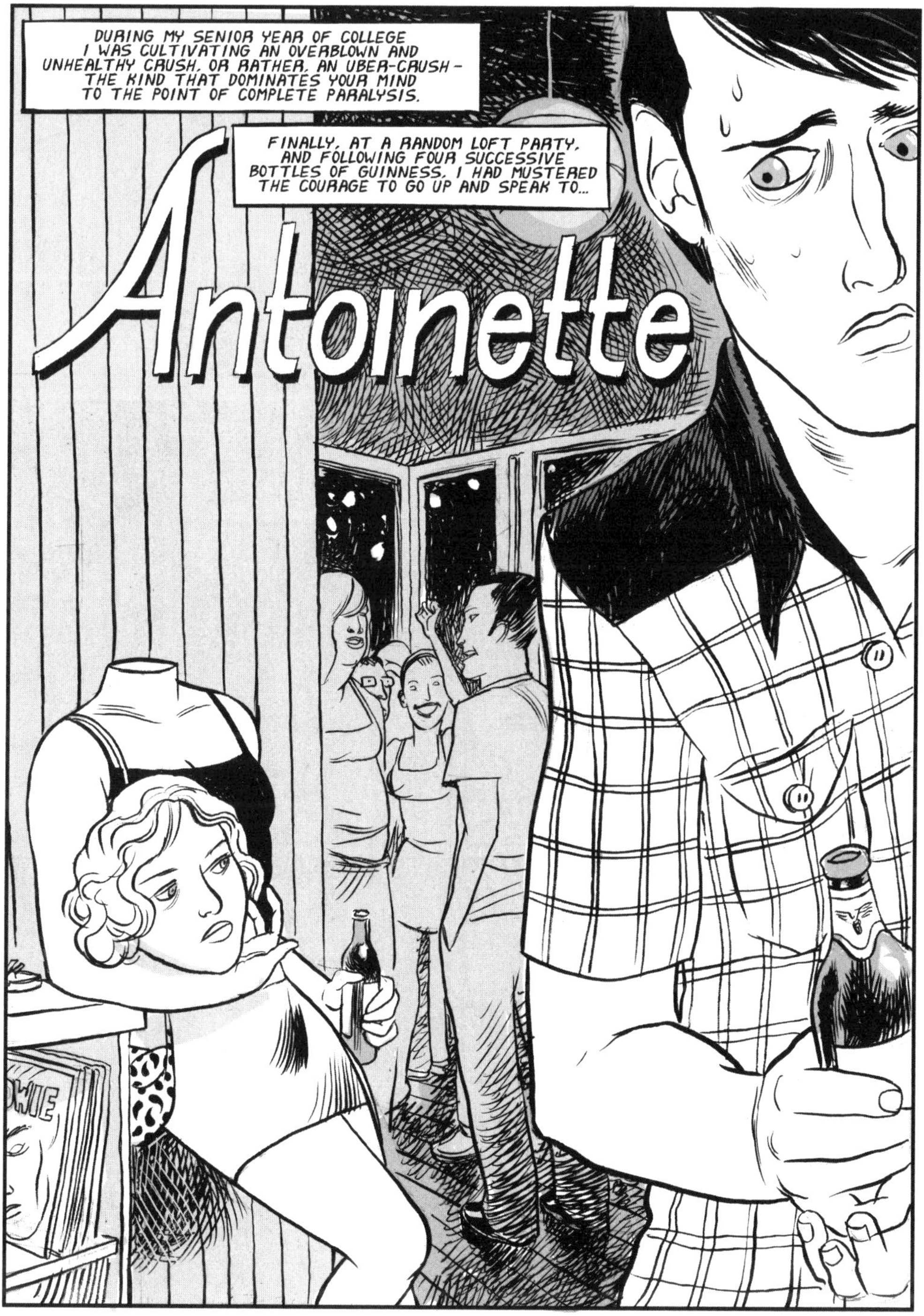
DURING MY SENIOR YEAR OF COLLEGE I WAS CULTIVATING AN OVERBLOWN AND UNHEALTHY CRUSH, OR RATHER, AN UBER-CRUSH – THE KIND THAT DOMINATES YOUR MIND TO THE POINT OF COMPLETE PARALYSIS.
FINALLY, AT A RANDOM LOFT PARTY, AND FOLLOWING FOUR SUCCESSIVE BOTTLES OF GUINNESS, I HAD MUSTERED THE COURAGE TO GO UP AND SPEAK TO...
Antoinette

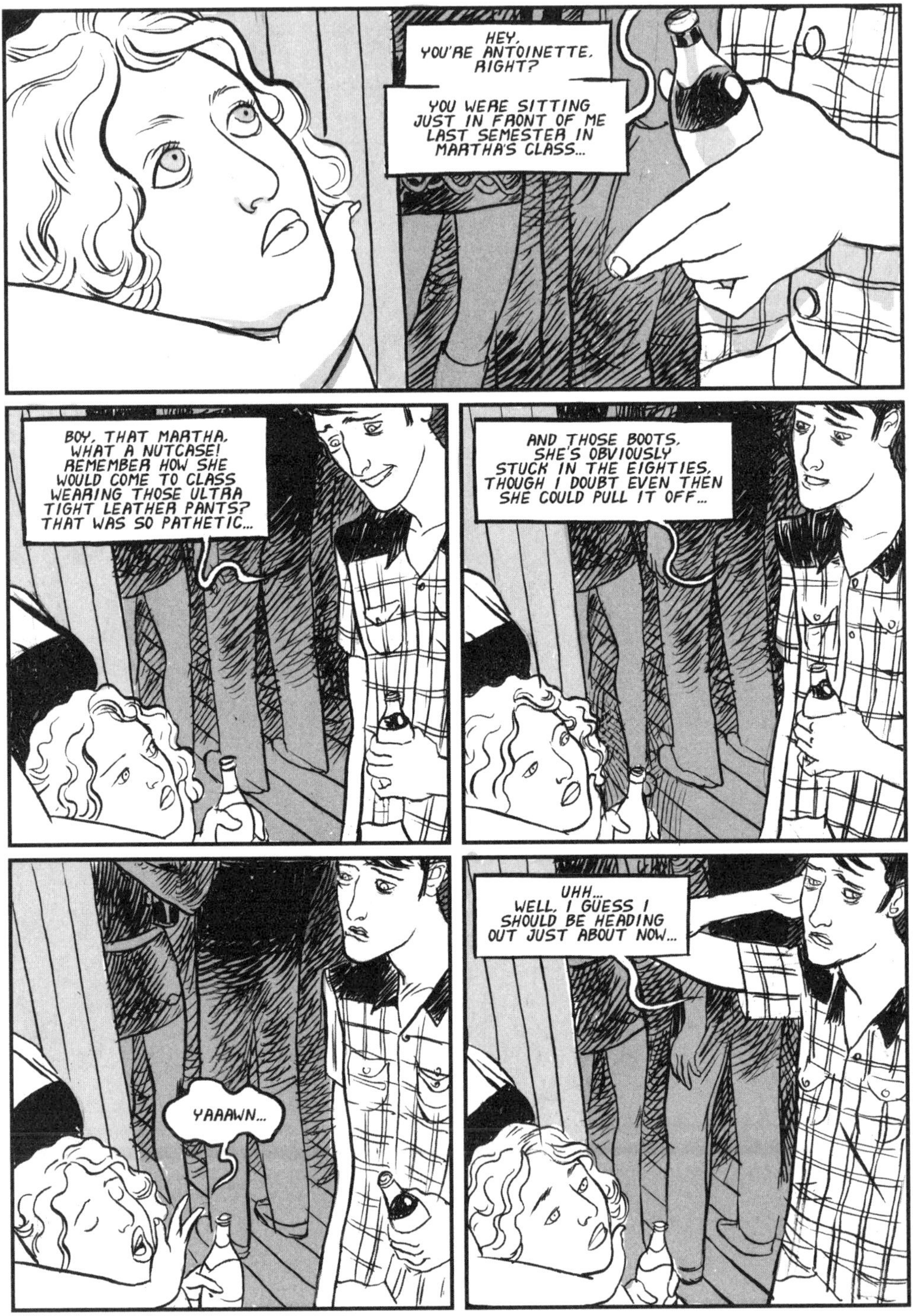
HEY, YOU'RE ANTOINETTE, RIGHT?
YOU WERE SITTING JUST IN FRONT OF ME LAST SEMESTER IN MARTHA'S CLASS...
BOY, THAT MARTHA, WHAT A NUTCASE! REMEMBER HOW SHE WOULD COME TO CLASS WEARING THOSE ULTRA TIGHT LEATHER PANTS? THAT WAS SO PATHETIC...
AND THOSE BOOTS, SHE'S OBVIOUSLY STUCK IN THE EIGHTIES, THOUGH I DOUBT EVEN THEN SHE COULD PULL IT OFF...
YAAAWN...
UHH... WELL, I GUESS I SHOULD BE HEADING OUT JUST ABOUT NOW...

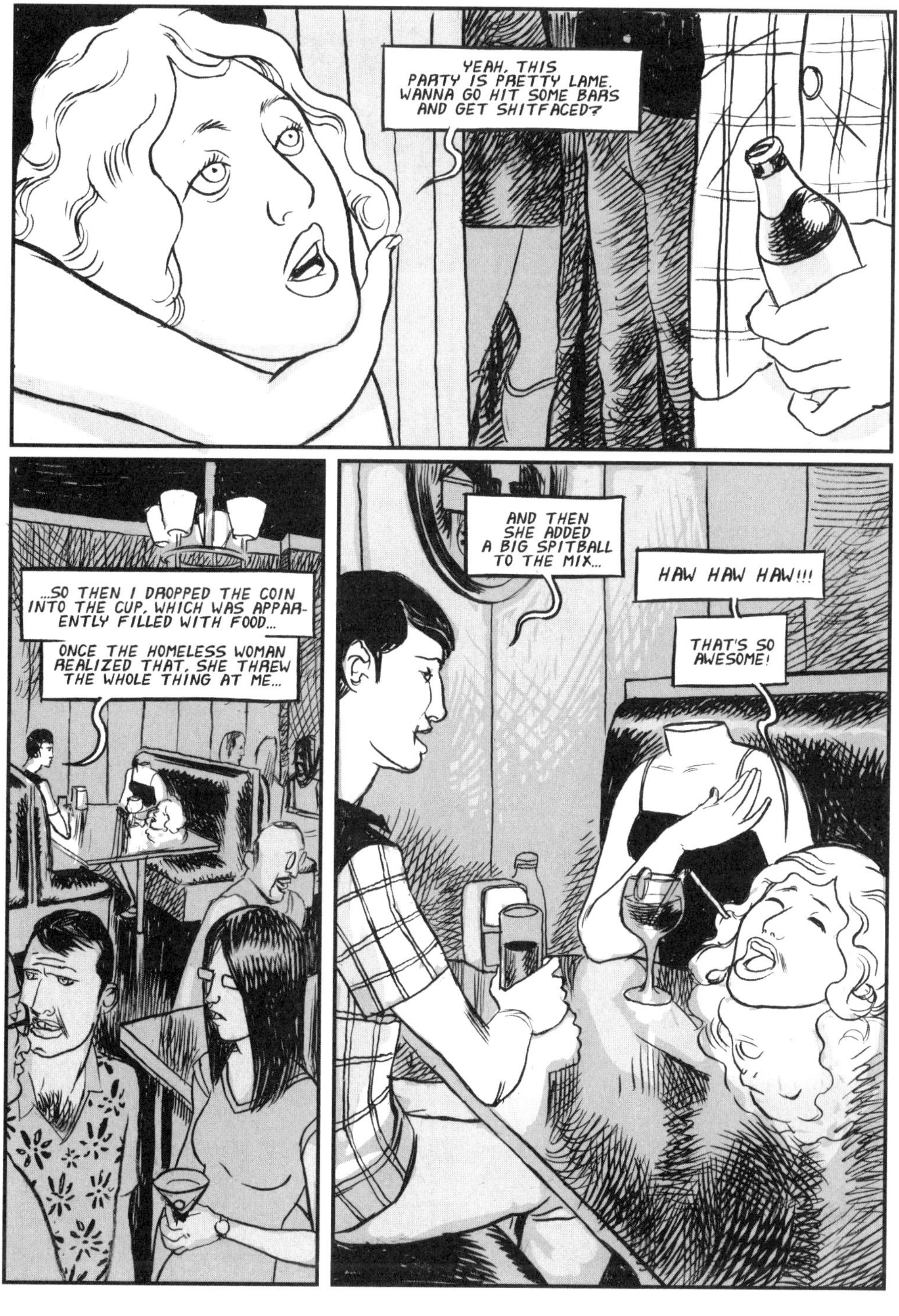
YEAH, THIS PARTY IS PRETTY LAME. WANNA GO HIT SOME BARS AND GET SHITFACED?
...SO THEN I DROPPED THE COIN INTO THE CUP, WHICH WAS APPARENTLY FILLED WITH FOOD...
ONCE THE HOMELESS WOMAN REALIZED THAT, SHE THREW THE WHOLE THING AT ME...
AND THEN SHE ADDED A BIG SPITBALL TO THE MIX...
HAW HAW HAW!!!
THAT'S SO AWESOME!

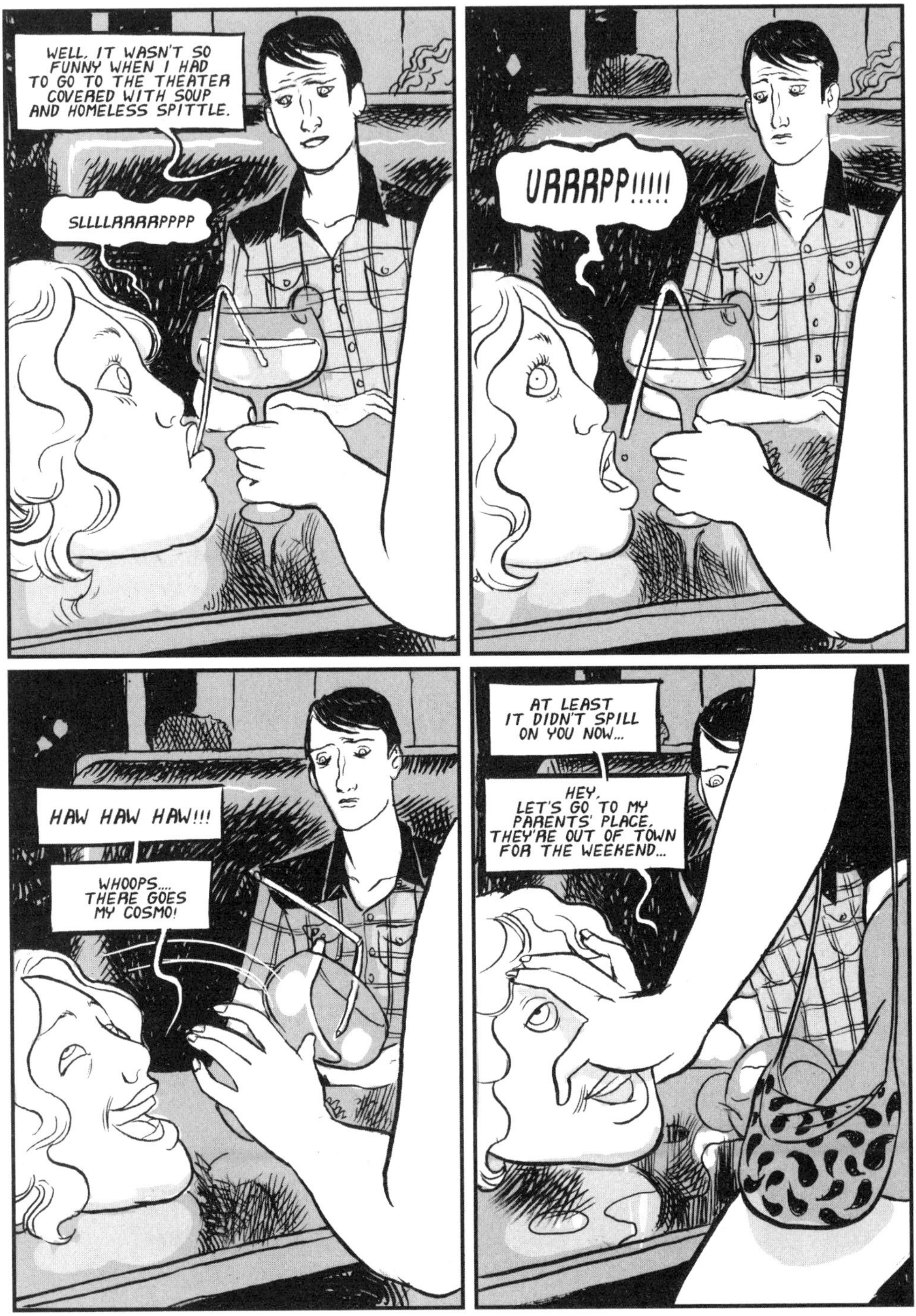
WELL, IT WASN'T SO FUNNY WHEN I HAD TO GO TO THE THEATER COVERED WITH SOUP AND HOMELESS SPITTLE.
SLLLLRRRRPPPP
URRRPP!!!!!
HAW HAW HAW!!!
WHOOPS.... THERE GOES MY COSMO!
AT LEAST IT DIDN'T SPILL ON YOU NOW...
HEY, LET'S GO TO MY PARENTS' PLACE, THEY'RE OUT OF TOWN FOR THE WEEKEND...

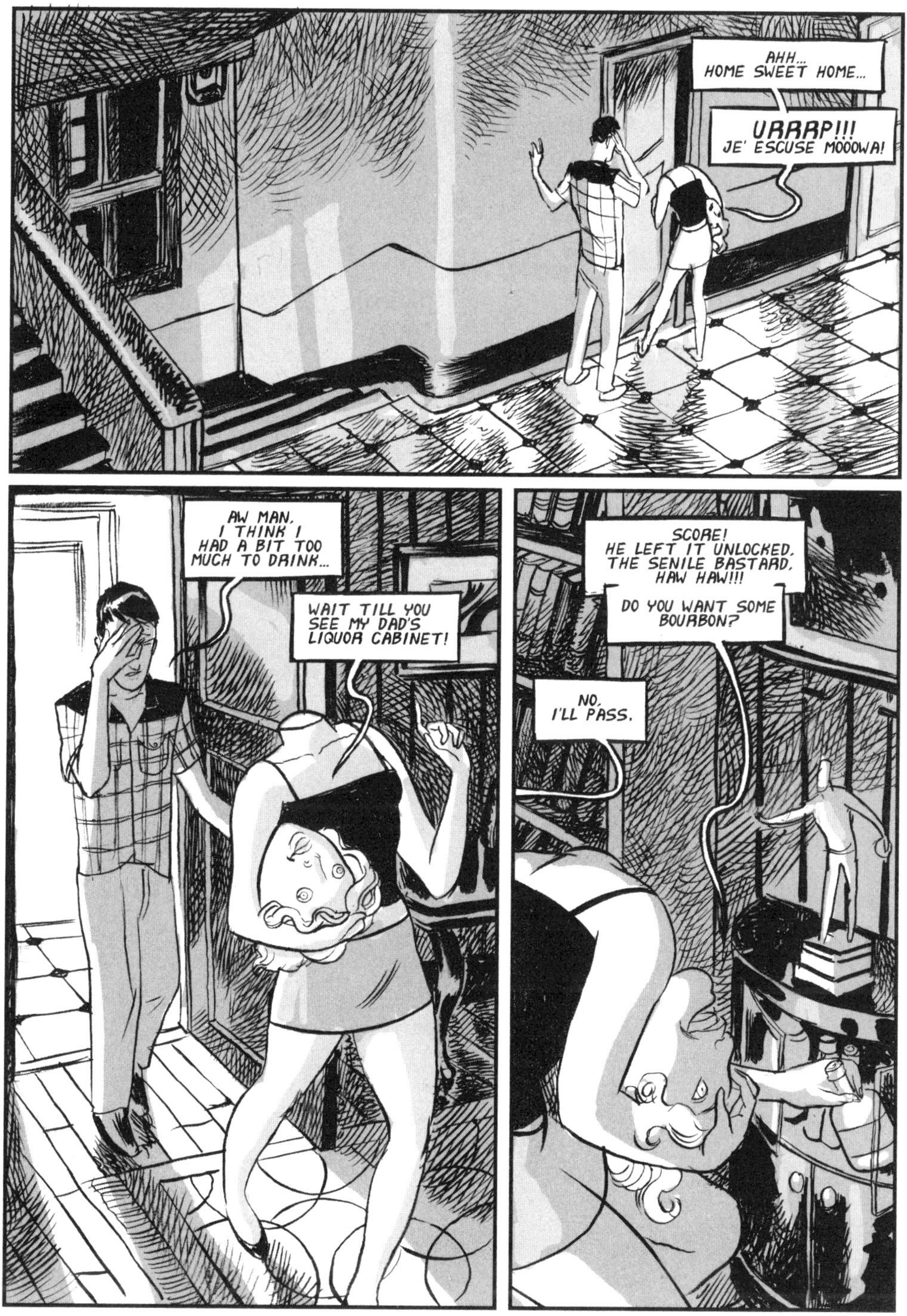
AHH... HOME SWEET HOME...
URRRP!!! JE' ESCUSE MOOOWA!
AW MAN, I THINK I HAD A BIT TOO MUCH TO DRINK...
WAIT TILL YOU SEE MY DAD'S LIQUOR CABINET!
SCORE! HE LEFT IT UNLOCKED, THE SENILE BASTARD, HAW HAW!!!
DO YOU WANT SOME BOURBON?
NO, I'LL PASS.

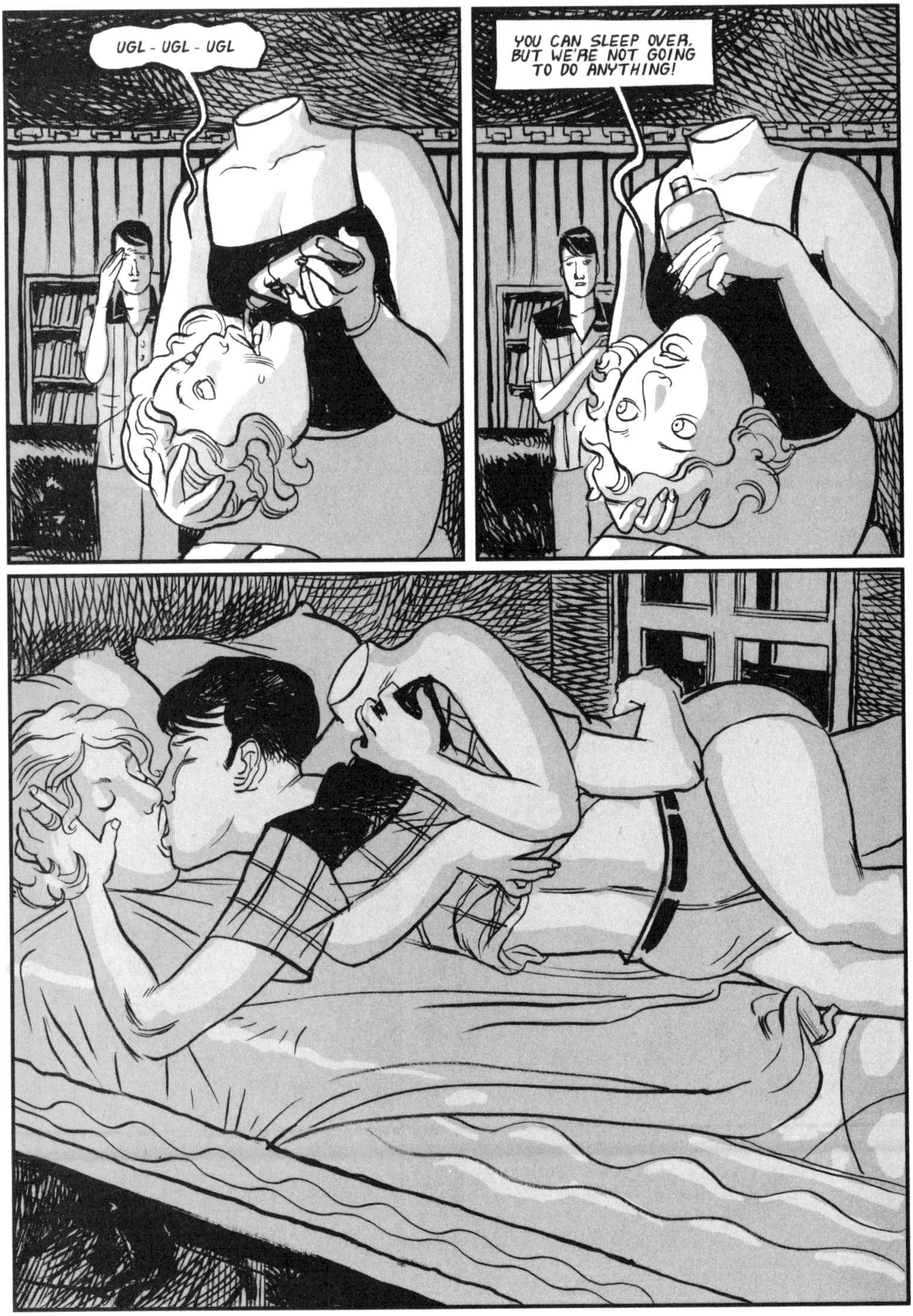
UGL - UGL - UGL
YOU CAN SLEEP OVER. BUT WE'RE NOT GOING TO DO ANYTHING!

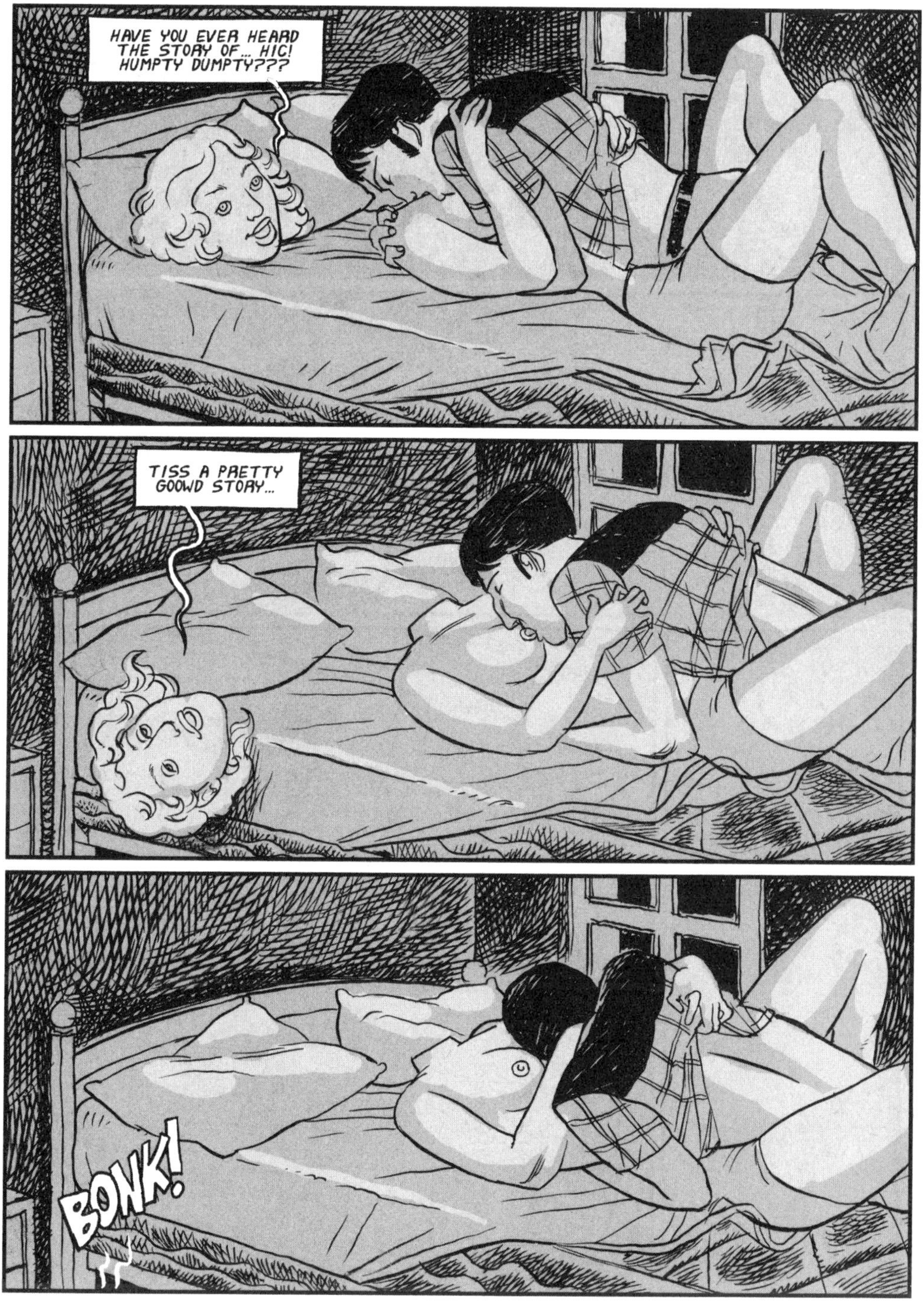
HAVE YOU EVER HEARD THE STORY OF... HIC! HUMPTY DUMPTY???
TISS A PRETTY GOOWD STORY...
BONK!

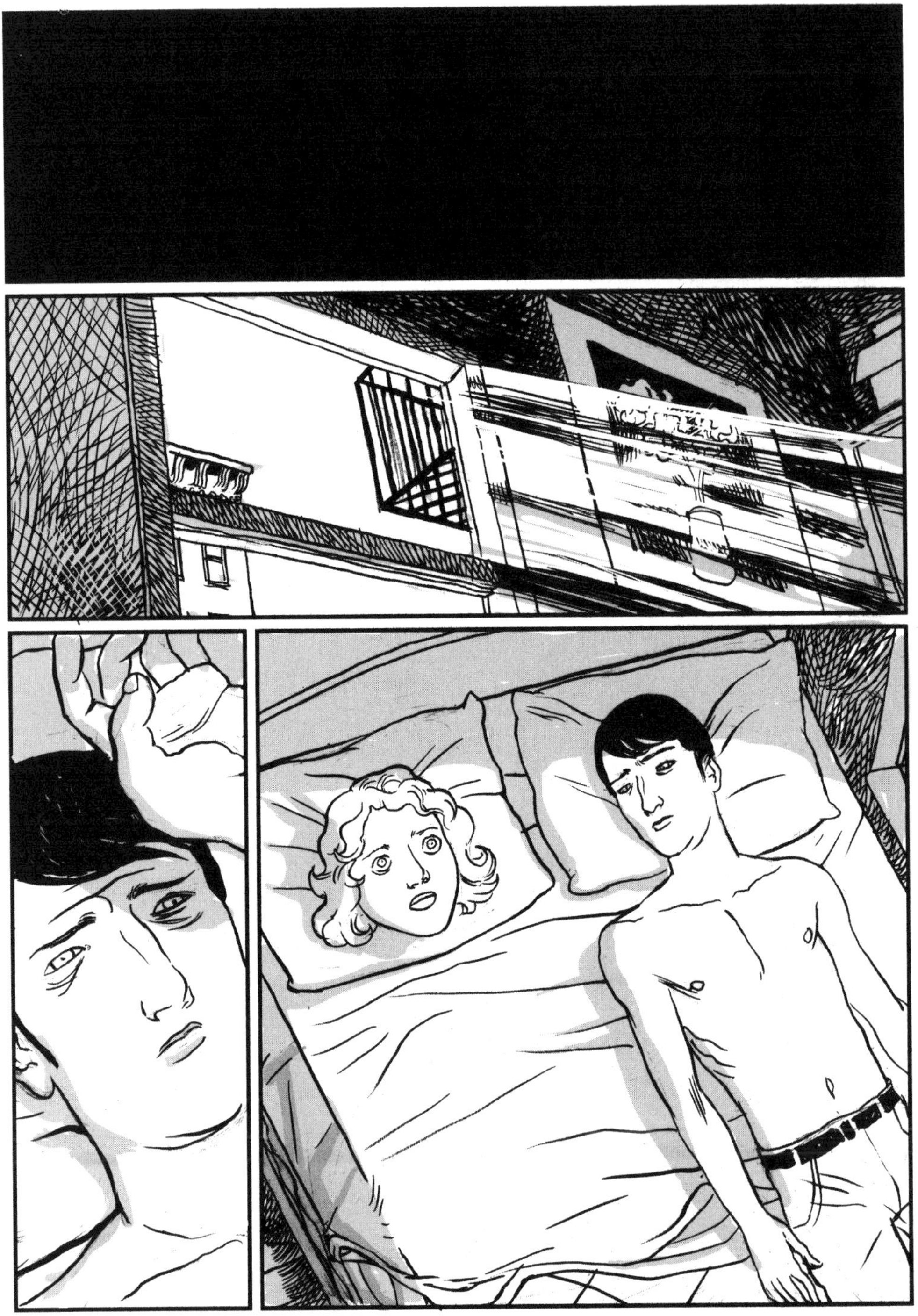

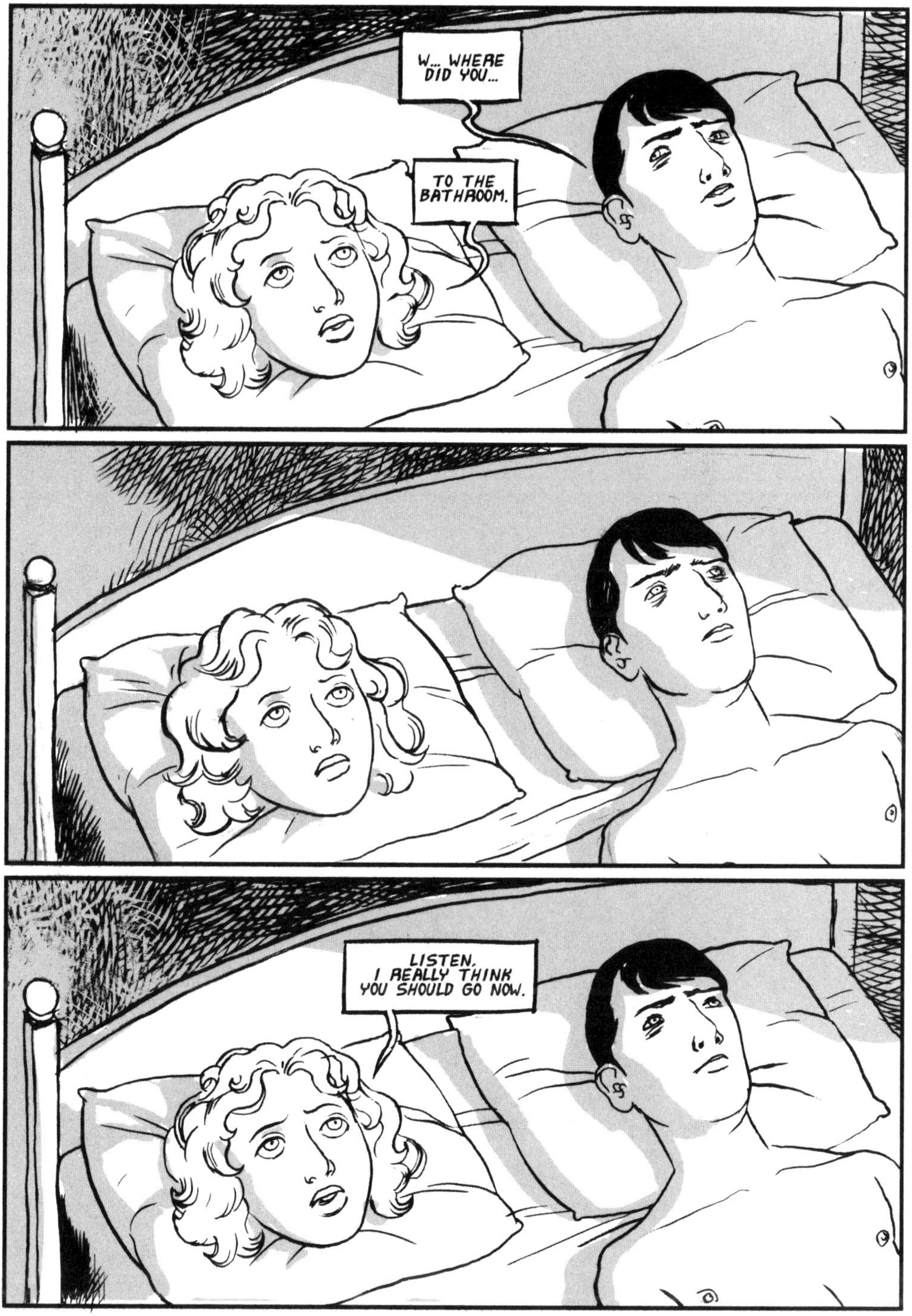
W... WHERE DID YOU...
TO THE BATHROOM.
LISTEN, I REALLY THINK YOU SHOULD GO NOW.

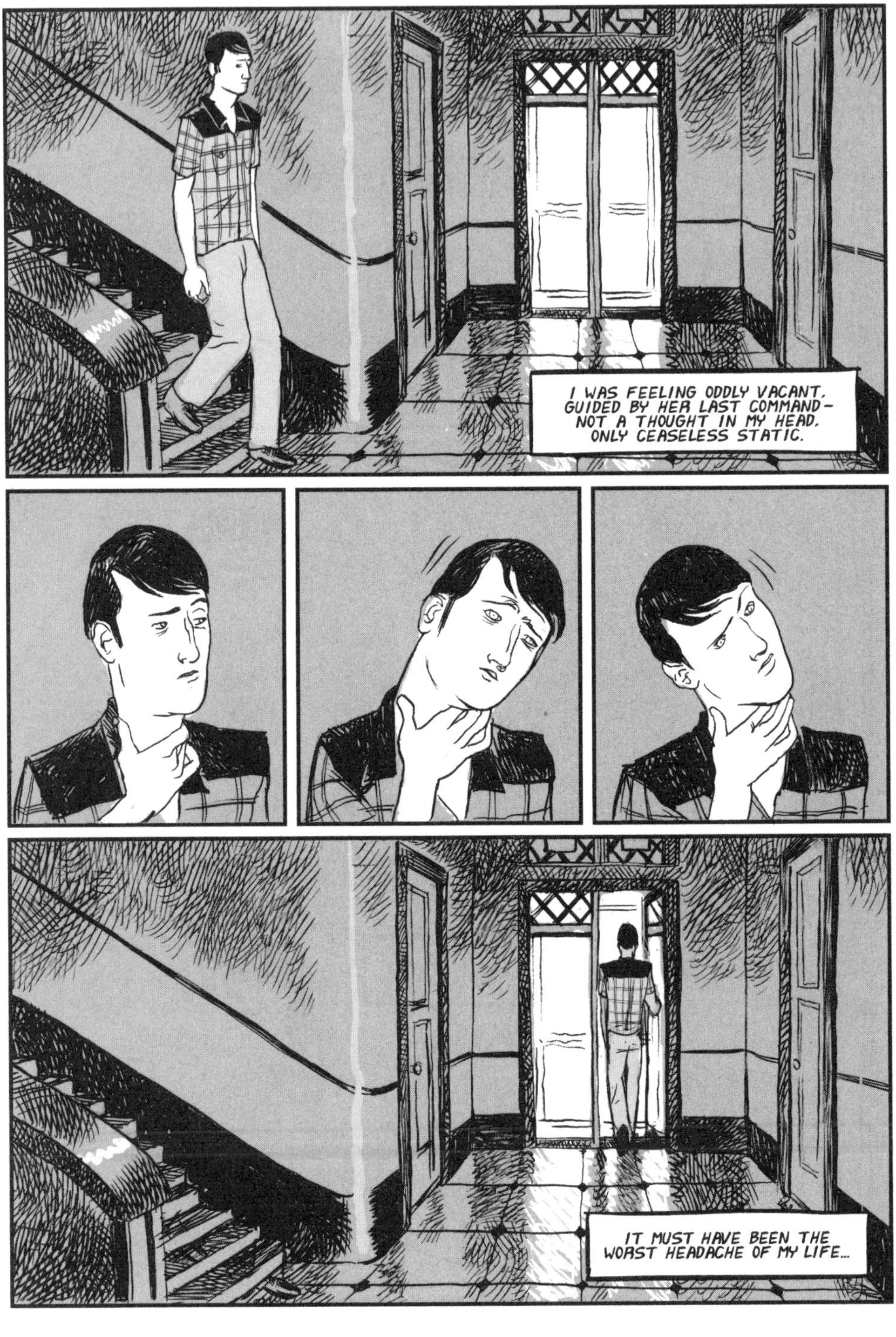
I WAS FEELING ODDLY VACANT, GUIDED BY HER LAST COMMAND–NOT A THOUGHT IN MY HEAD, ONLY CEASELESS STATIC.
IT MUST HAVE BEEN THE WORST HEADACHE OF MY LIFE...

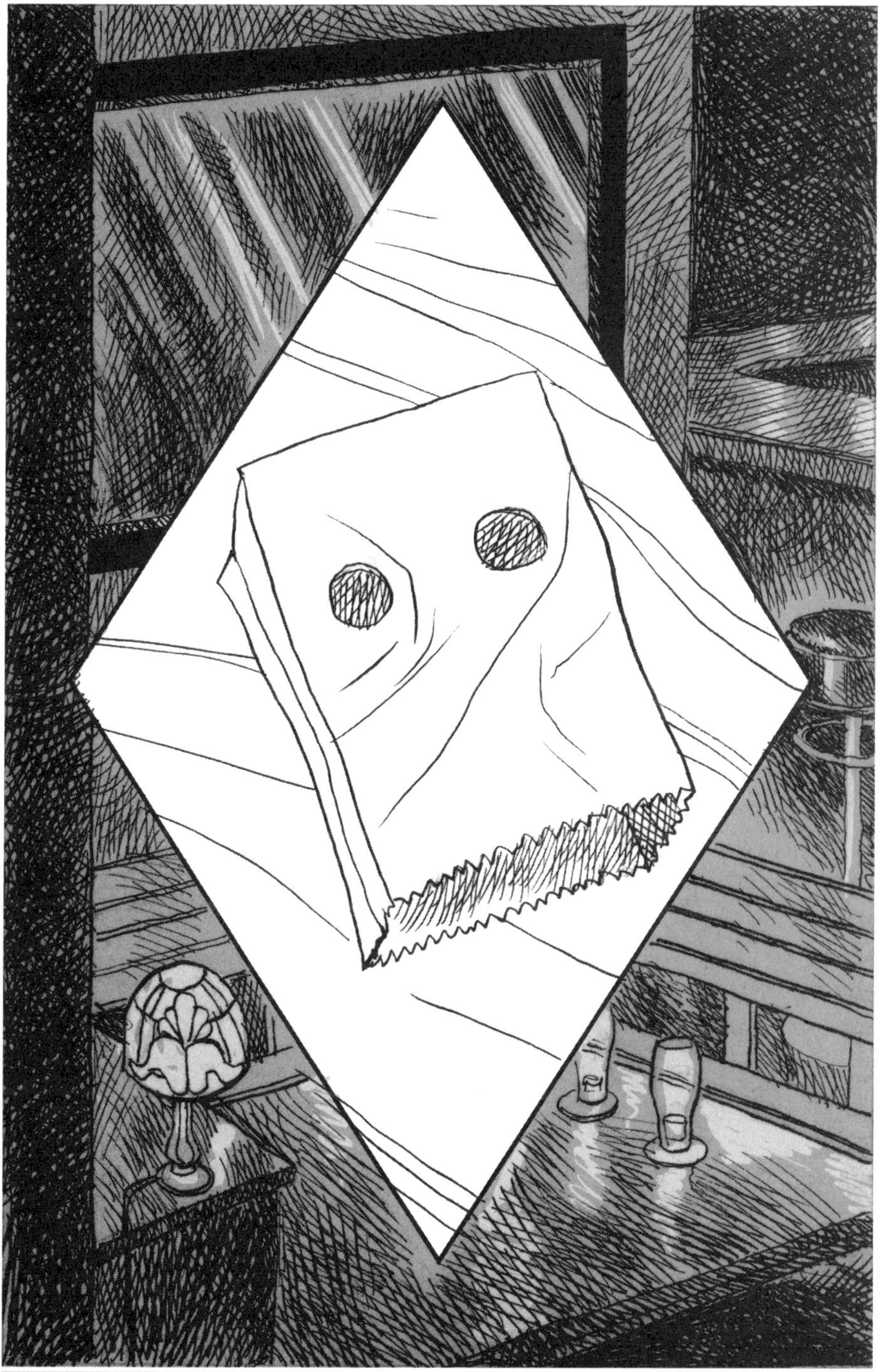

· A DATE ·

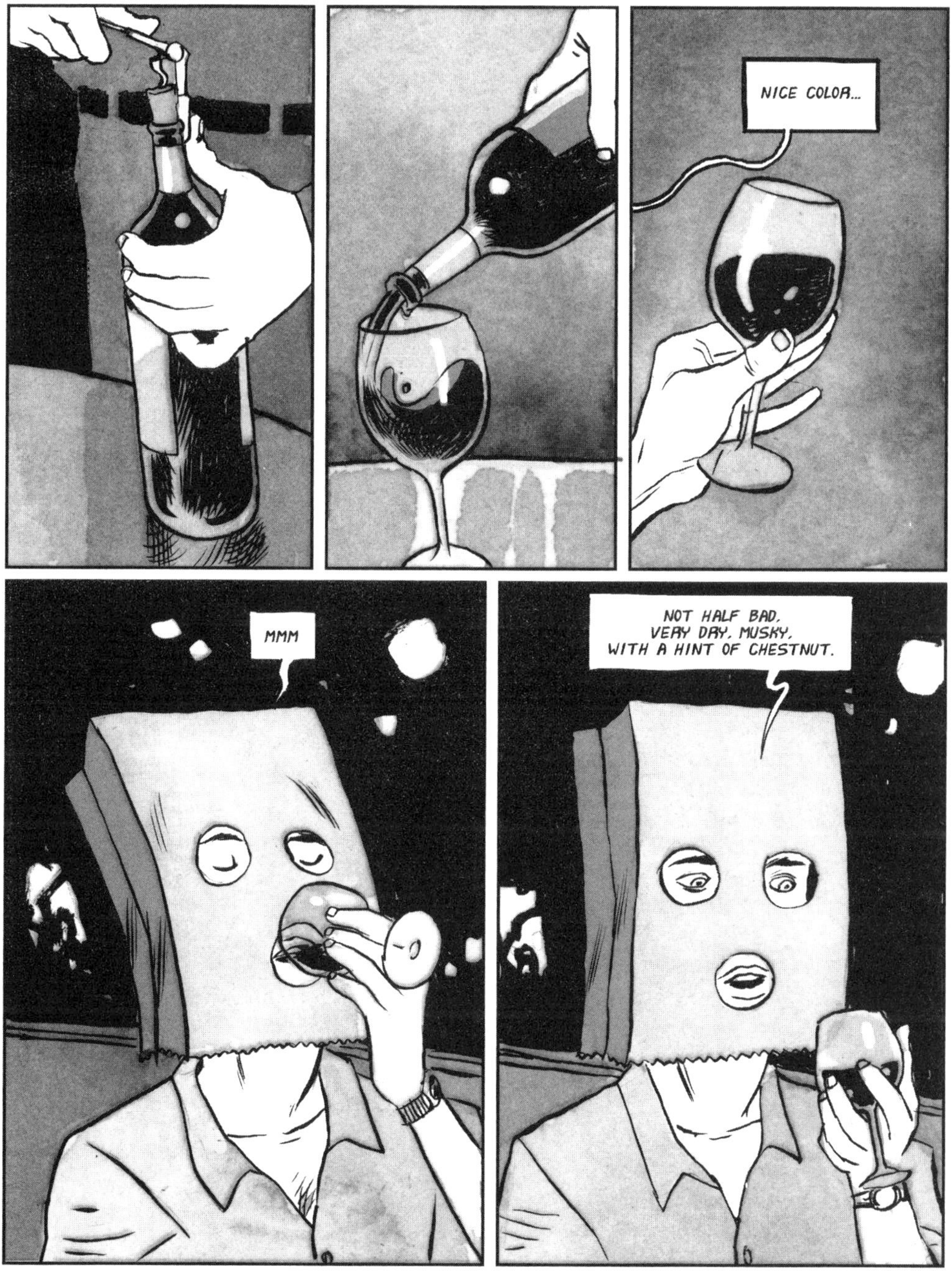
NICE COLOR...
MMM
NOT HALF BAD, VERY DRY, MUSKY, WITH A HINT OF CHESTNUT.

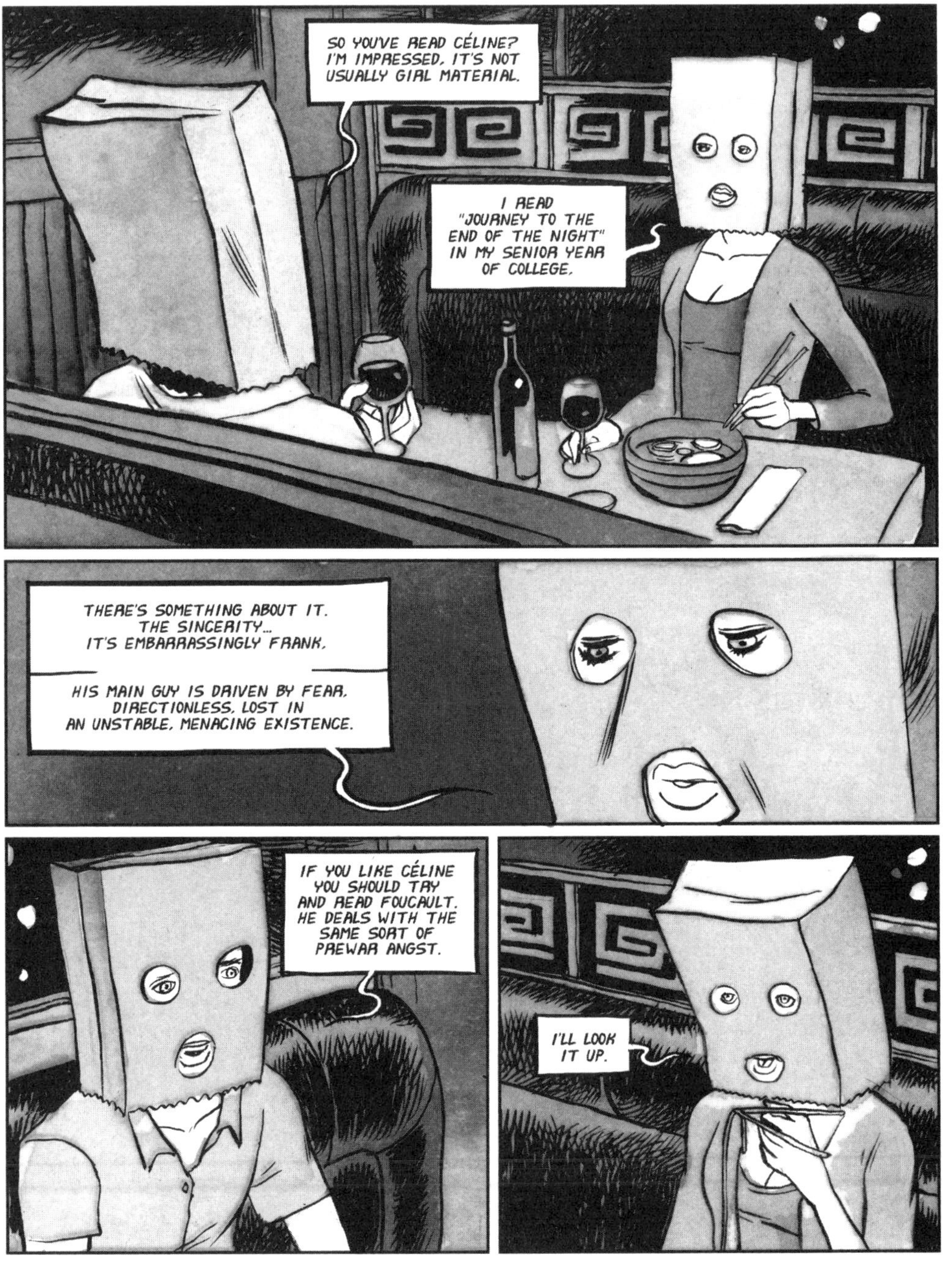
SO YOU'VE READ CÉLINE? I'M IMPRESSED. IT'S NOT USUALLY GIRL MATERIAL.
I READ "JOURNEY TO THE END OF THE NIGHT" IN MY SENIOR YEAR OF COLLEGE.
THERE'S SOMETHING ABOUT IT. THE SINCERITY... IT'S EMBARRASSINGLY FRANK.
HIS MAIN GUY IS DRIVEN BY FEAR, DIRECTIONLESS, LOST IN AN UNSTABLE, MENACING EXISTENCE.
IF YOU LIKE CÉLINE YOU SHOULD TRY AND READ FOUCAULT. HE DEALS WITH THE SAME SORT OF PREWAR ANGST.
I'LL LOOK IT UP.

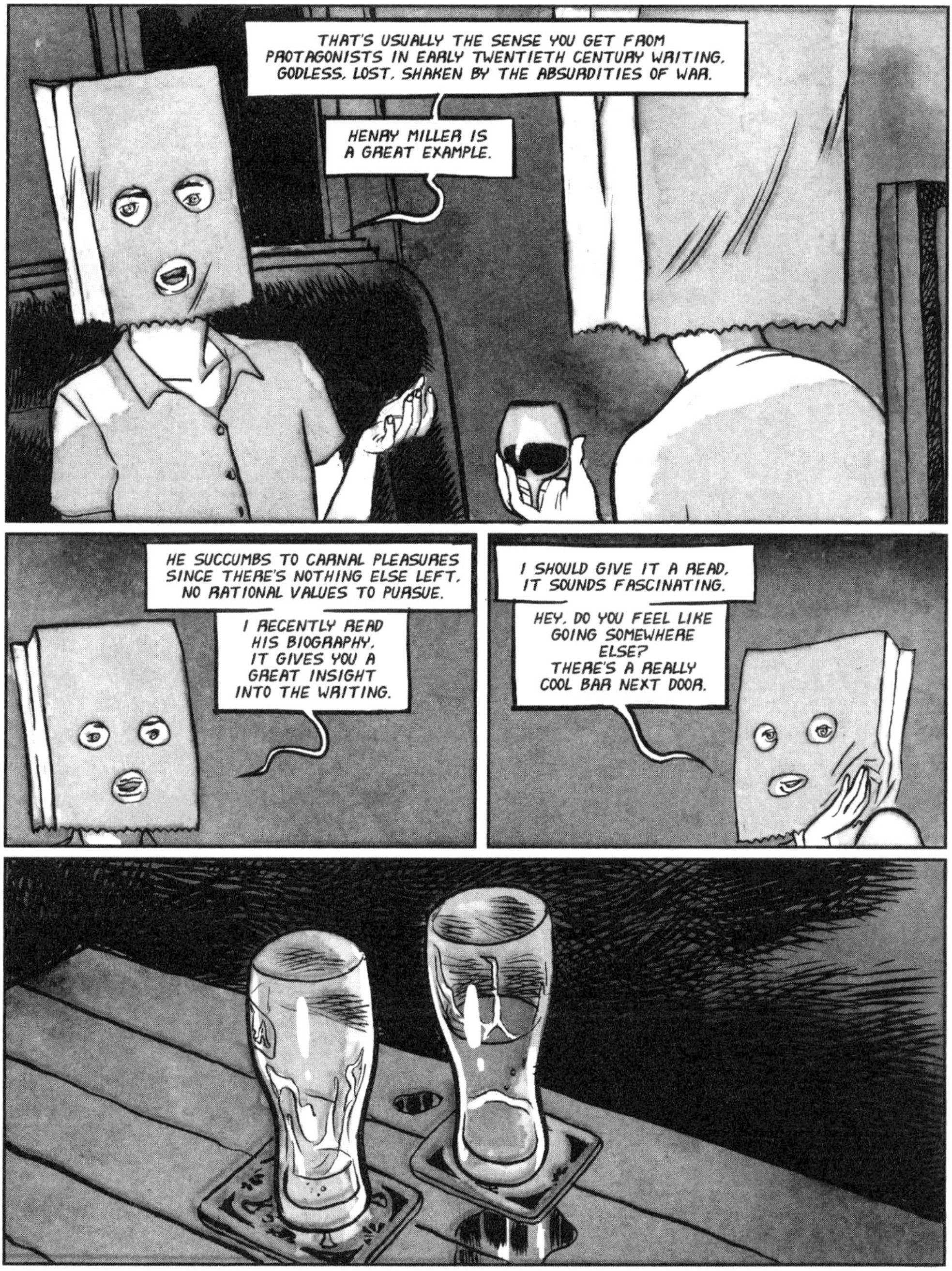
THAT'S USUALLY THE SENSE YOU GET FROM PROTAGONISTS IN EARLY TWENTIETH CENTURY WRITING. GODLESS, LOST, SHAKEN BY THE ABSURDITIES OF WAR.
HENRY MILLER IS A GREAT EXAMPLE.
HE SUCCUMBS TO CARNAL PLEASURES SINCE THERE'S NOTHING ELSE LEFT, NO RATIONAL VALUES TO PURSUE.
I RECENTLY READ HIS BIOGRAPHY, IT GIVES YOU A GREAT INSIGHT INTO THE WRITING.
I SHOULD GIVE IT A READ, IT SOUNDS FASCINATING.
HEY, DO YOU FEEL LIKE GOING SOMEWHERE ELSE? THERE'S A REALLY COOL BAR NEXT DOOR.

EHHHMM.

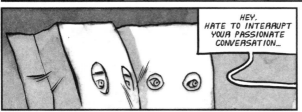

HEY,
HATE TO INTERRUPT
YOUR PASSIONATE
CONVERSATION...

COME ON, LET'S GET OUT OF HERE,
DO YOU WANT ME TO WALK YOU HOME?

AH..SURE,
WHY NOT?

WE KIND OF NEED A SPACE TO SIT IN,
WOULD YOU GUYS MIND MOVING TO A SMALLER SPOT?
IT'LL ALSO BE COZIER FOR YOU...

TEE-HEE!

VIRGINIA WOOLF
MM... WAIT A SECOND

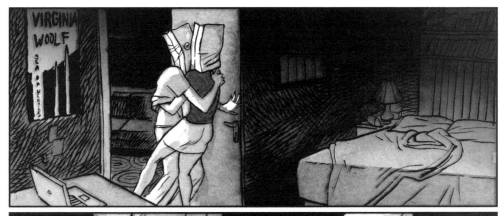

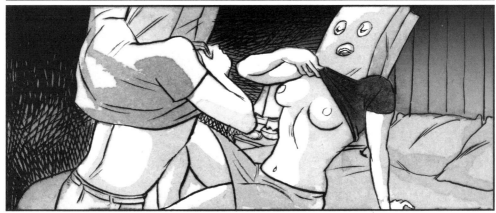

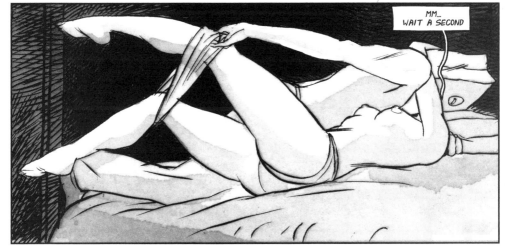

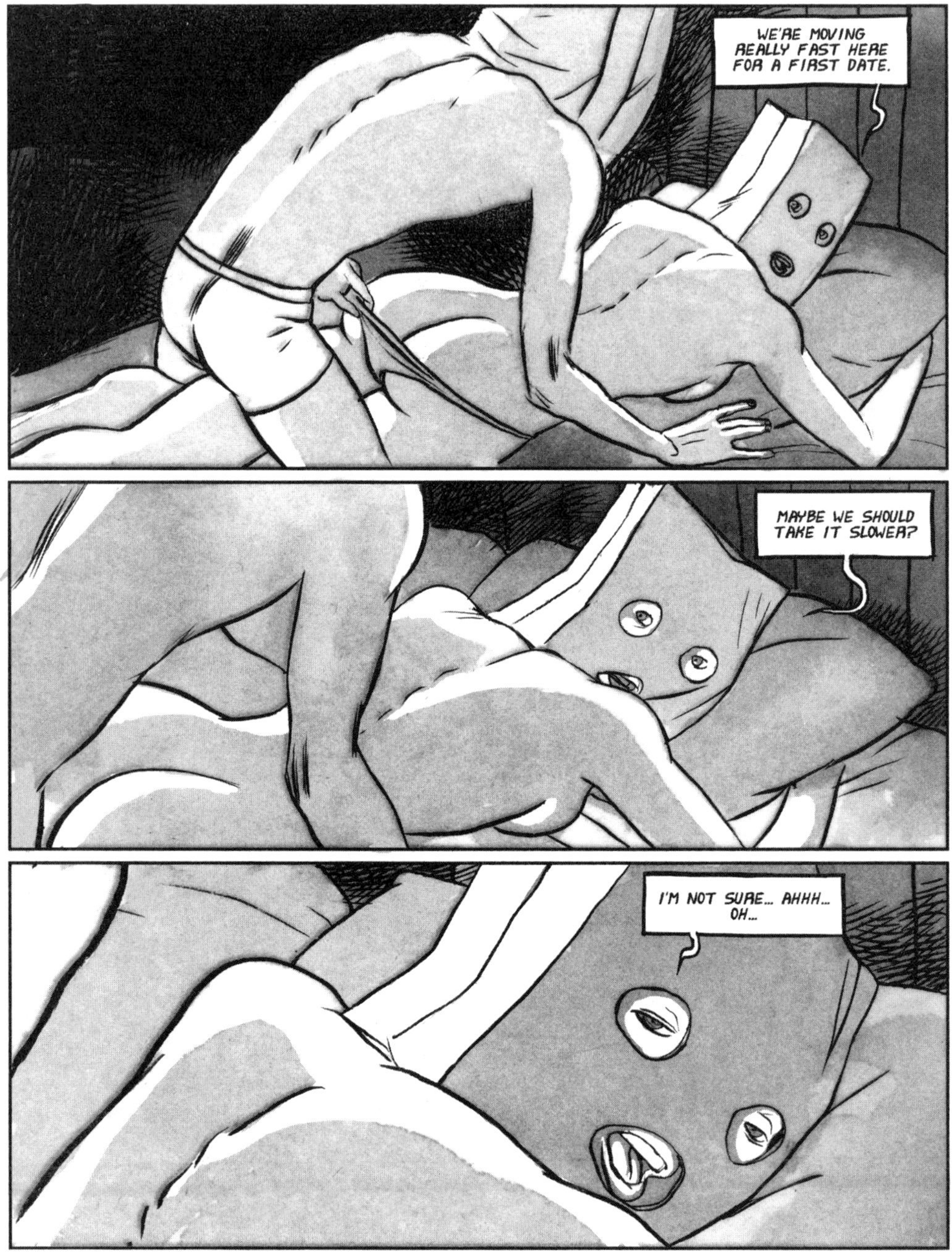
WE'RE MOVING REALLY FAST HERE FOR A FIRST DATE.
MAYBE WE SHOULD TAKE IT SLOWER?
I'M NOT SURE... AHHH... OH...

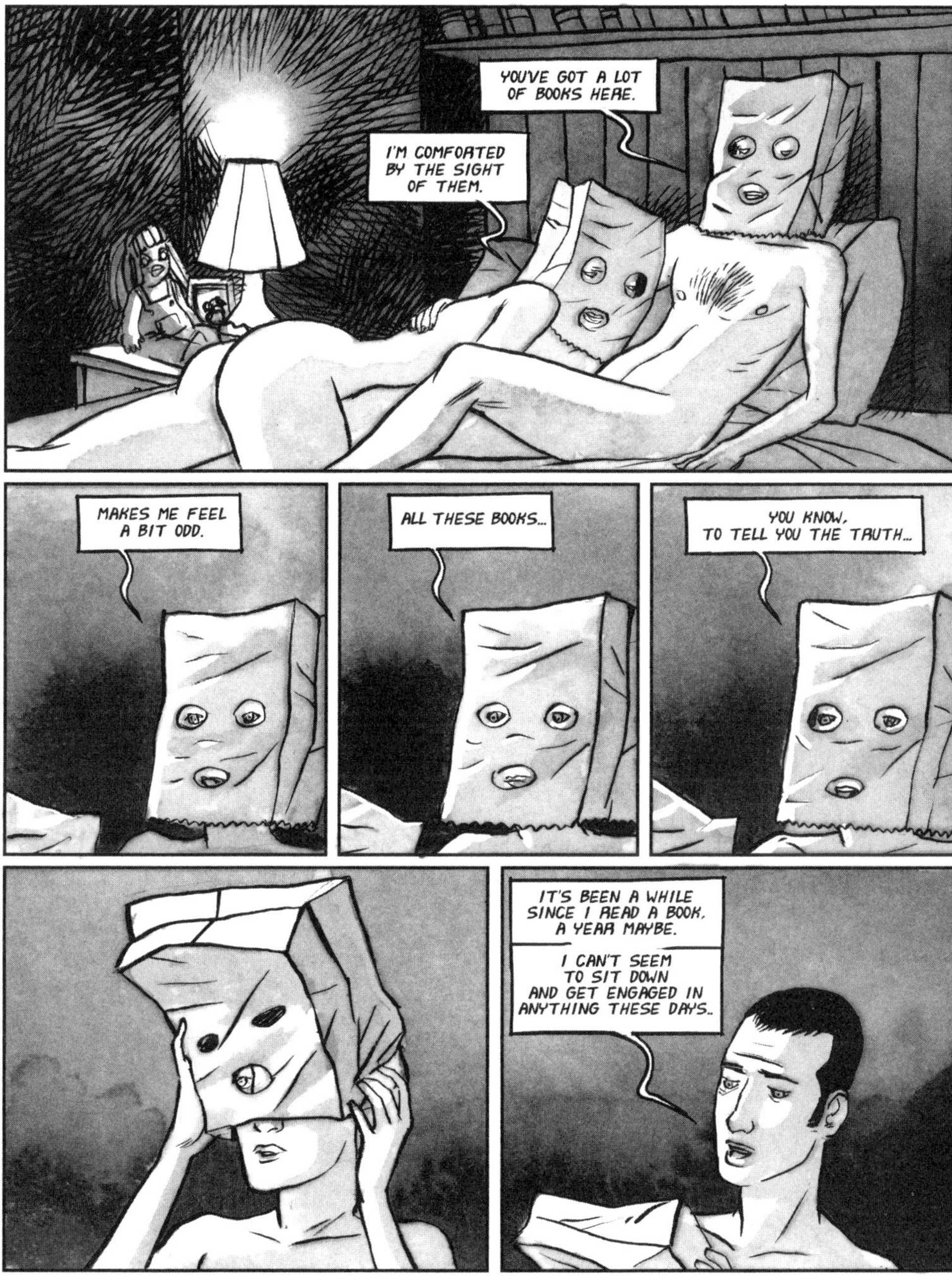
YOU'VE GOT A LOT OF BOOKS HERE.
I'M COMFORTED BY THE SIGHT OF THEM.
MAKES ME FEEL A BIT ODD.
ALL THESE BOOKS...
YOU KNOW, TO TELL YOU THE TRUTH...
IT'S BEEN A WHILE SINCE I READ A BOOK, A YEAR MAYBE.
I CAN'T SEEM TO SIT DOWN AND GET ENGAGED IN ANYTHING THESE DAYS..

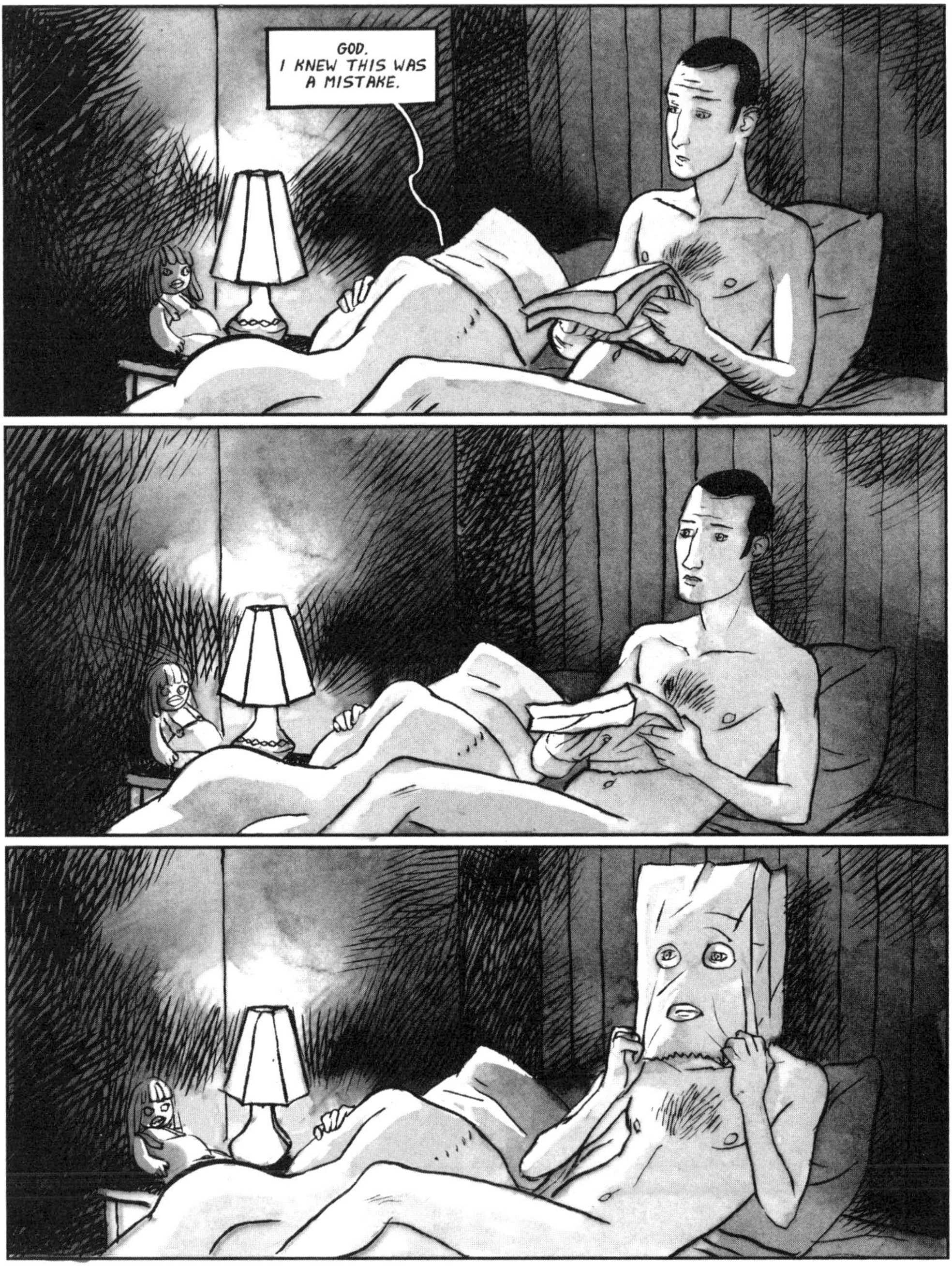
GOD. I KNEW THIS WAS A MISTAKE.

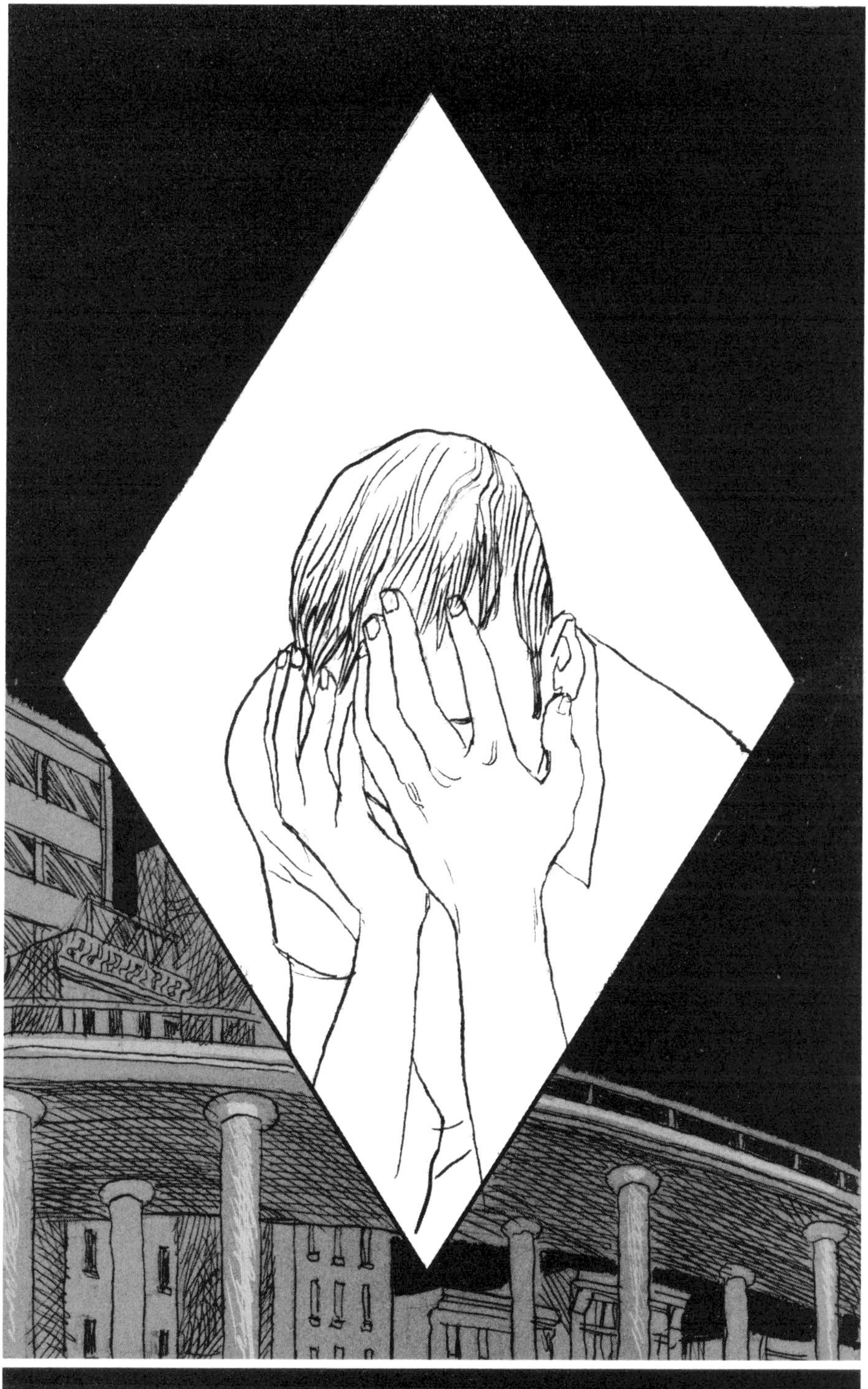
WHAT IS WRONG WITH ME?

WHAT IS WRONG WITH ME?

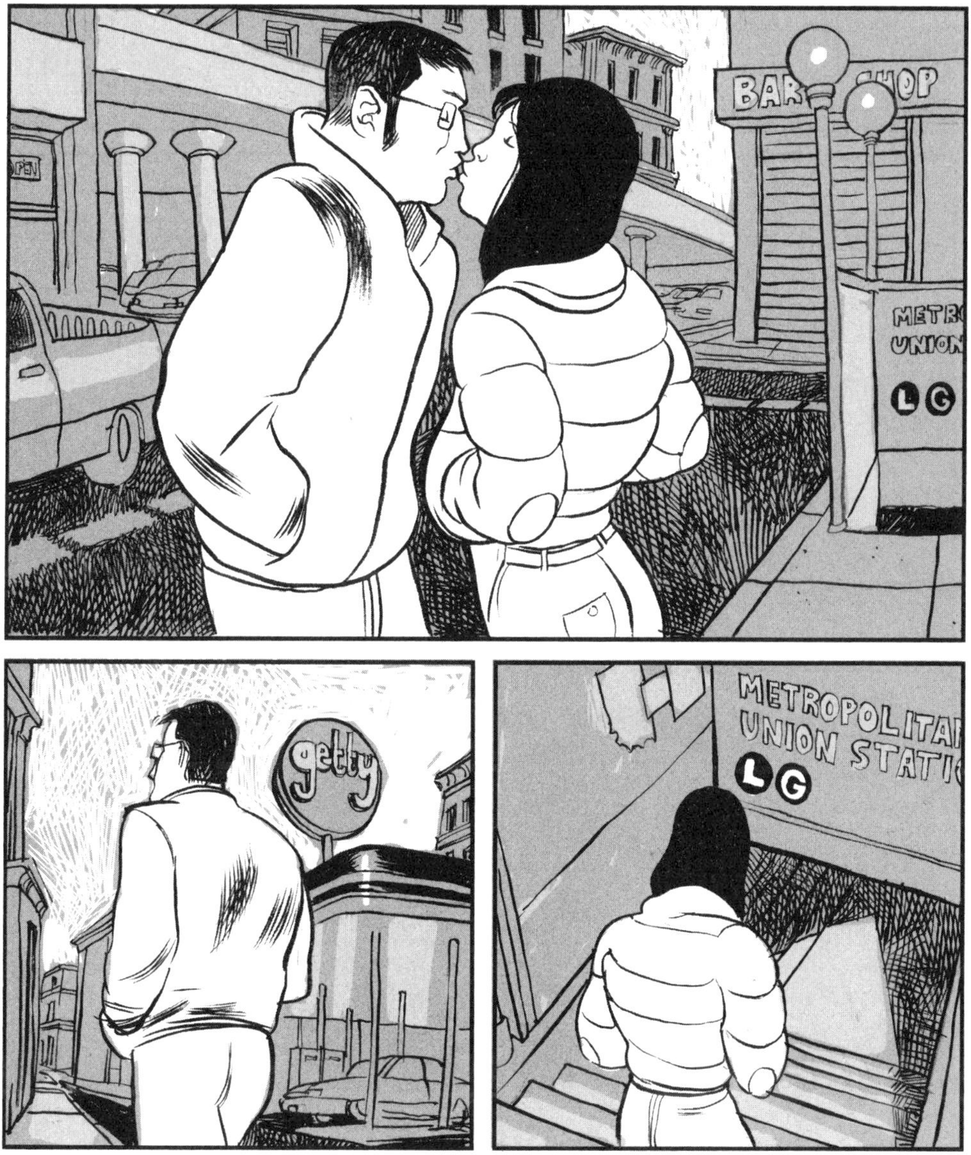
METRO
UNION
LG
getty
METROPOLITA
UNION STATI
LG

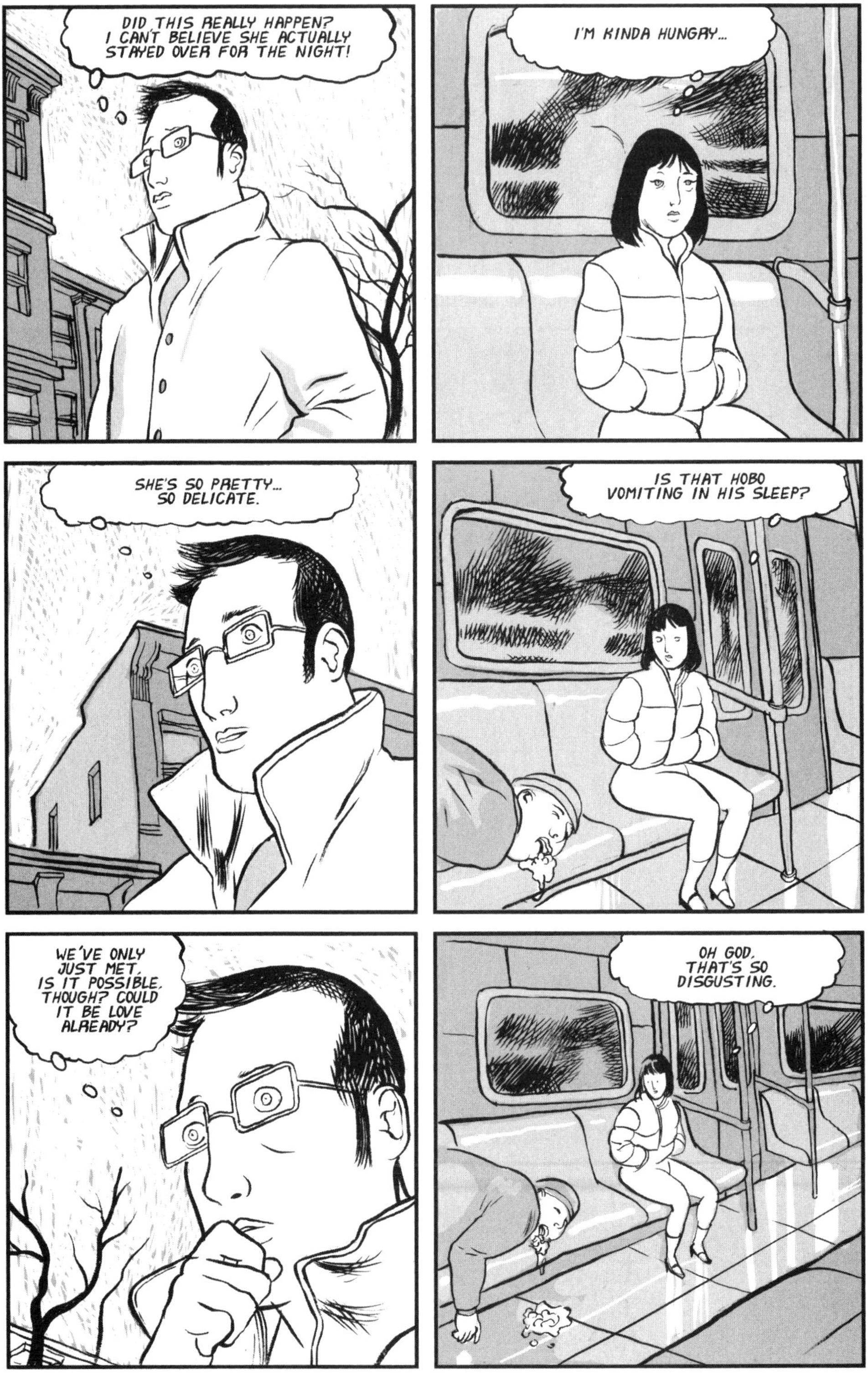
DID THIS REALLY HAPPEN? I CAN'T BELIEVE SHE ACTUALLY STAYED OVER FOR THE NIGHT!
I'M KINDA HUNGRY...
SHE'S SO PRETTY... SO DELICATE.
IS THAT HOBO VOMITING IN HIS SLEEP?
WE'VE ONLY JUST MET. IS IT POSSIBLE, THOUGH? COULD IT BE LOVE ALREADY?
OH GOD, THAT'S SO DISGUSTING.

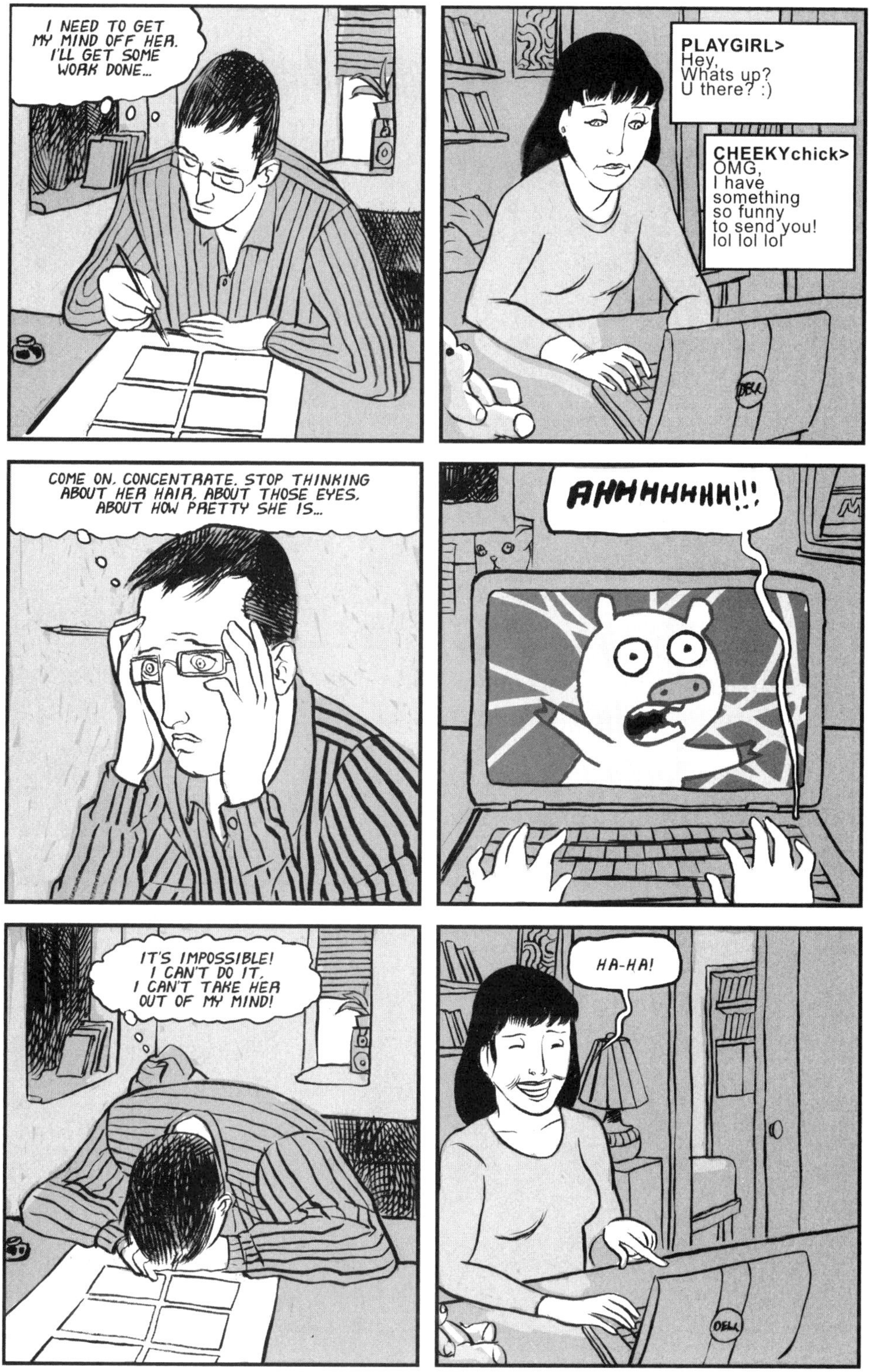
I NEED TO GET MY MIND OFF HER. I'LL GET SOME WORK DONE...
PLAYGIRL> Hey, Whats up? U there? :)
CHEEKYchick> OMG, I have something so funny to send you! lol lol lol
COME ON, CONCENTRATE. STOP THINKING ABOUT HER HAIR, ABOUT THOSE EYES, ABOUT HOW PRETTY SHE IS...
AHHHHHHH!!!
IT'S IMPOSSIBLE! I CAN'T DO IT. I CAN'T TAKE HER OUT OF MY MIND!
HA-HA!

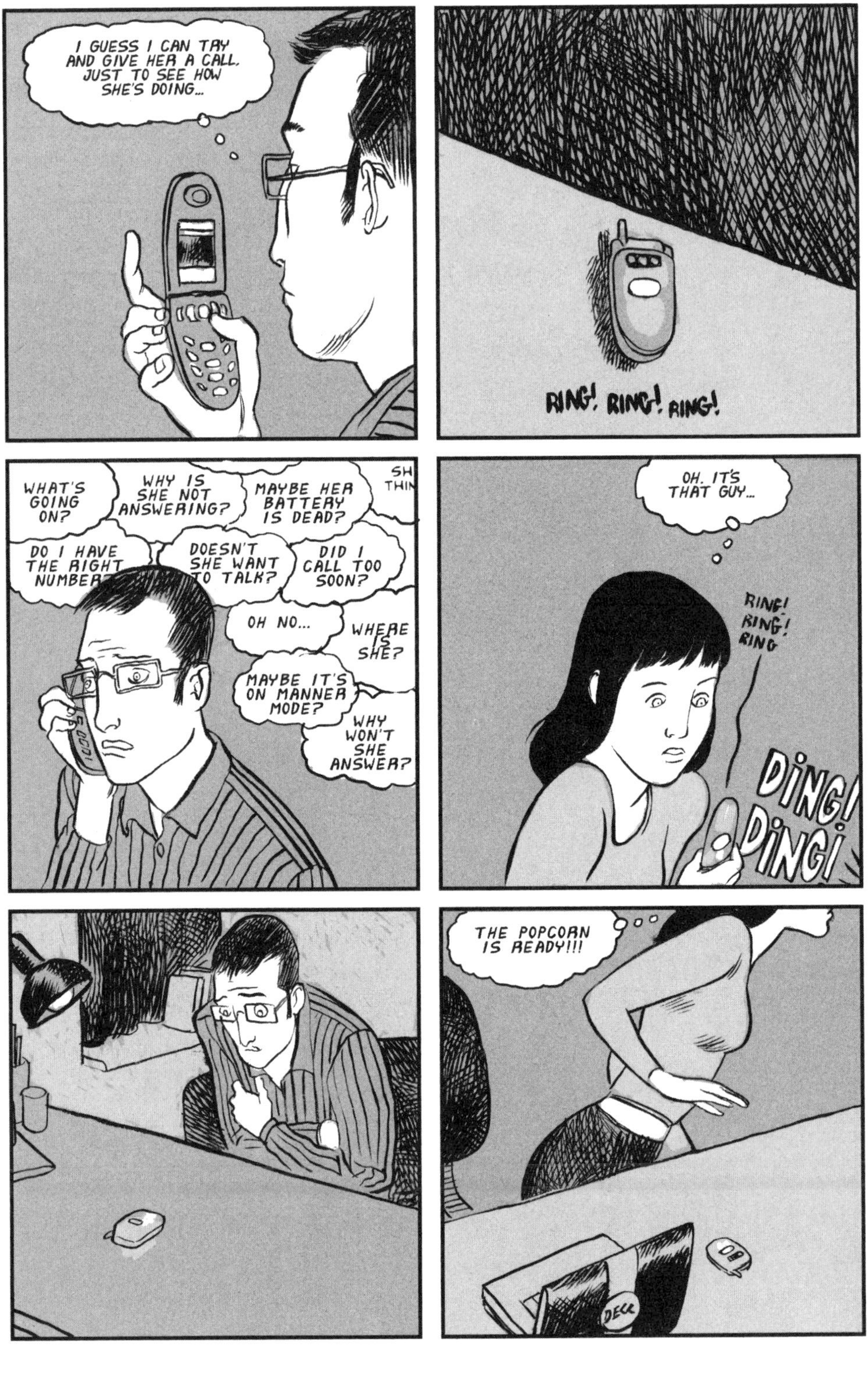
I GUESS I CAN TRY AND GIVE HER A CALL, JUST TO SEE HOW SHE'S DOING...
RING! RING! RING!
WHAT'S GOING ON?
WHY IS SHE NOT ANSWERING?
MAYBE HER BATTERY IS DEAD?
DO I HAVE THE RIGHT NUMBE
DOESN'T SHE WANT TO TALK?
DID I CALL TOO SOON?
OH NO...
WHERE IS SHE?
MAYBE IT'S ON MANNER MODE?
WHY WON'T SHE ANSWER?
OH. IT'S THAT GUY...
RING! RING! RING
DING! DING!
THE POPCORN IS READY!!!

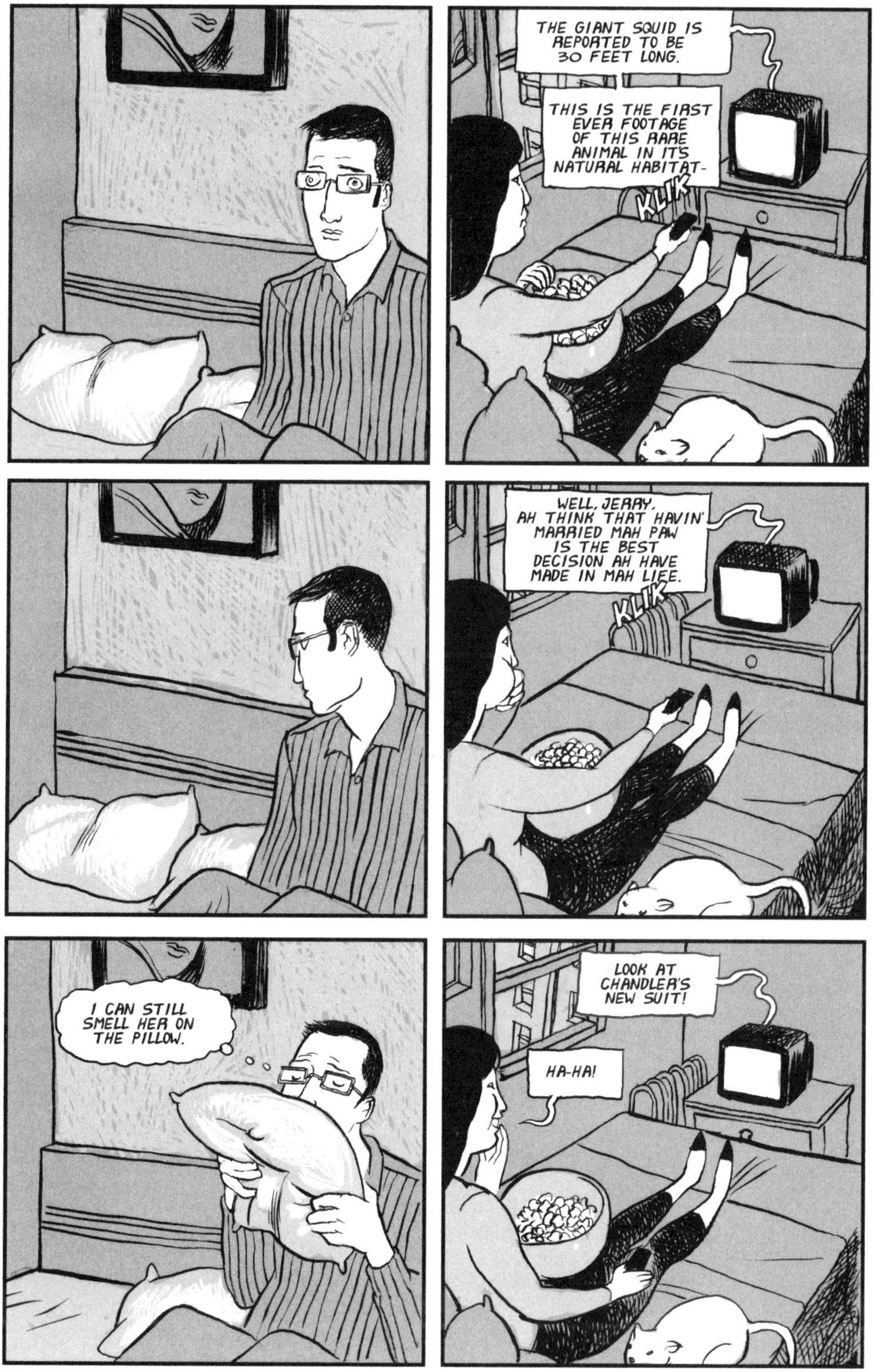
THE GIANT SQUID IS REPORTED TO BE 30 FEET LONG.
THIS IS THE FIRST EVER FOOTAGE OF THIS RARE ANIMAL IN IT'S NATURAL HABITAT-
KLIK
WELL, JERRY, AH THINK THAT HAVIN' MARRIED MAH PAW IS THE BEST DECISION AH HAVE MADE IN MAH LIFE.
KLIK
I CAN STILL SMELL HER ON THE PILLOW.
LOOK AT CHANDLER'S NEW SUIT!
HA-HA!

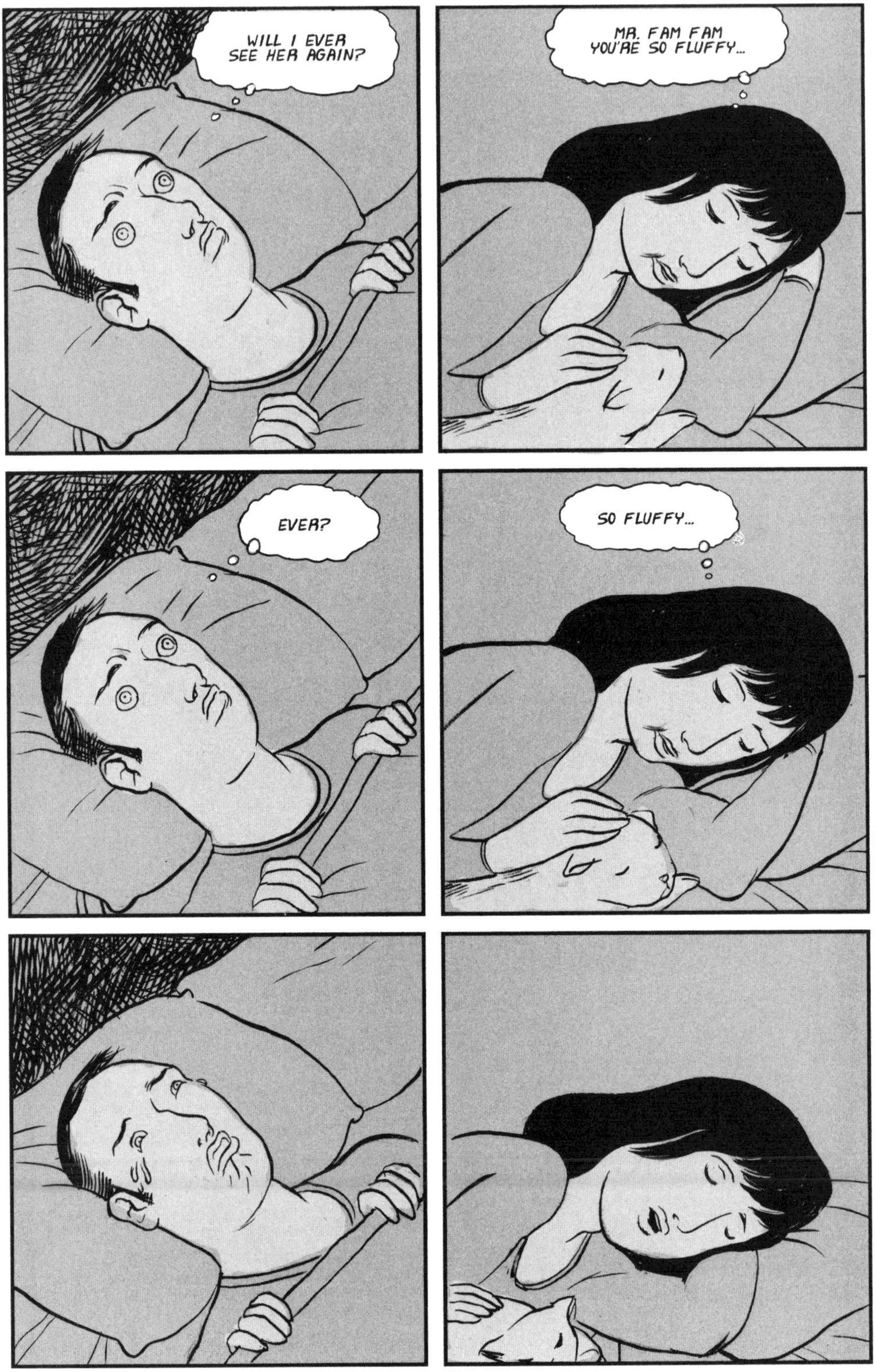
WILL I EVER SEE HER AGAIN?
MR. FAM FAM YOU'RE SO FLUFFY...
EVER?
SO FLUFFY...

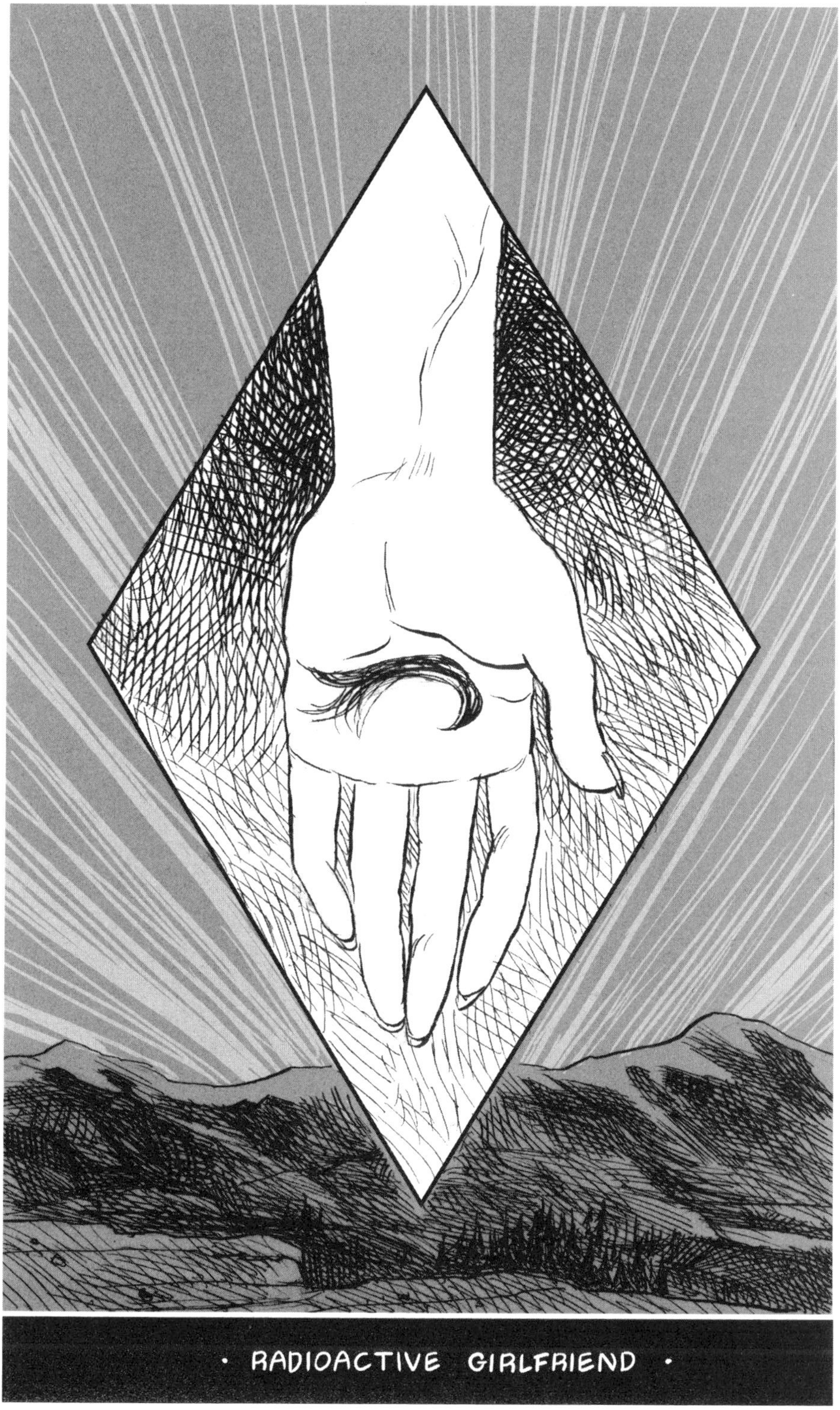

· RADIOACTIVE GIRLFRIEND ·

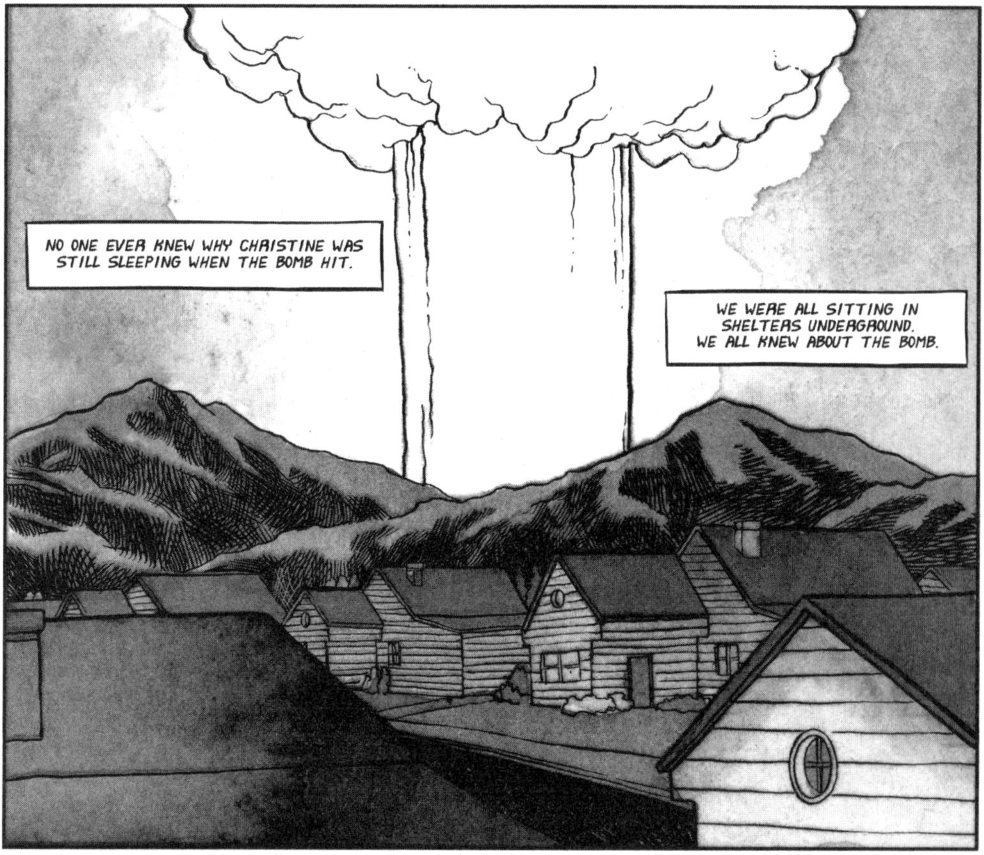
NO ONE EVER KNEW WHY CHRISTINE WAS STILL SLEEPING WHEN THE BOMB HIT.
WE WERE ALL SITTING IN SHELTERS UNDERGROUND. WE ALL KNEW ABOUT THE BOMB.

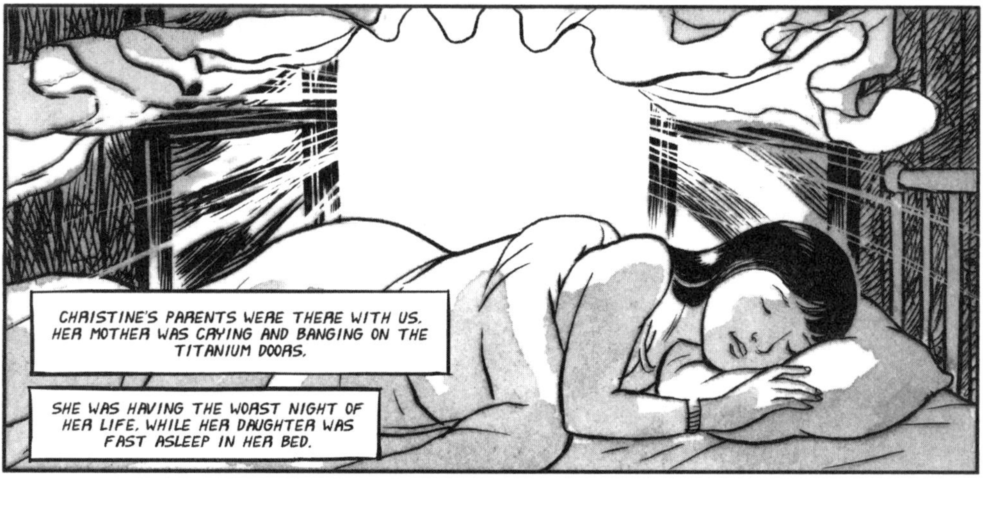
CHRISTINE'S PARENTS WERE THERE WITH US. HER MOTHER WAS CRYING AND BANGING ON THE TITANIUM DOORS.
SHE WAS HAVING THE WORST NIGHT OF HER LIFE, WHILE HER DAUGHTER WAS FAST ASLEEP IN HER BED.

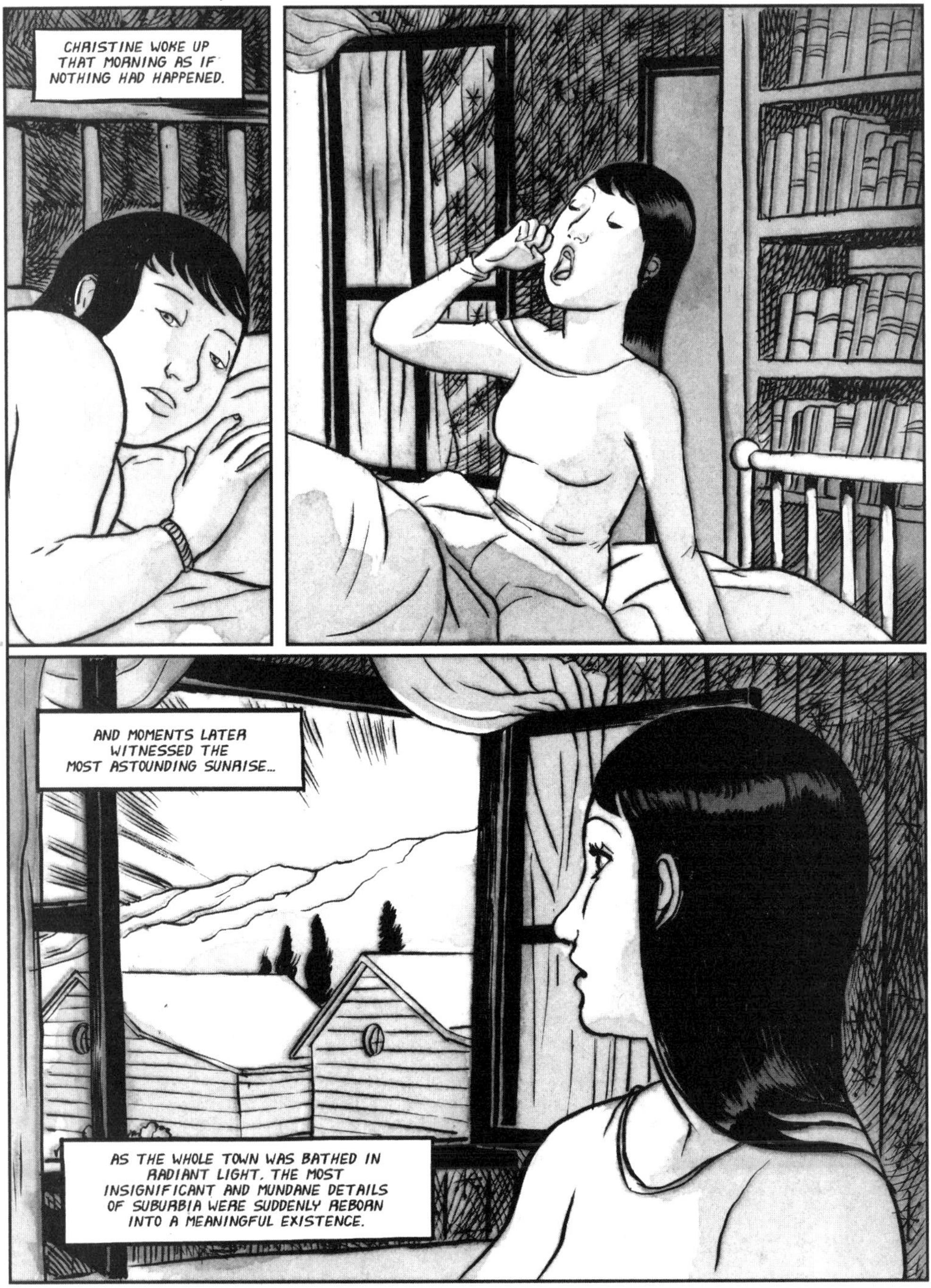
CHRISTINE WOKE UP THAT MORNING AS IF NOTHING HAD HAPPENED.
AND MOMENTS LATER WITNESSED THE MOST ASTOUNDING SUNRISE...
AS THE WHOLE TOWN WAS BATHED IN RADIANT LIGHT, THE MOST INSIGNIFICANT AND MUNDANE DETAILS OF SUBURBIA WERE SUDDENLY REBORN INTO A MEANINGFUL EXISTENCE.

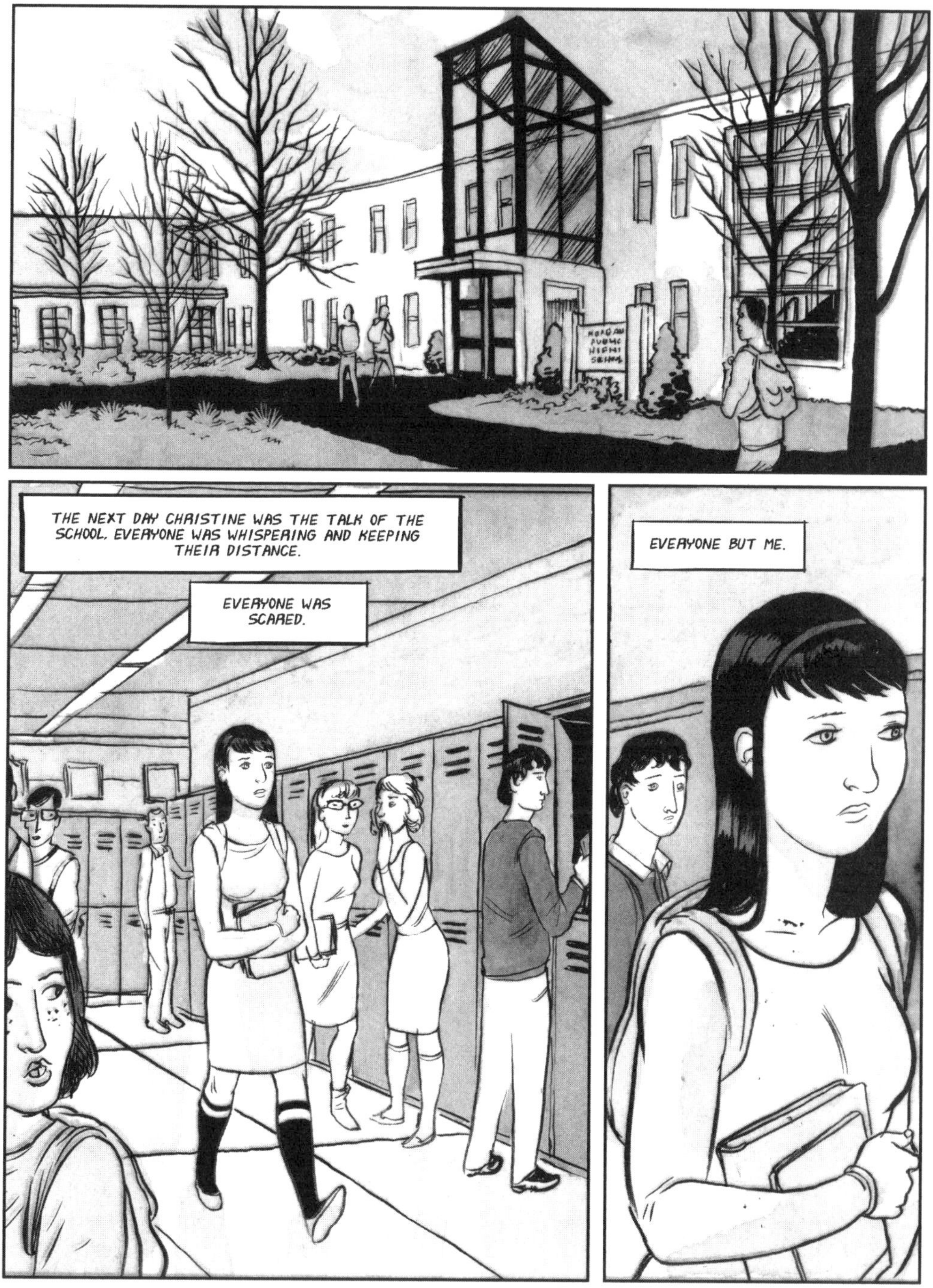
THE NEXT DAY CHRISTINE WAS THE TALK OF THE SCHOOL, EVERYONE WAS WHISPERING AND KEEPING THEIR DISTANCE.
EVERYONE WAS SCARED.
EVERYONE BUT ME.

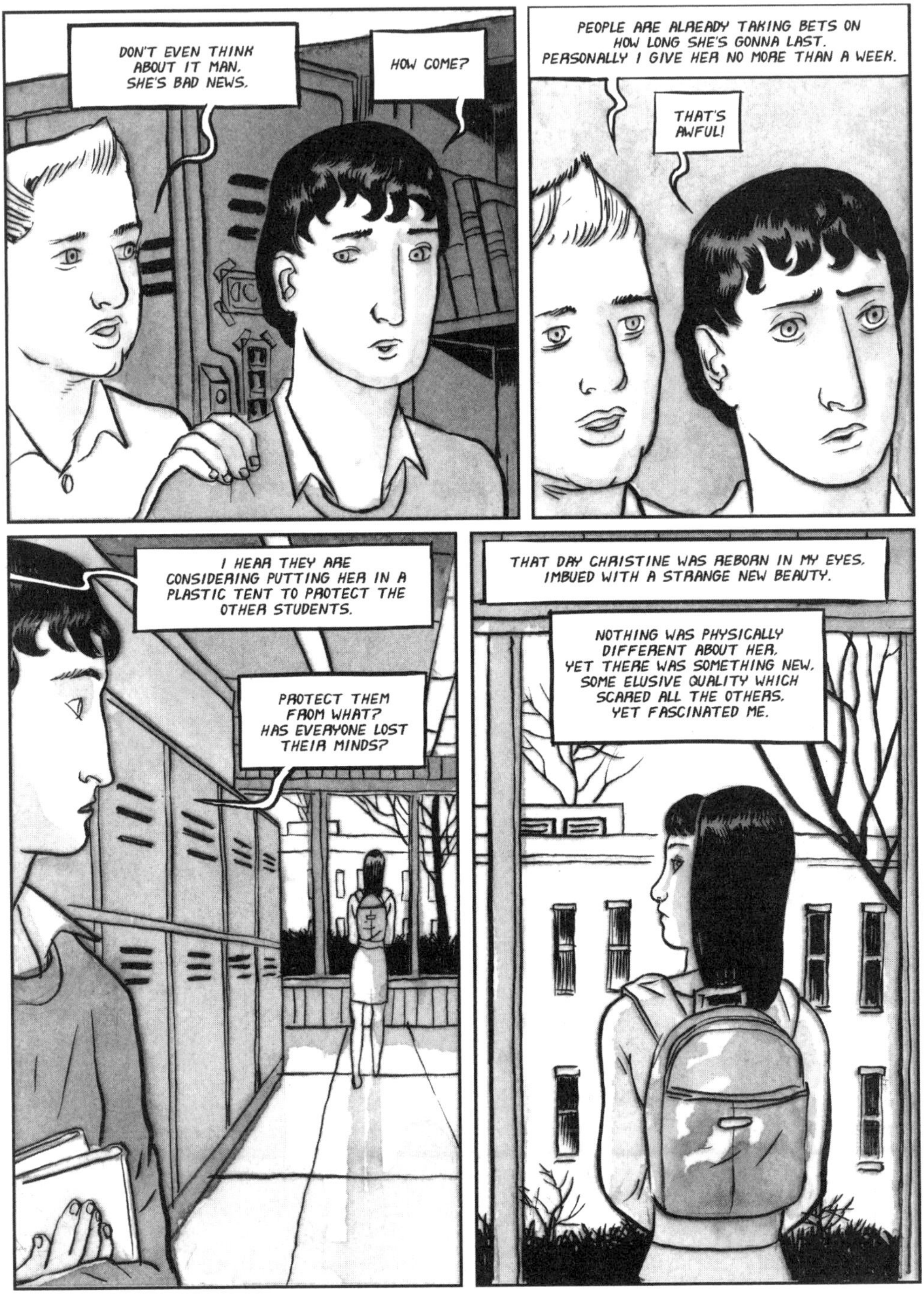
DON'T EVEN THINK ABOUT IT MAN, SHE'S BAD NEWS.
HOW COME?
PEOPLE ARE ALREADY TAKING BETS ON HOW LONG SHE'S GONNA LAST. PERSONALLY I GIVE HER NO MORE THAN A WEEK.
THAT'S AWFUL!
I HEAR THEY ARE CONSIDERING PUTTING HER IN A PLASTIC TENT TO PROTECT THE OTHER STUDENTS.
PROTECT THEM FROM WHAT? HAS EVERYONE LOST THEIR MINDS?
THAT DAY CHRISTINE WAS REBORN IN MY EYES, IMBUED WITH A STRANGE NEW BEAUTY.
NOTHING WAS PHYSICALLY DIFFERENT ABOUT HER, YET THERE WAS SOMETHING NEW, SOME ELUSIVE QUALITY WHICH SCARED ALL THE OTHERS, YET FASCINATED ME.

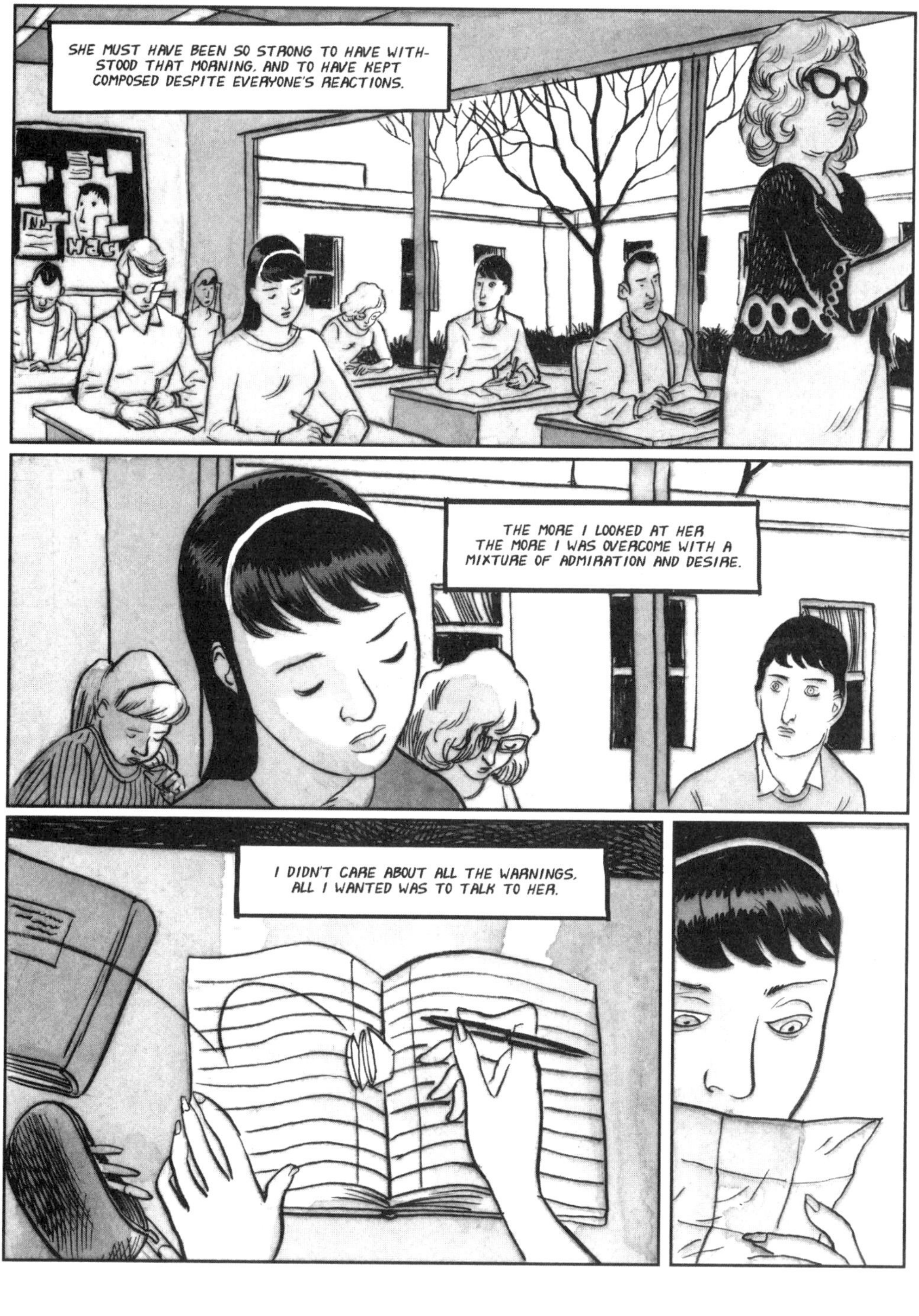
SHE MUST HAVE BEEN SO STRONG TO HAVE WITH-STOOD THAT MORNING, AND TO HAVE KEPT COMPOSED DESPITE EVERYONE'S REACTIONS.
THE MORE I LOOKED AT HER THE MORE I WAS OVERCOME WITH A MIXTURE OF ADMIRATION AND DESIRE.
I DIDN'T CARE ABOUT ALL THE WARNINGS, ALL I WANTED WAS TO TALK TO HER.

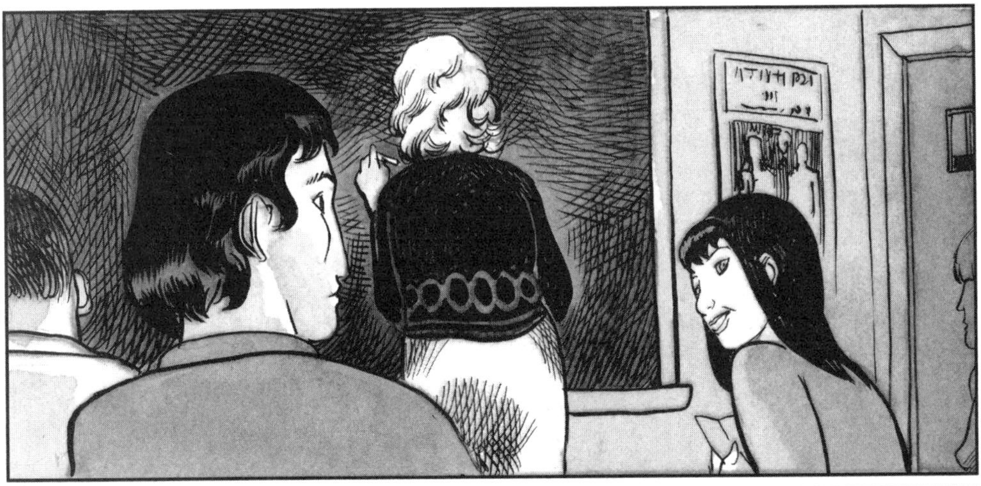

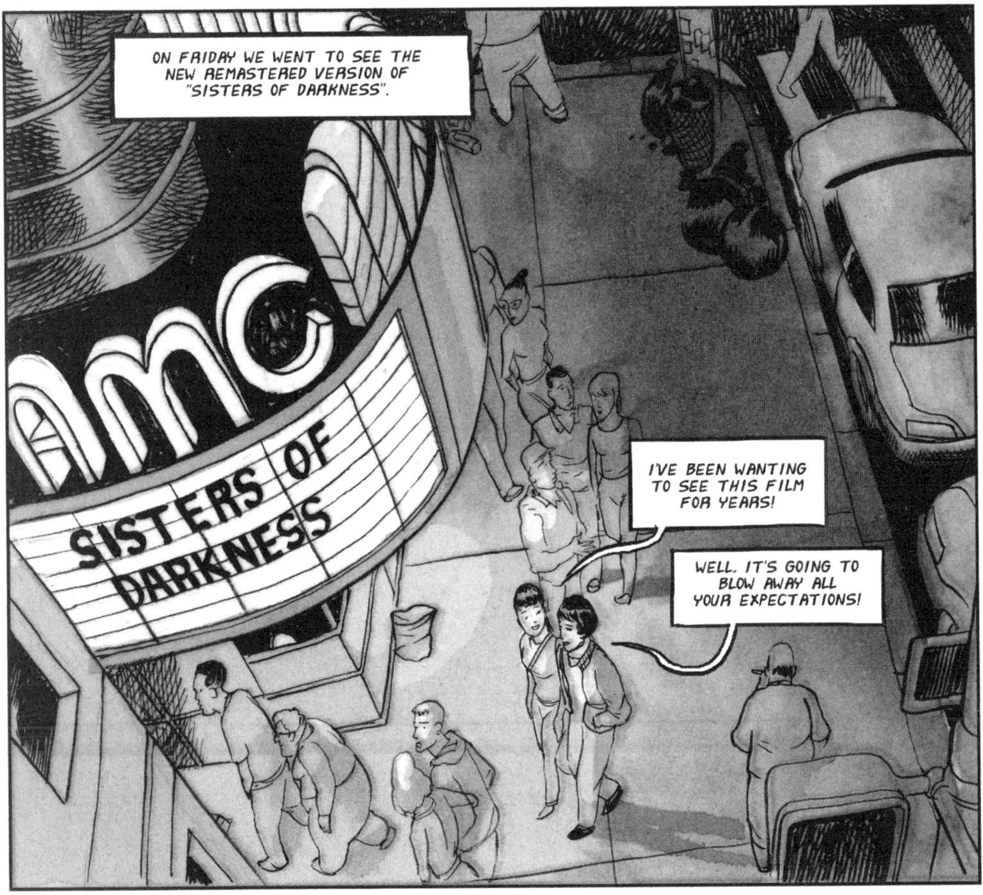

ON FRIDAY WE WENT TO SEE THE NEW REMASTERED VERSION OF "SISTERS OF DARKNESS".
SISTERS OF DARKNESS
I'VE BEEN WANTING TO SEE THIS FILM FOR YEARS!
WELL, IT'S GOING TO BLOW AWAY ALL YOUR EXPECTATIONS!

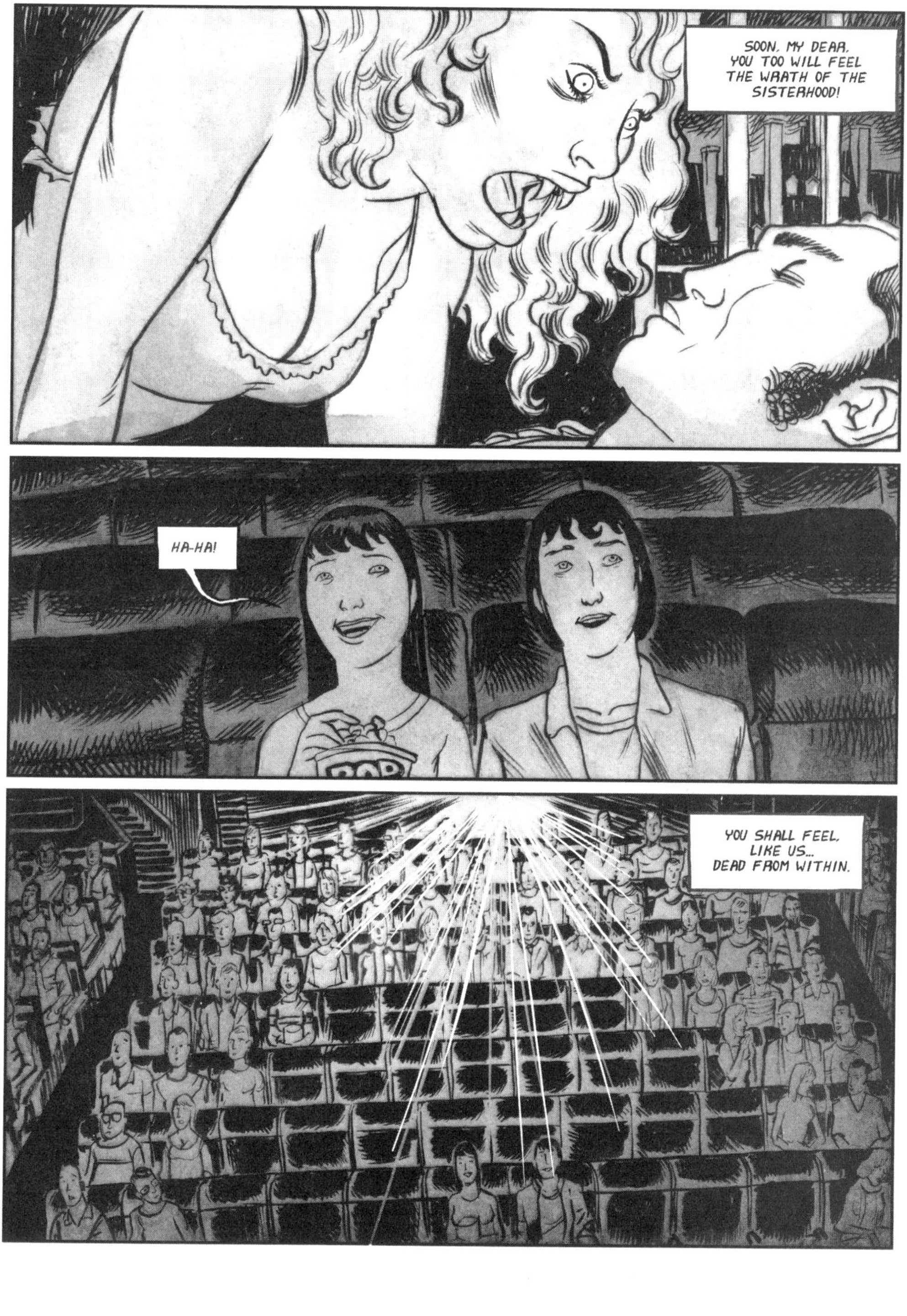
SOON, MY DEAR, YOU TOO WILL FEEL THE WRATH OF THE SISTERHOOD!
HA-HA!
POP
YOU SHALL FEEL, LIKE US... DEAD FROM WITHIN.

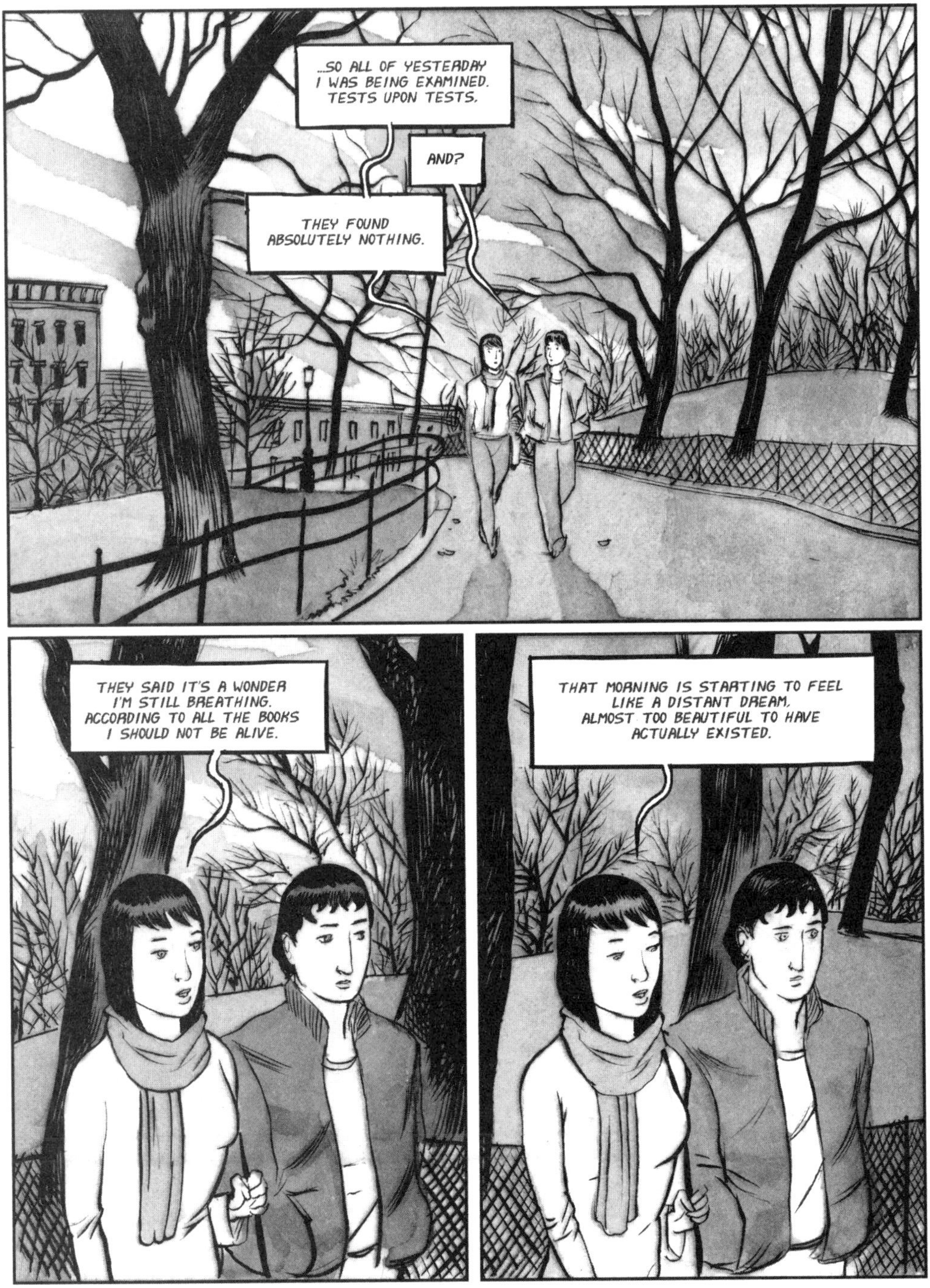
...SO ALL OF YESTERDAY I WAS BEING EXAMINED. TESTS UPON TESTS.
AND?
THEY FOUND ABSOLUTELY NOTHING.
THEY SAID IT'S A WONDER I'M STILL BREATHING. ACCORDING TO ALL THE BOOKS I SHOULD NOT BE ALIVE.
THAT MORNING IS STARTING TO FEEL LIKE A DISTANT DREAM, ALMOST TOO BEAUTIFUL TO HAVE ACTUALLY EXISTED.

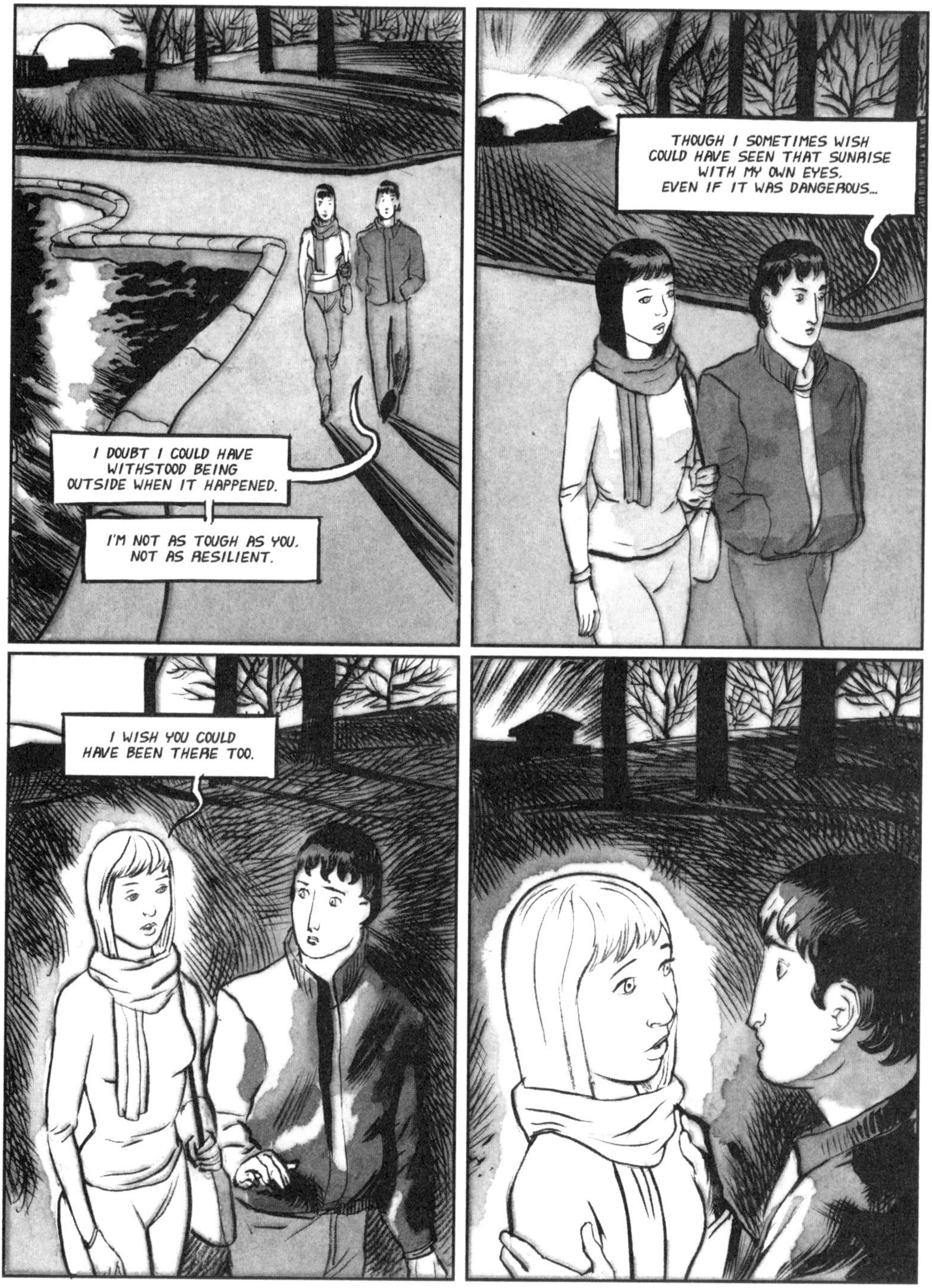
I DOUBT I COULD HAVE WITHSTOOD BEING OUTSIDE WHEN IT HAPPENED.
I'M NOT AS TOUGH AS YOU. NOT AS RESILIENT.
THOUGH I SOMETIMES WISH COULD HAVE SEEN THAT SUNRISE WITH MY OWN EYES. EVEN IF IT WAS DANGEROUS...
I WISH YOU COULD HAVE BEEN THERE TOO.

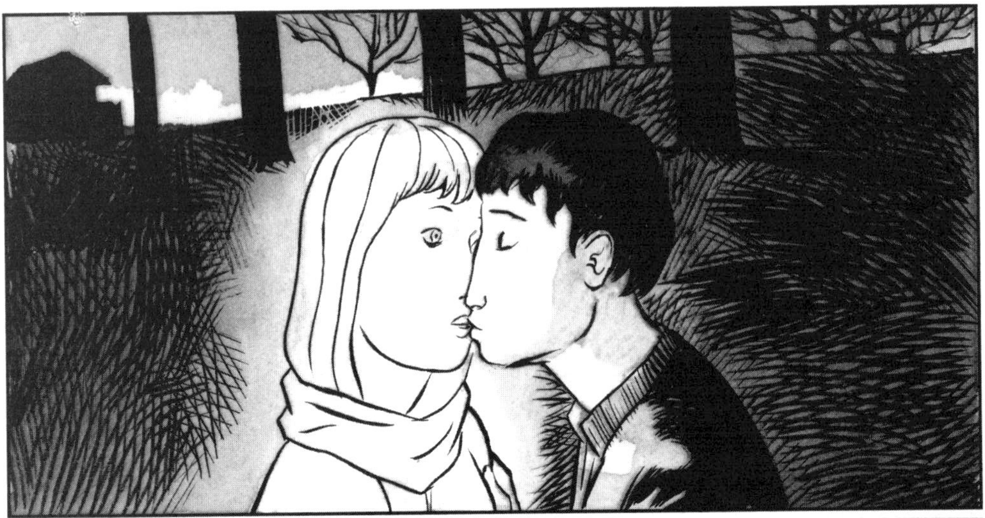

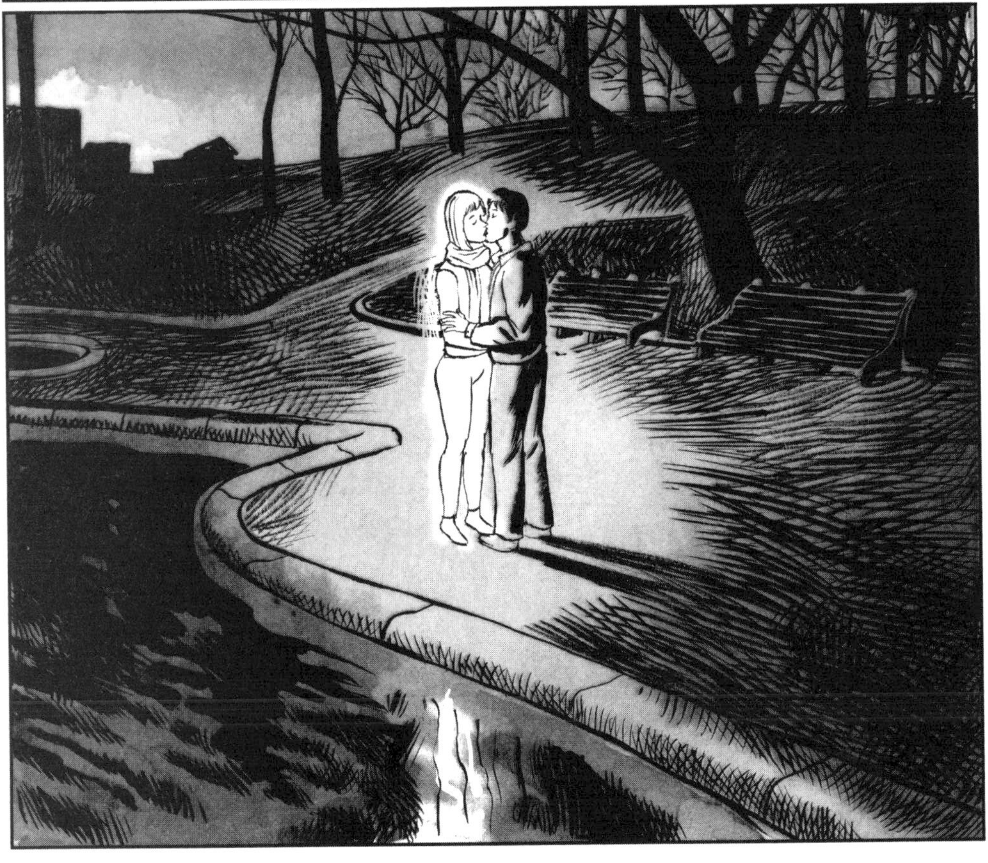

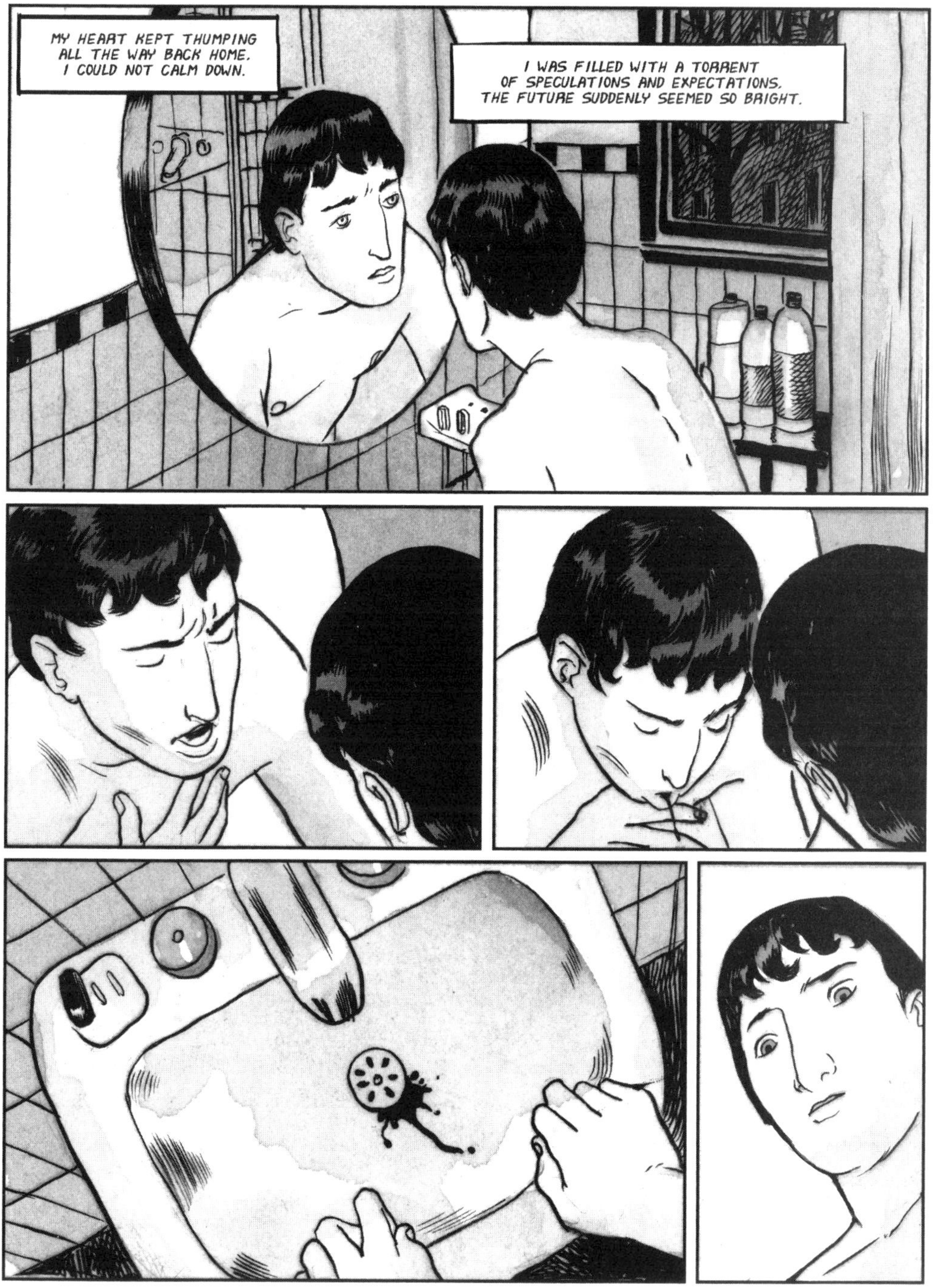
MY HEART KEPT THUMPING
ALL THE WAY BACK HOME.
I COULD NOT CALM DOWN.
I WAS FILLED WITH A TORRENT
OF SPECULATIONS AND EXPECTATIONS.
THE FUTURE SUDDENLY SEEMED SO BRIGHT.

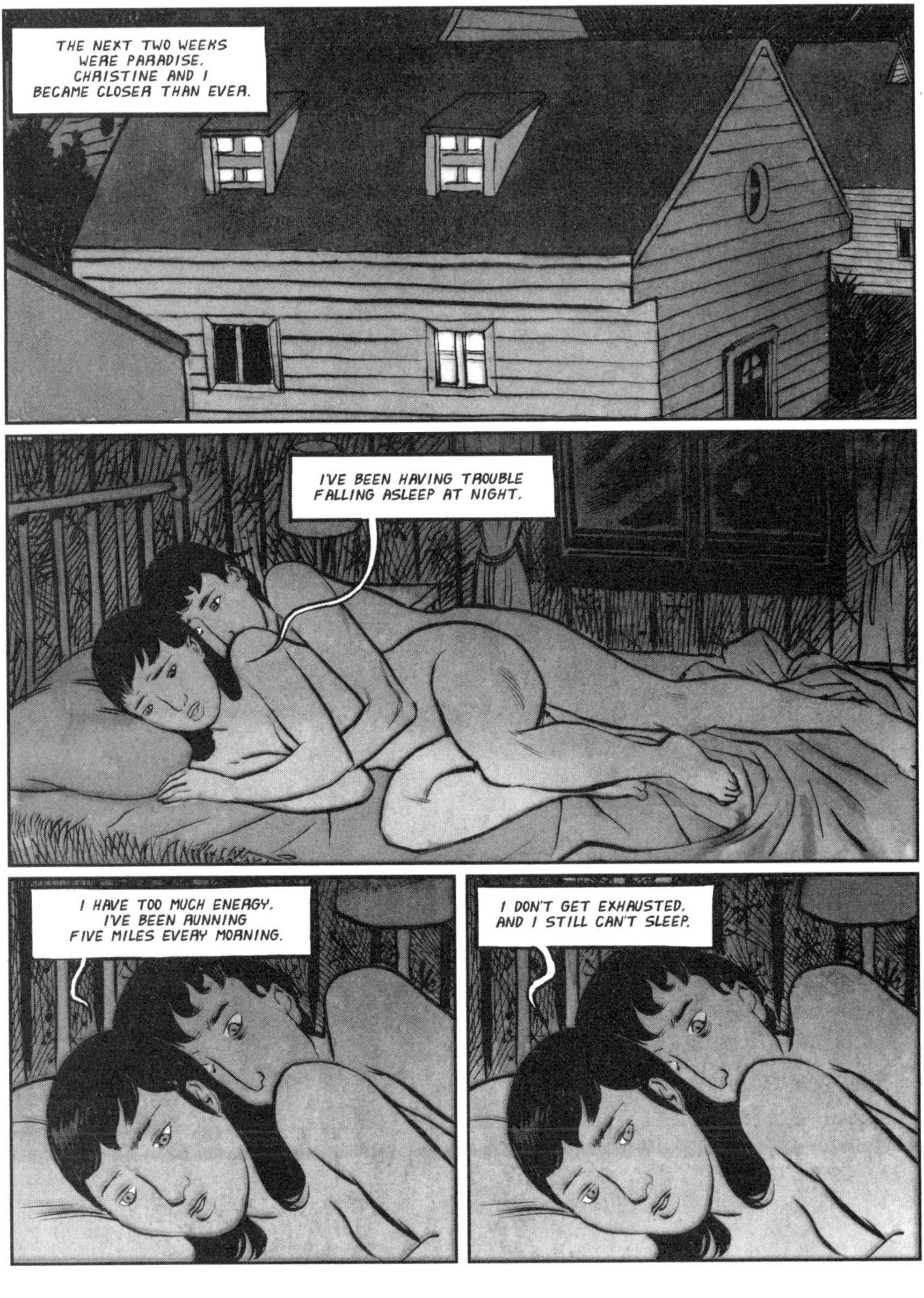
THE NEXT TWO WEEKS WERE PARADISE. CHRISTINE AND I BECAME CLOSER THAN EVER.
I'VE BEEN HAVING TROUBLE FALLING ASLEEP AT NIGHT.
I HAVE TOO MUCH ENERGY. I'VE BEEN RUNNING FIVE MILES EVERY MORNING.
I DON'T GET EXHAUSTED. AND I STILL CAN'T SLEEP.

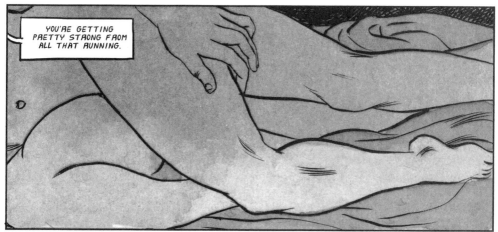

YOU'RE GETTING PRETTY STRONG FROM ALL THAT RUNNING.

I THINK YOU LOOK GREAT, HEALTHIER THAN EVER.

AHHK! AHKK!

ARE YOU ALL RIGHT?

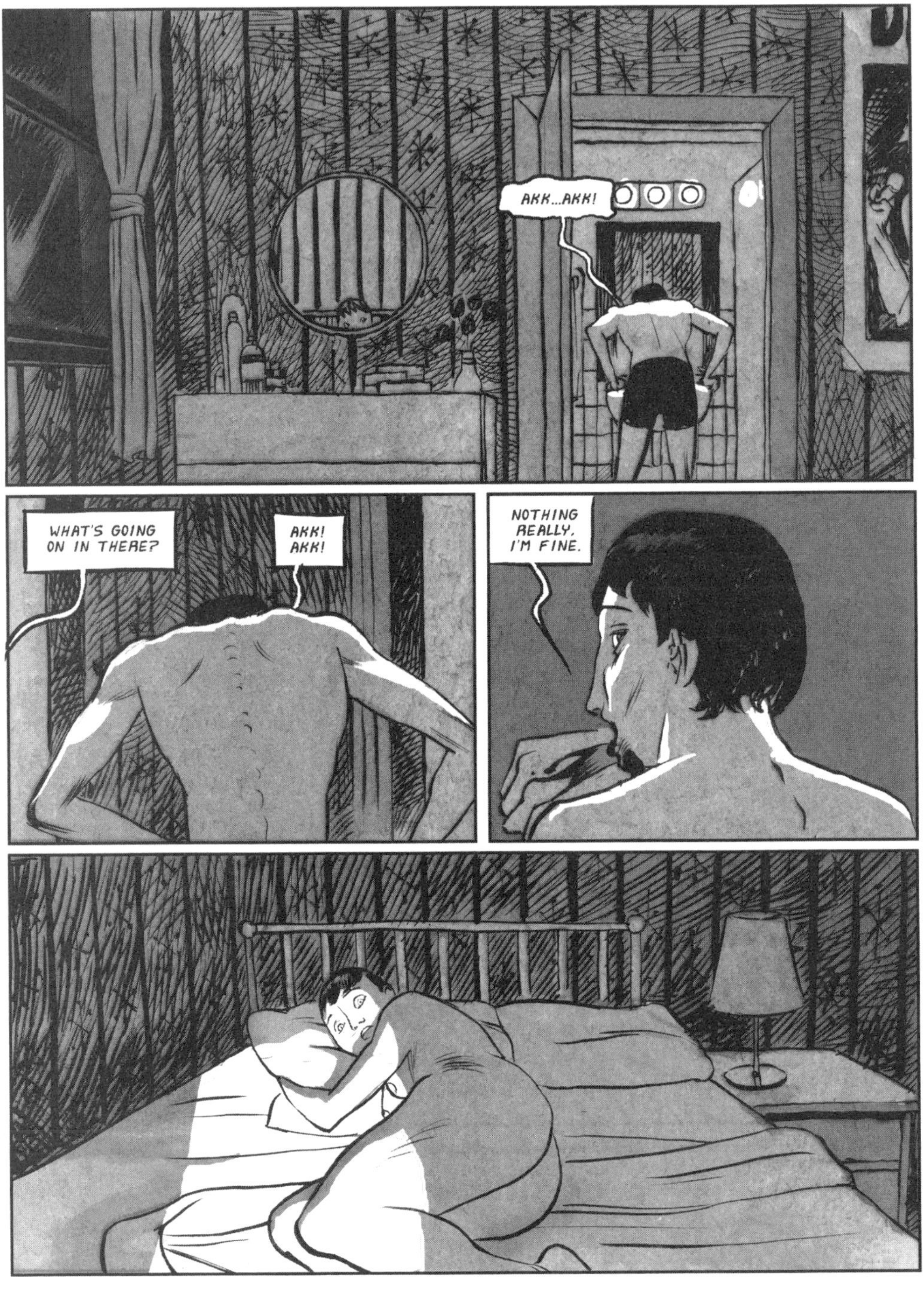
AKK...AKK!
WHAT'S GOING ON IN THERE?
AKK! AKK!
NOTHING REALLY, I'M FINE.

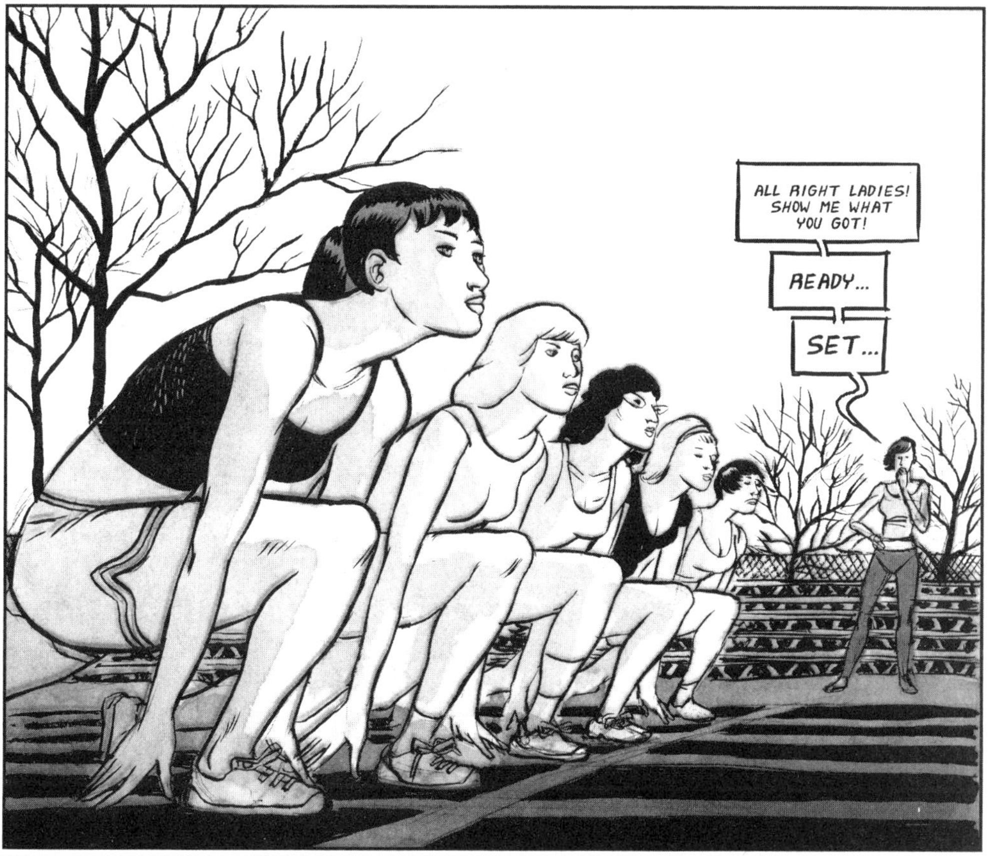
ALL RIGHT LADIES! SHOW ME WHAT YOU GOT!
READY...
SET...

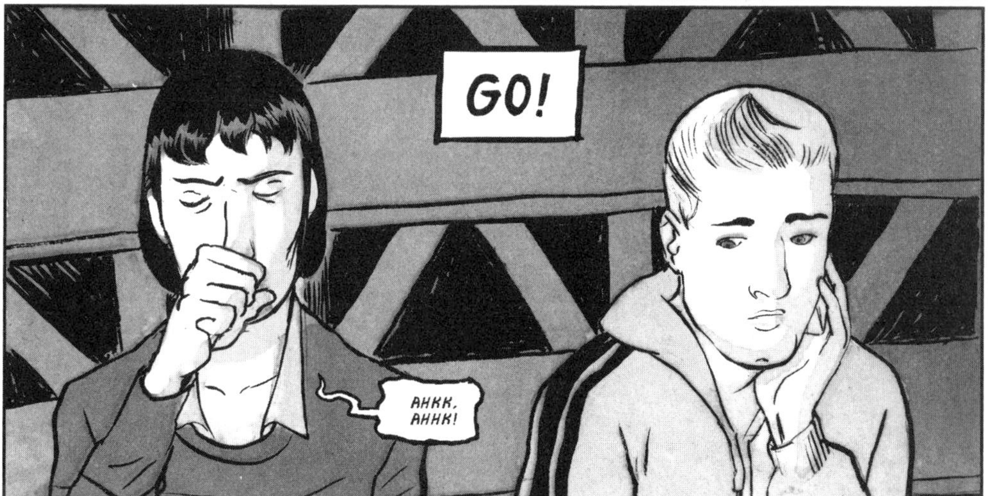
GO!
AHKK, AHHK!

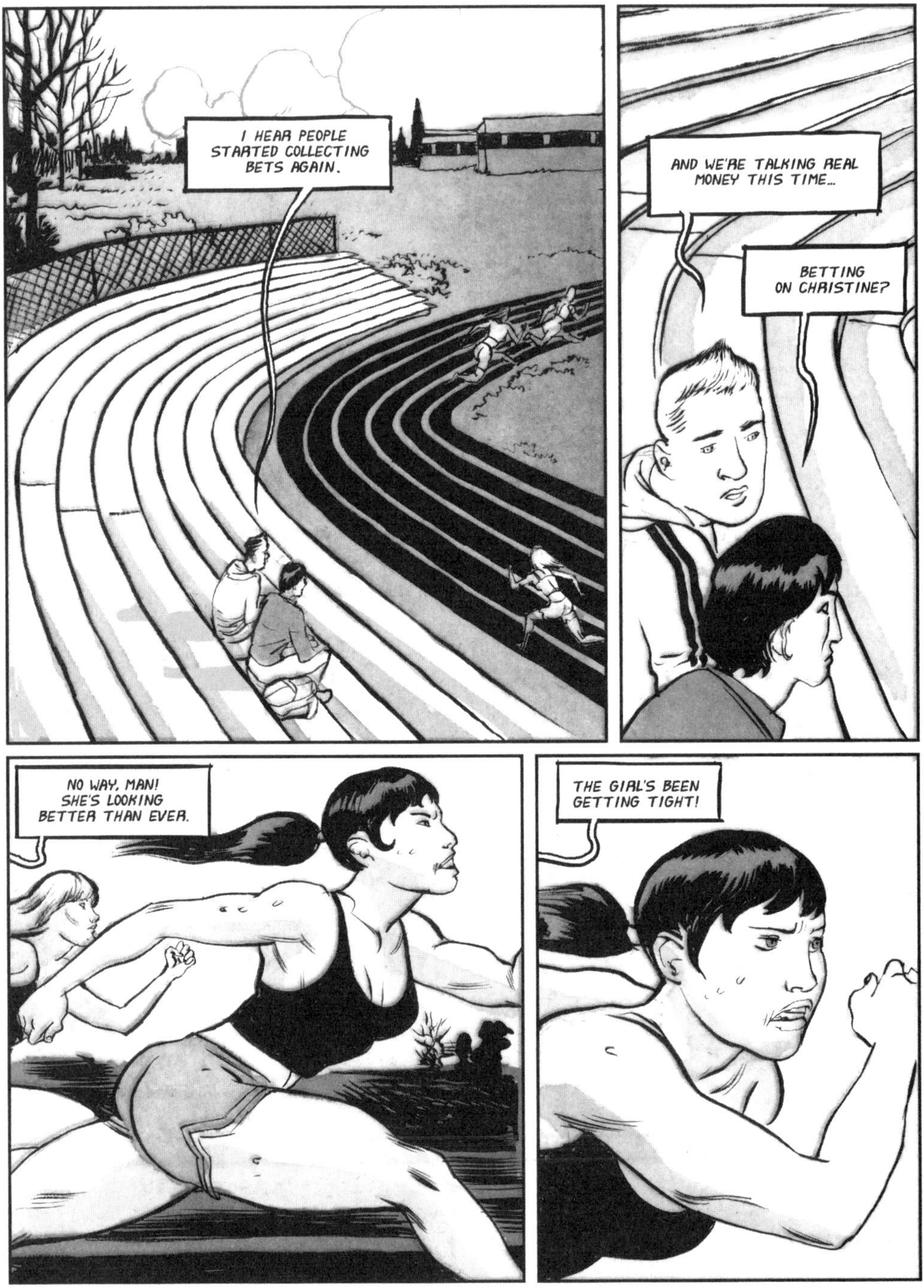
I HEAR PEOPLE STARTED COLLECTING BETS AGAIN.
AND WE'RE TALKING REAL MONEY THIS TIME...
BETTING ON CHRISTINE?
NO WAY, MAN! SHE'S LOOKING BETTER THAN EVER.
THE GIRL'S BEEN GETTING TIGHT!

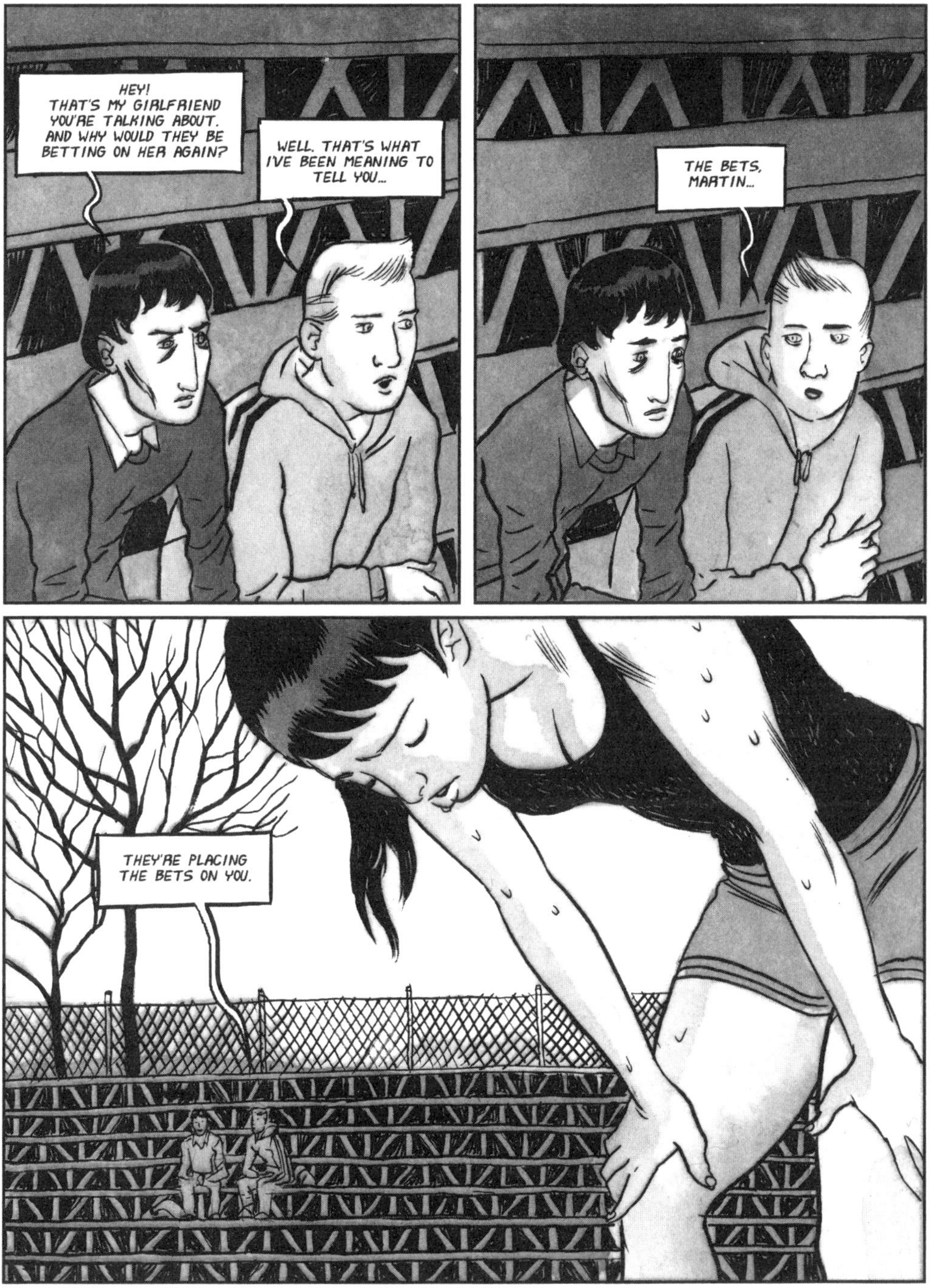
HEY!
THAT'S MY GIRLFRIEND YOU'RE TALKING ABOUT. AND WHY WOULD THEY BE BETTING ON HER AGAIN?
WELL. THAT'S WHAT I'VE BEEN MEANING TO TELL YOU...
THE BETS, MARTIN...
THEY'RE PLACING THE BETS ON YOU.

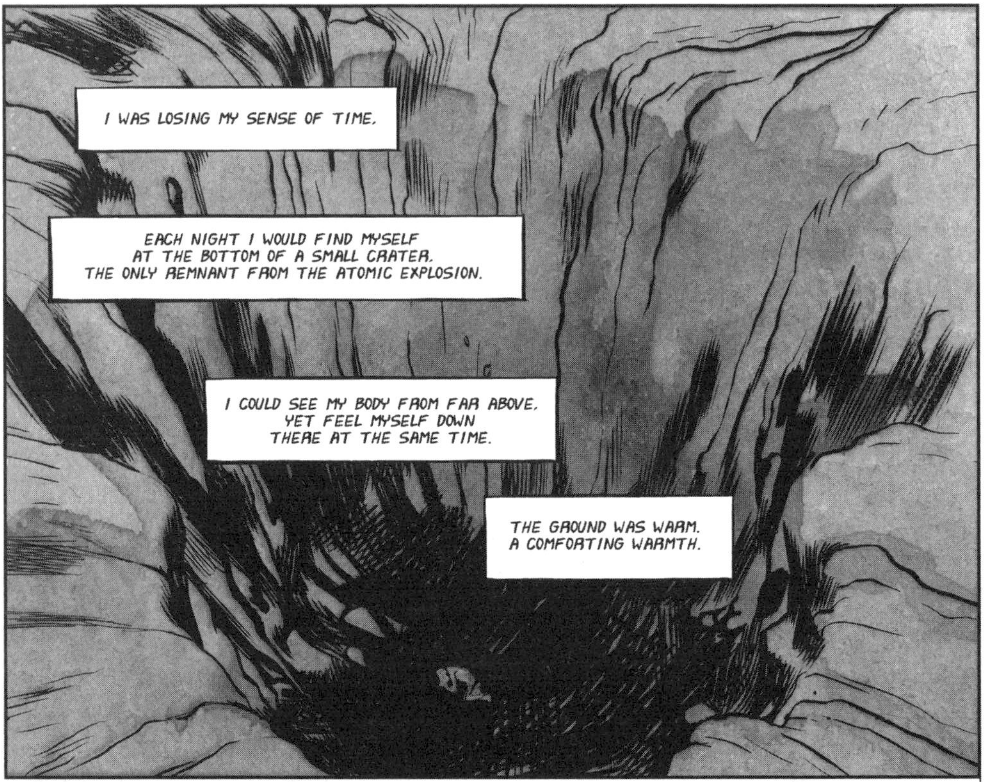
I WAS LOSING MY SENSE OF TIME.
EACH NIGHT I WOULD FIND MYSELF AT THE BOTTOM OF A SMALL CRATER. THE ONLY REMNANT FROM THE ATOMIC EXPLOSION.
I COULD SEE MY BODY FROM FAR ABOVE, YET FEEL MYSELF DOWN THERE AT THE SAME TIME.
THE GROUND WAS WARM. A COMFORTING WARMTH.

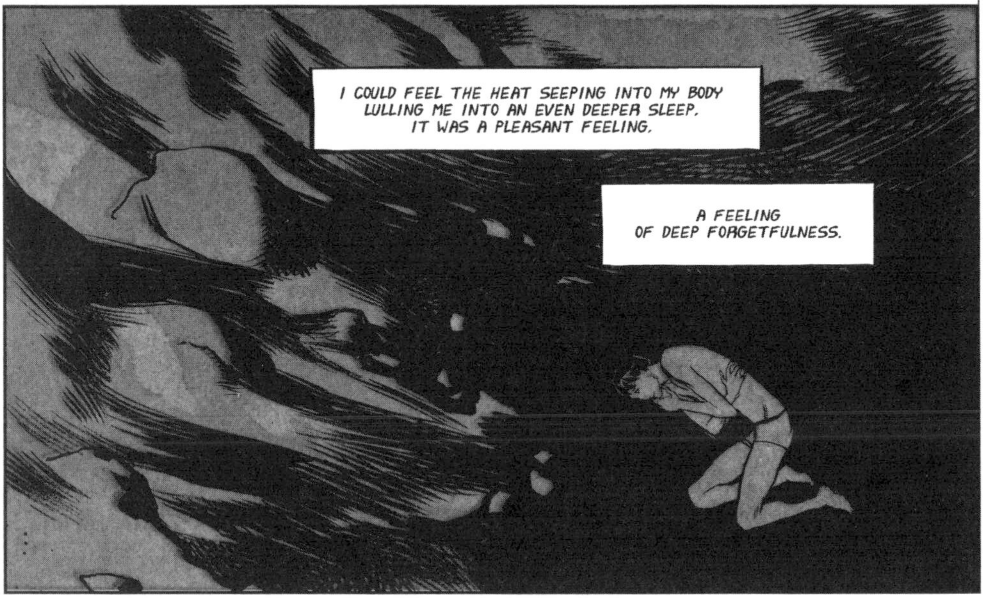
I COULD FEEL THE HEAT SEEPING INTO MY BODY LULLING ME INTO AN EVEN DEEPER SLEEP. IT WAS A PLEASANT FEELING.
A FEELING OF DEEP FORGETFULNESS.

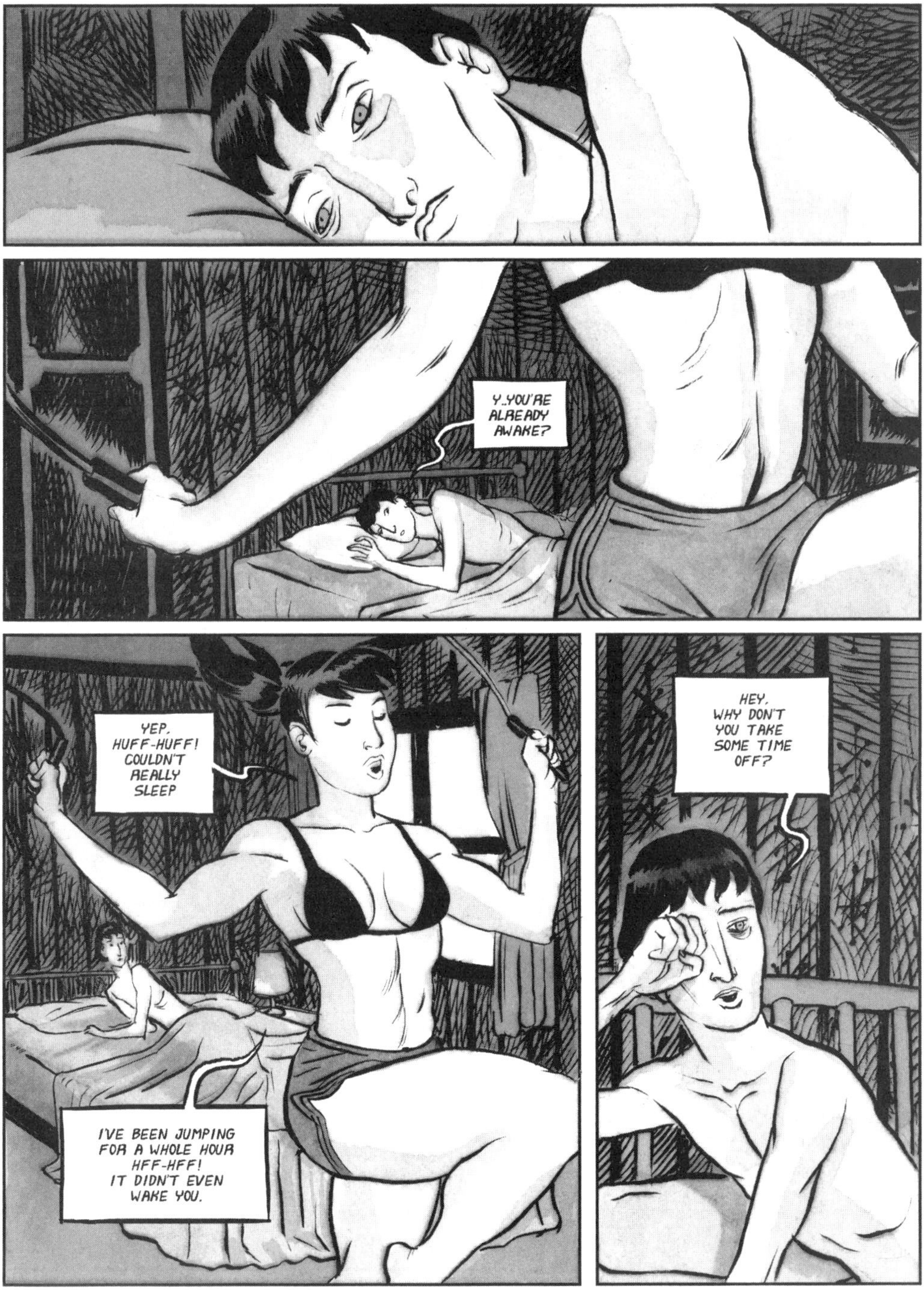
Y..YOU'RE ALREADY AWAKE?
YEP. HUFF-HUFF! COULDN'T REALLY SLEEP
I'VE BEEN JUMPING FOR A WHOLE HOUR HFF-HFF! IT DIDN'T EVEN WAKE YOU.
HEY, WHY DON'T YOU TAKE SOME TIME OFF?

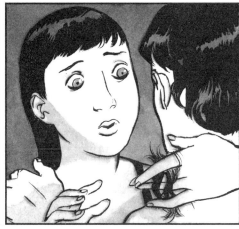

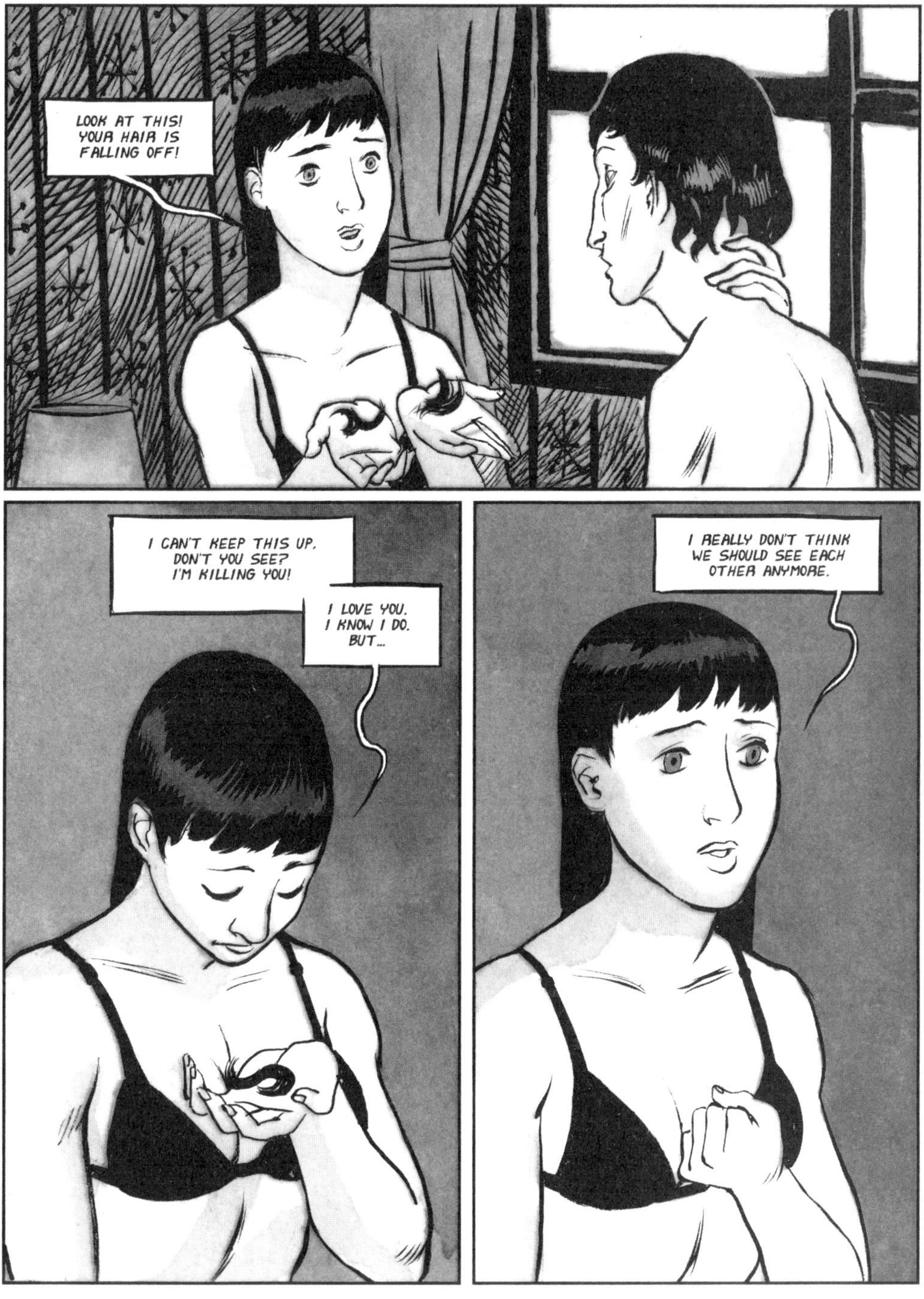
LOOK AT THIS! YOUR HAIR IS FALLING OFF!
I CAN'T KEEP THIS UP. DON'T YOU SEE? I'M KILLING YOU!
I LOVE YOU. I KNOW I DO. BUT...
I REALLY DON'T THINK WE SHOULD SEE EACH OTHER ANYMORE.

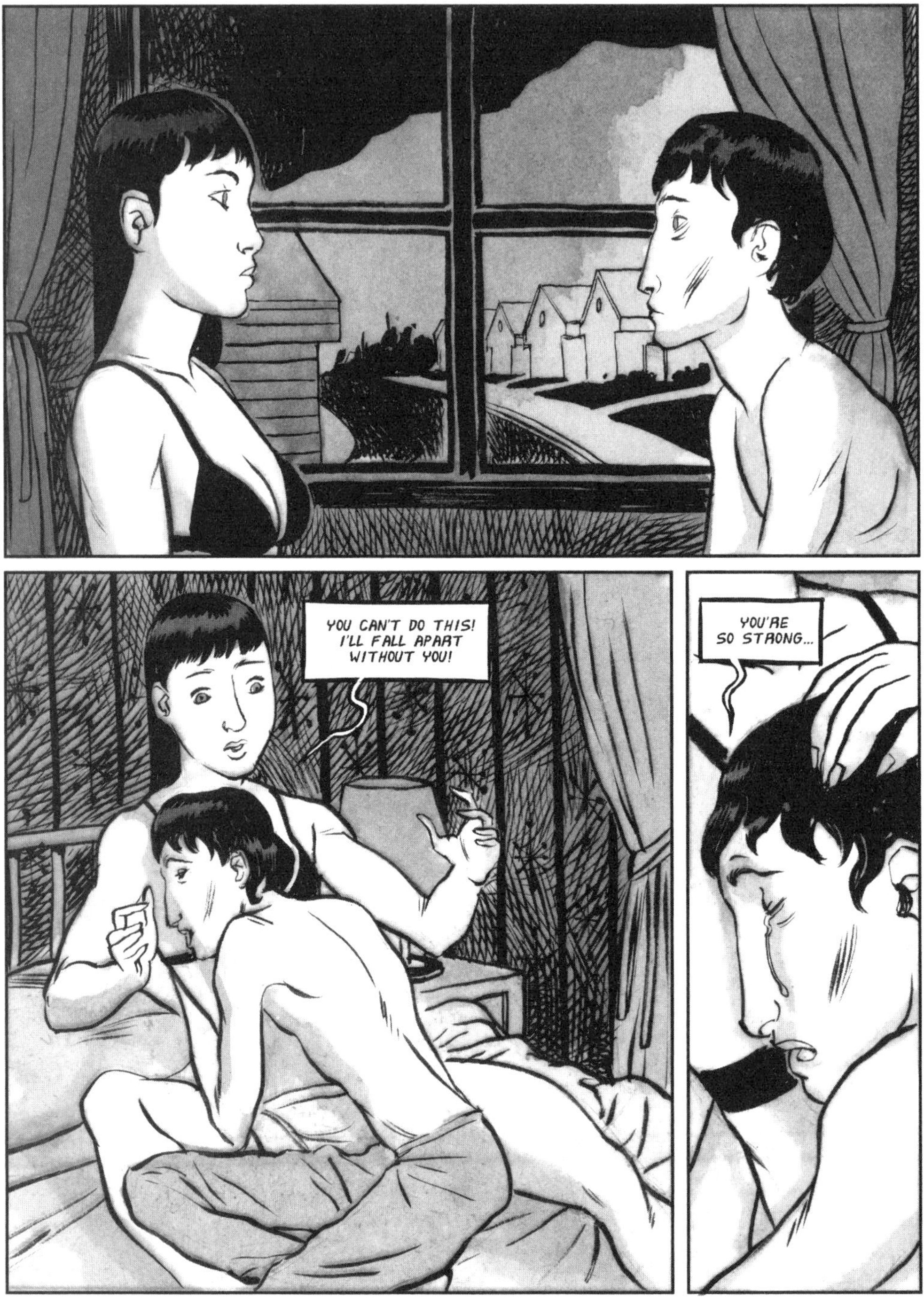
YOU CAN'T DO THIS! I'LL FALL APART WITHOUT YOU!
YOU'RE SO STRONG...

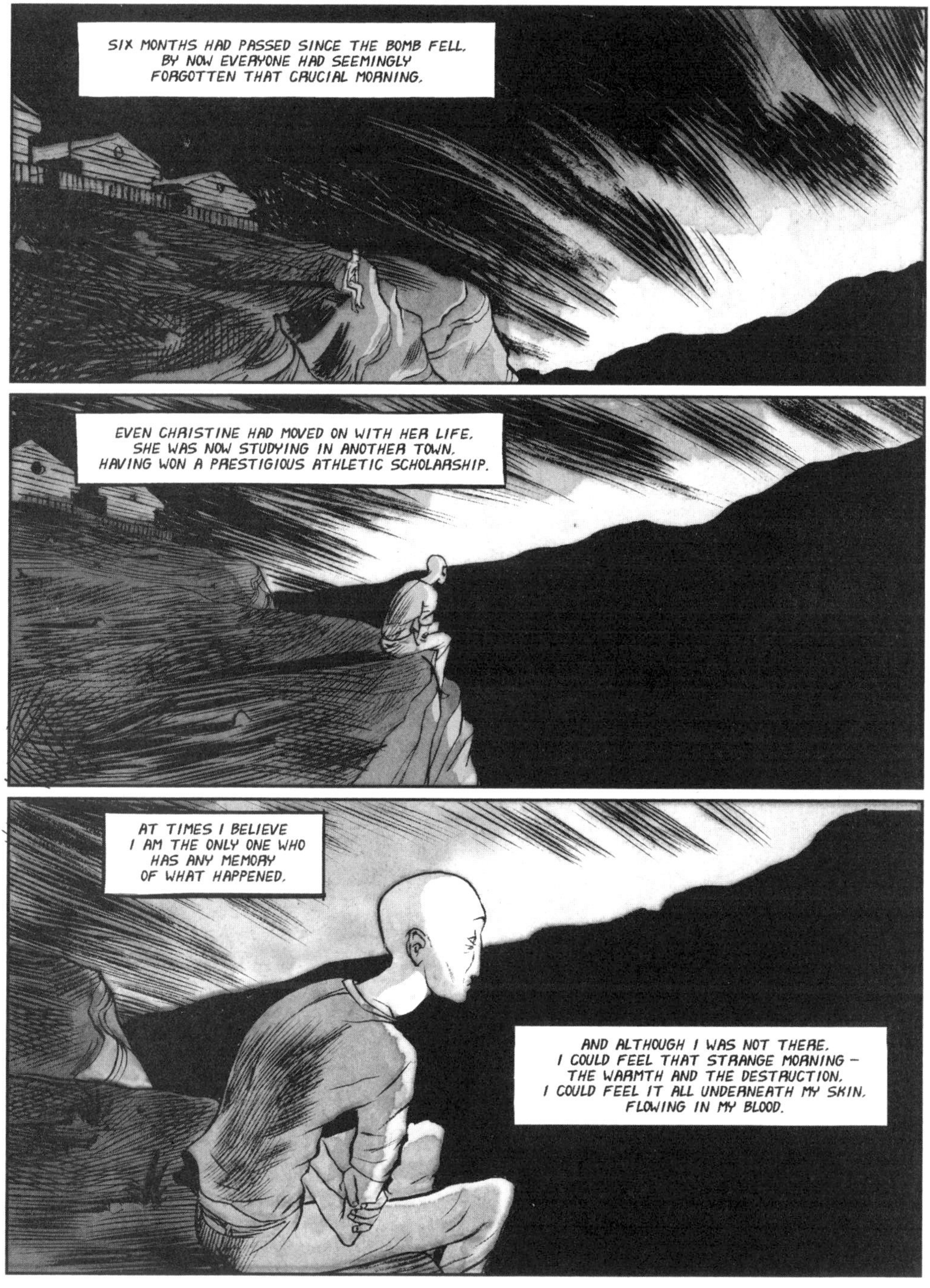
SIX MONTHS HAD PASSED SINCE THE BOMB FELL. BY NOW EVERYONE HAD SEEMINGLY FORGOTTEN THAT CRUCIAL MORNING.
EVEN CHRISTINE HAD MOVED ON WITH HER LIFE. SHE WAS NOW STUDYING IN ANOTHER TOWN, HAVING WON A PRESTIGIOUS ATHLETIC SCHOLARSHIP.
AT TIMES I BELIEVE I AM THE ONLY ONE WHO HAS ANY MEMORY OF WHAT HAPPENED.
AND ALTHOUGH I WAS NOT THERE, I COULD FEEL THAT STRANGE MORNING — THE WARMTH AND THE DESTRUCTION. I COULD FEEL IT ALL UNDERNEATH MY SKIN, FLOWING IN MY BLOOD.

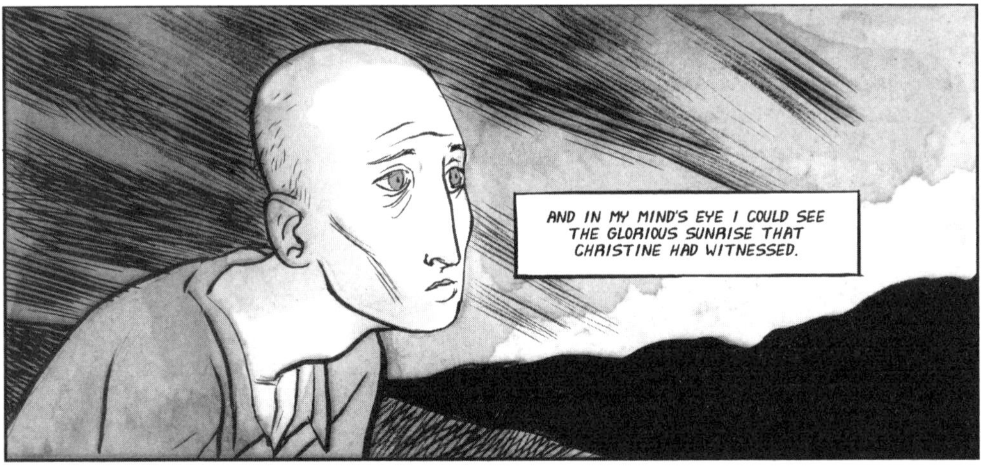
AND IN MY MIND'S EYE I COULD SEE THE GLORIOUS SUNRISE THAT CHRISTINE HAD WITNESSED.

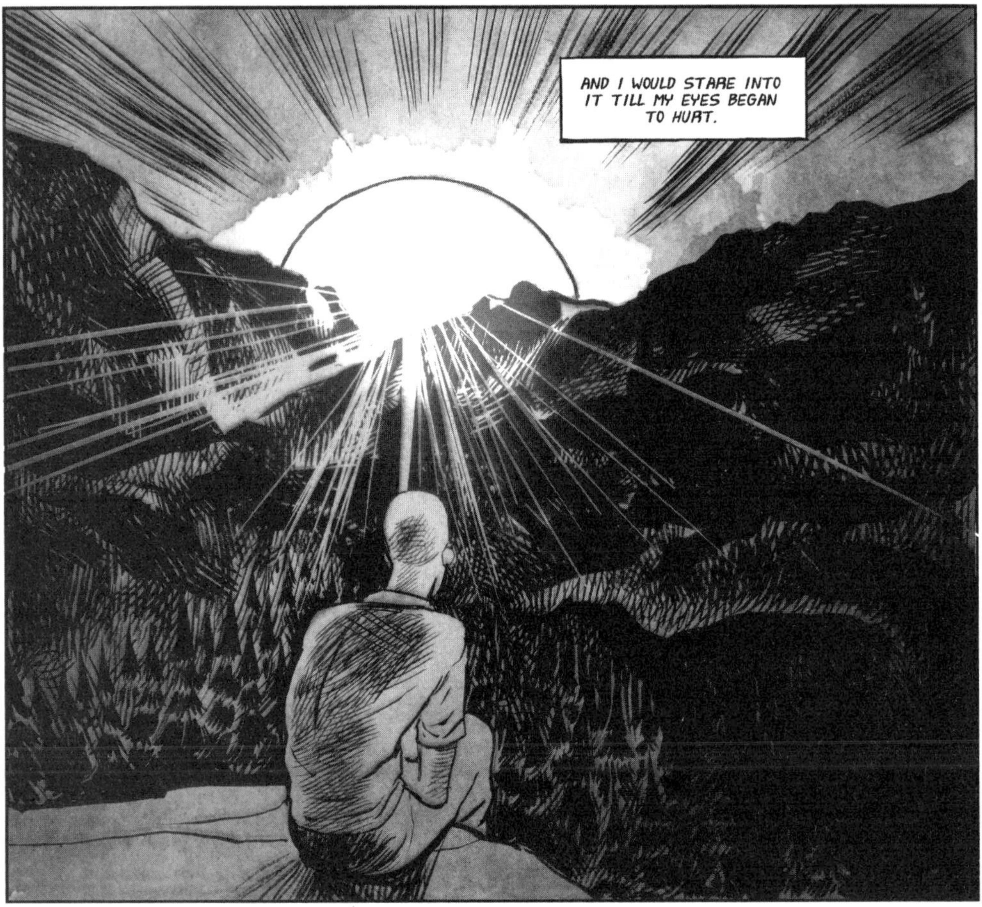
AND I WOULD STARE INTO IT TILL MY EYES BEGAN TO HURT.

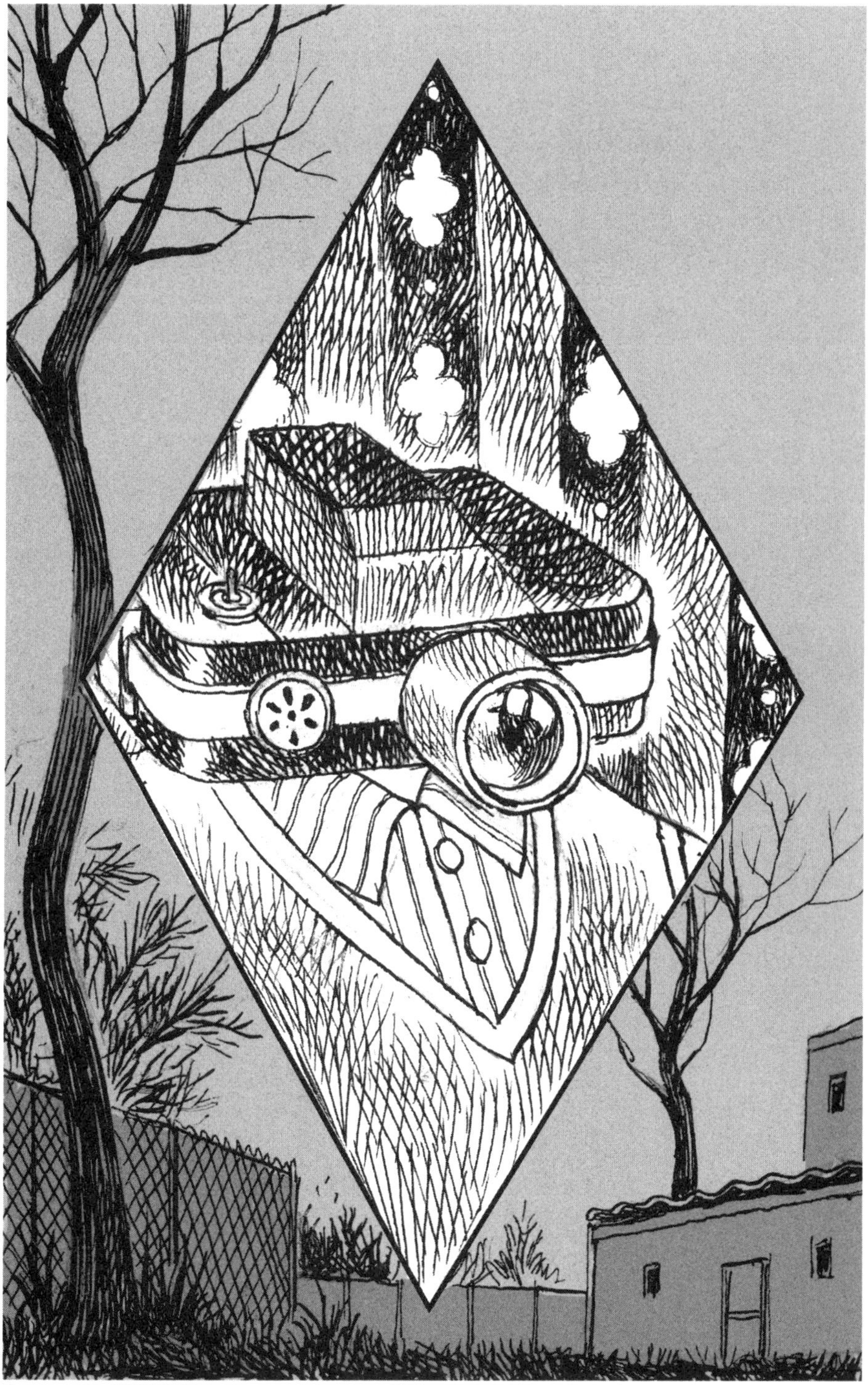

• GRANDPA MINOLTA •

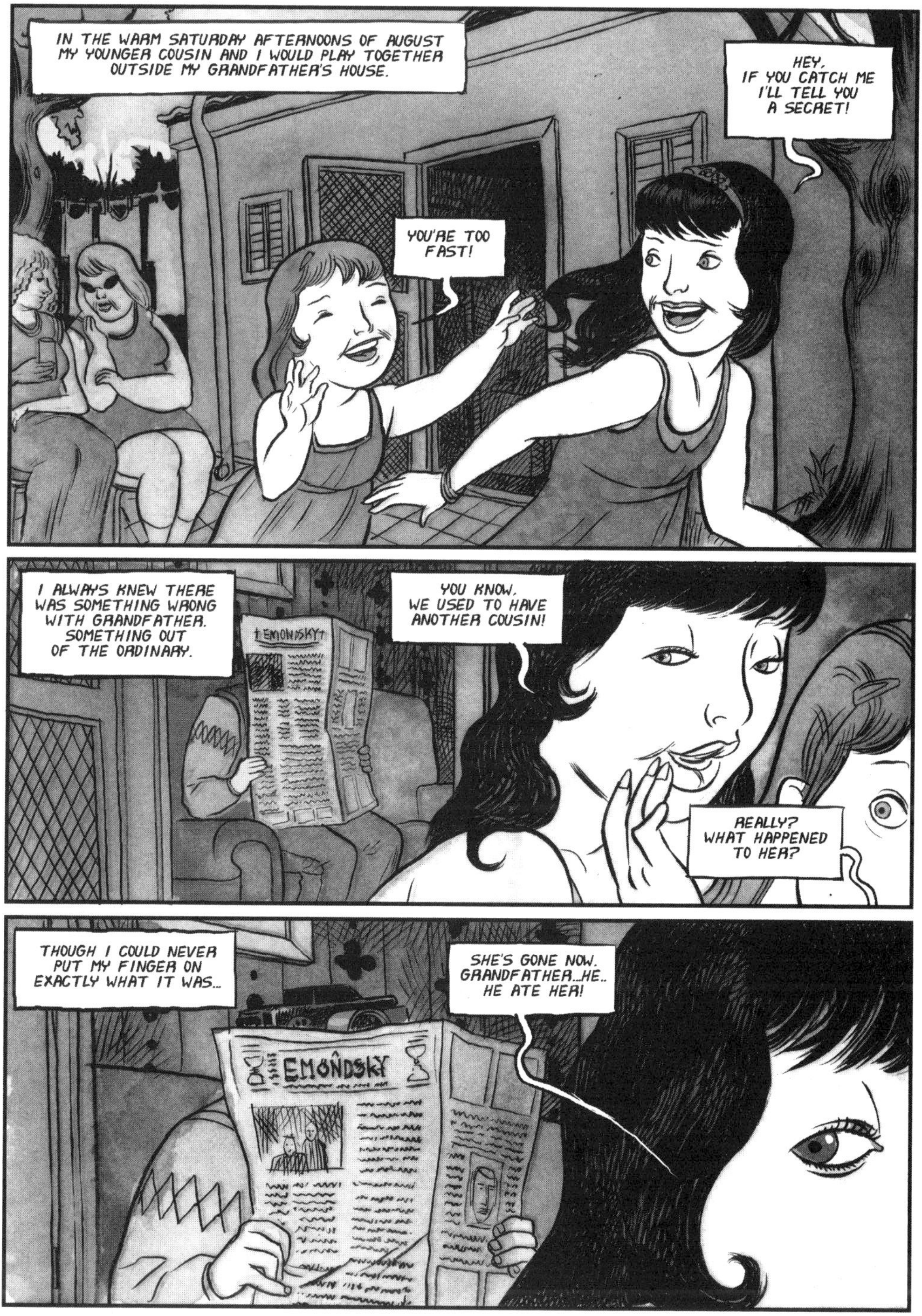
IN THE WARM SATURDAY AFTERNOONS OF AUGUST MY YOUNGER COUSIN AND I WOULD PLAY TOGETHER OUTSIDE MY GRANDFATHER'S HOUSE.
HEY, IF YOU CATCH ME I'LL TELL YOU A SECRET!
YOU'RE TOO FAST!
I ALWAYS KNEW THERE WAS SOMETHING WRONG WITH GRANDFATHER. SOMETHING OUT OF THE ORDINARY.
EMONDSKY
YOU KNOW, WE USED TO HAVE ANOTHER COUSIN!
REALLY? WHAT HAPPENED TO HER?
THOUGH I COULD NEVER PUT MY FINGER ON EXACTLY WHAT IT WAS...
SHE'S GONE NOW. GRANDFATHER...HE.. HE ATE HER!
EMONDSKY

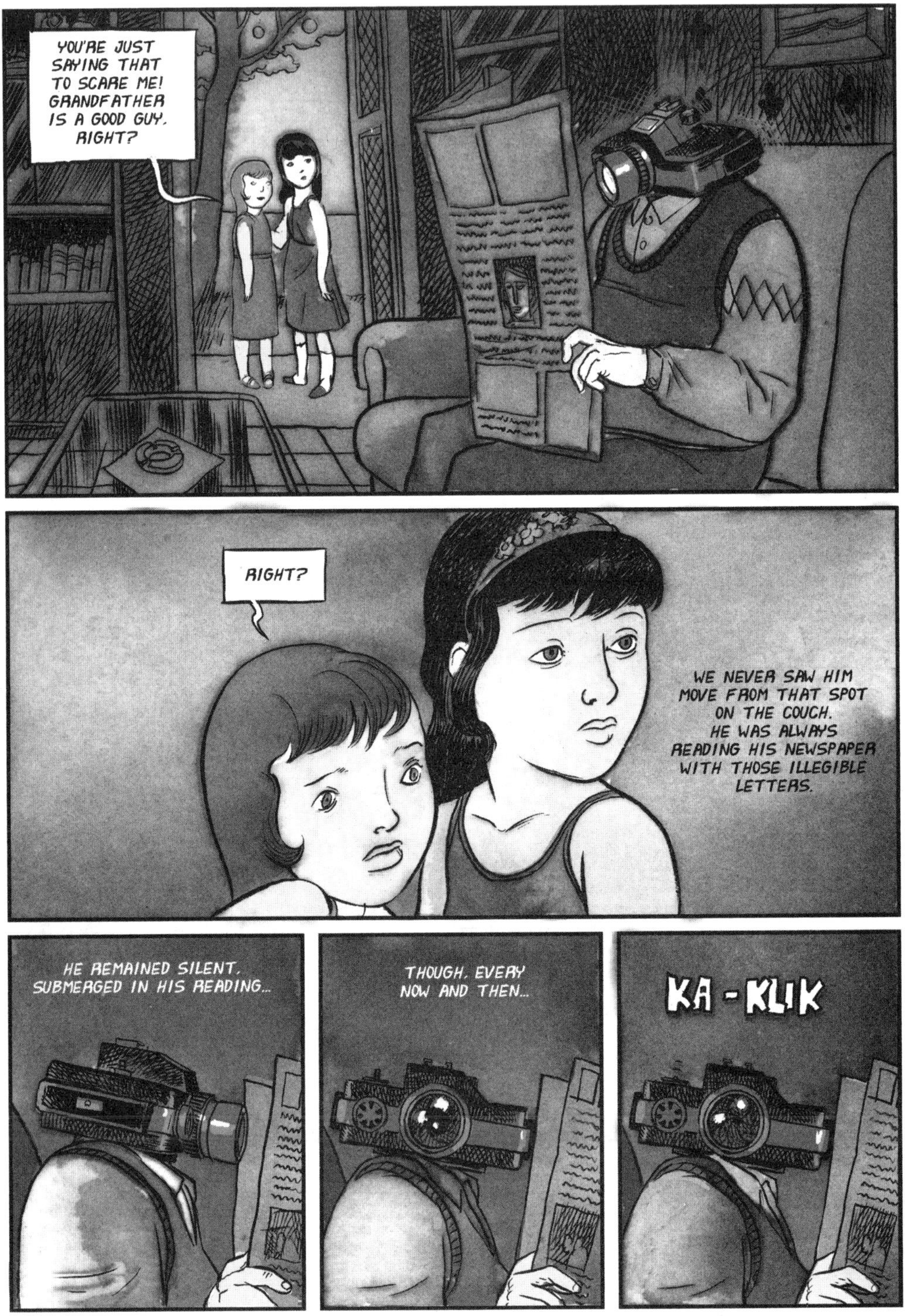
YOU'RE JUST SAYING THAT TO SCARE ME! GRANDFATHER IS A GOOD GUY, RIGHT?
RIGHT?
WE NEVER SAW HIM MOVE FROM THAT SPOT ON THE COUCH. HE WAS ALWAYS READING HIS NEWSPAPER WITH THOSE ILLEGIBLE LETTERS.
HE REMAINED SILENT, SUBMERGED IN HIS READING...
THOUGH, EVERY NOW AND THEN...
KA - KLIK

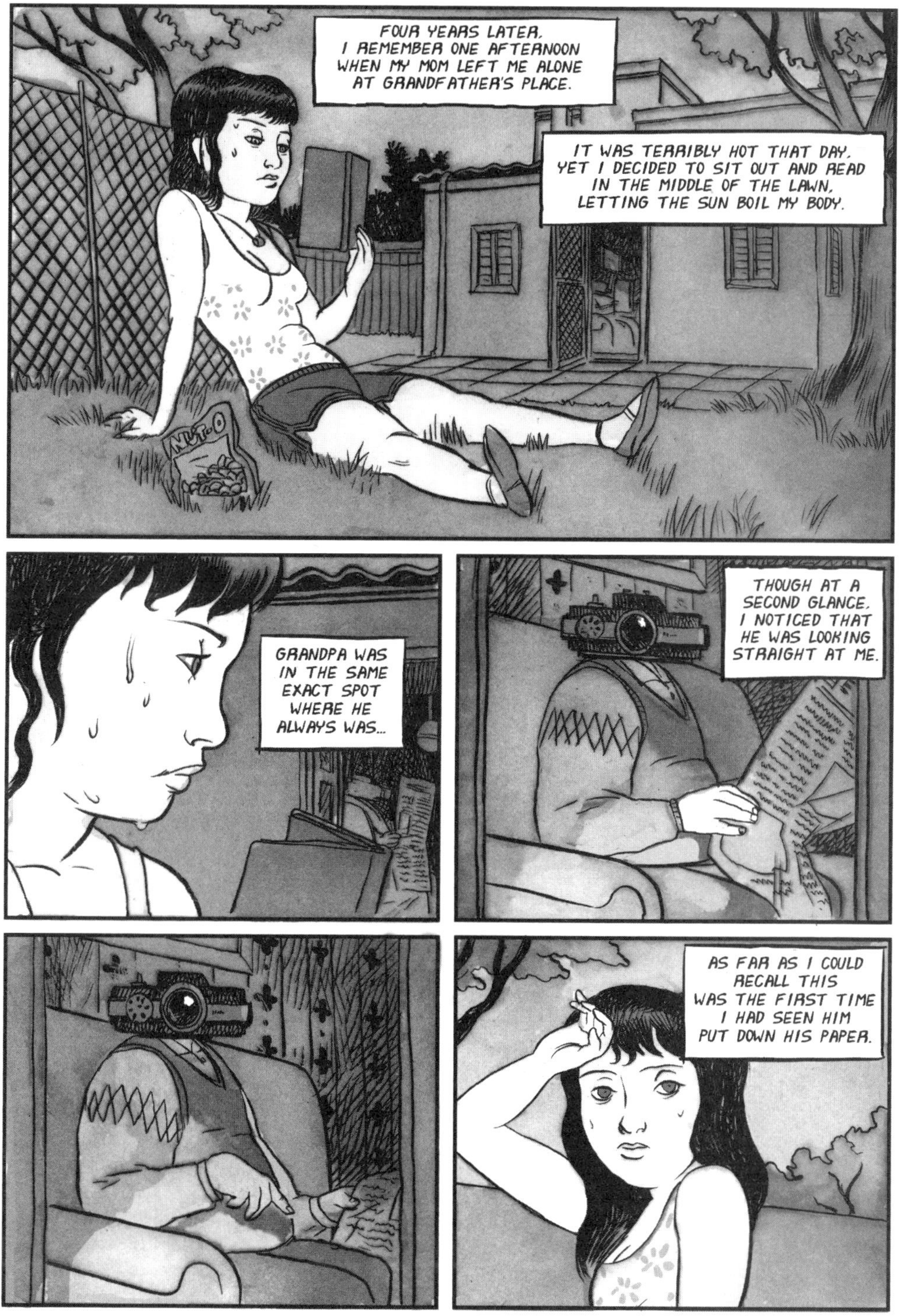
FOUR YEARS LATER, I REMEMBER ONE AFTERNOON WHEN MY MOM LEFT ME ALONE AT GRANDFATHER'S PLACE.
IT WAS TERRIBLY HOT THAT DAY. YET I DECIDED TO SIT OUT AND READ IN THE MIDDLE OF THE LAWN, LETTING THE SUN BOIL MY BODY.
NUT-O
GRANDPA WAS IN THE SAME EXACT SPOT WHERE HE ALWAYS WAS...
THOUGH AT A SECOND GLANCE, I NOTICED THAT HE WAS LOOKING STRAIGHT AT ME.
AS FAR AS I COULD RECALL THIS WAS THE FIRST TIME I HAD SEEN HIM PUT DOWN HIS PAPER.

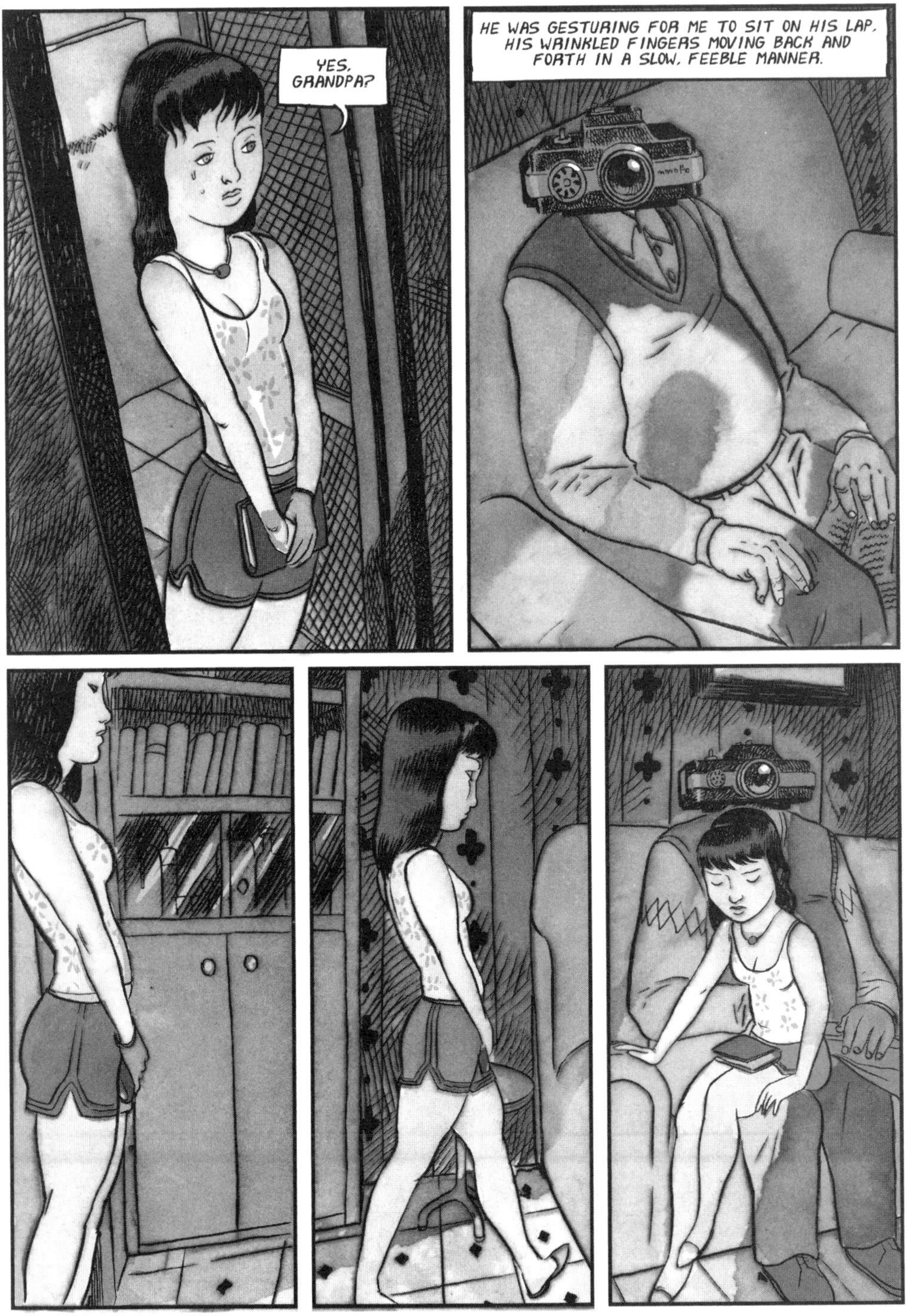
YES, GRANDPA?
HE WAS GESTURING FOR ME TO SIT ON HIS LAP, HIS WRINKLED FINGERS MOVING BACK AND FORTH IN A SLOW, FEEBLE MANNER.

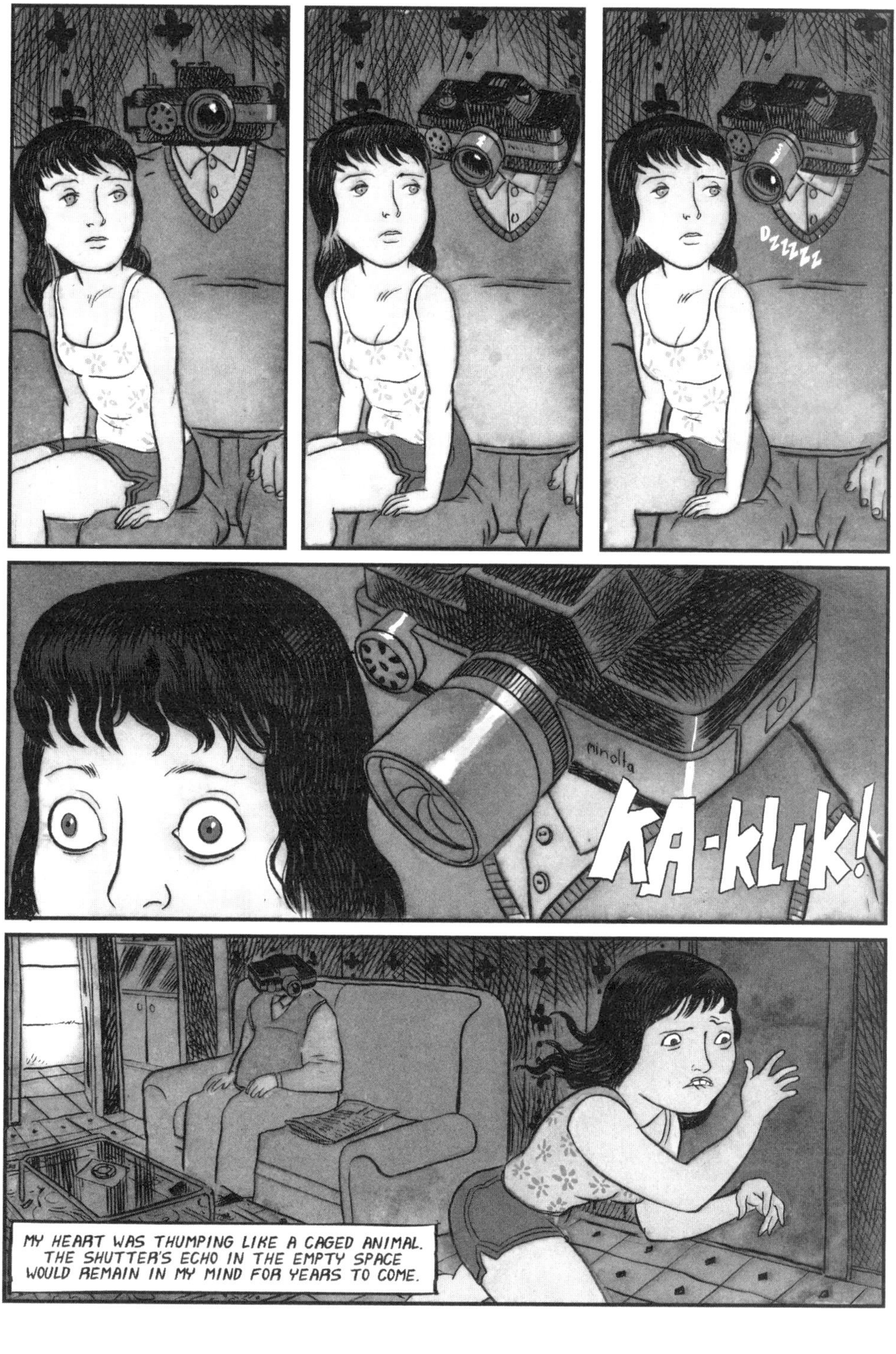
DZZZZZ
minolta
KA-KLIK!
MY HEART WAS THUMPING LIKE A CAGED ANIMAL. THE SHUTTER'S ECHO IN THE EMPTY SPACE WOULD REMAIN IN MY MIND FOR YEARS TO COME.

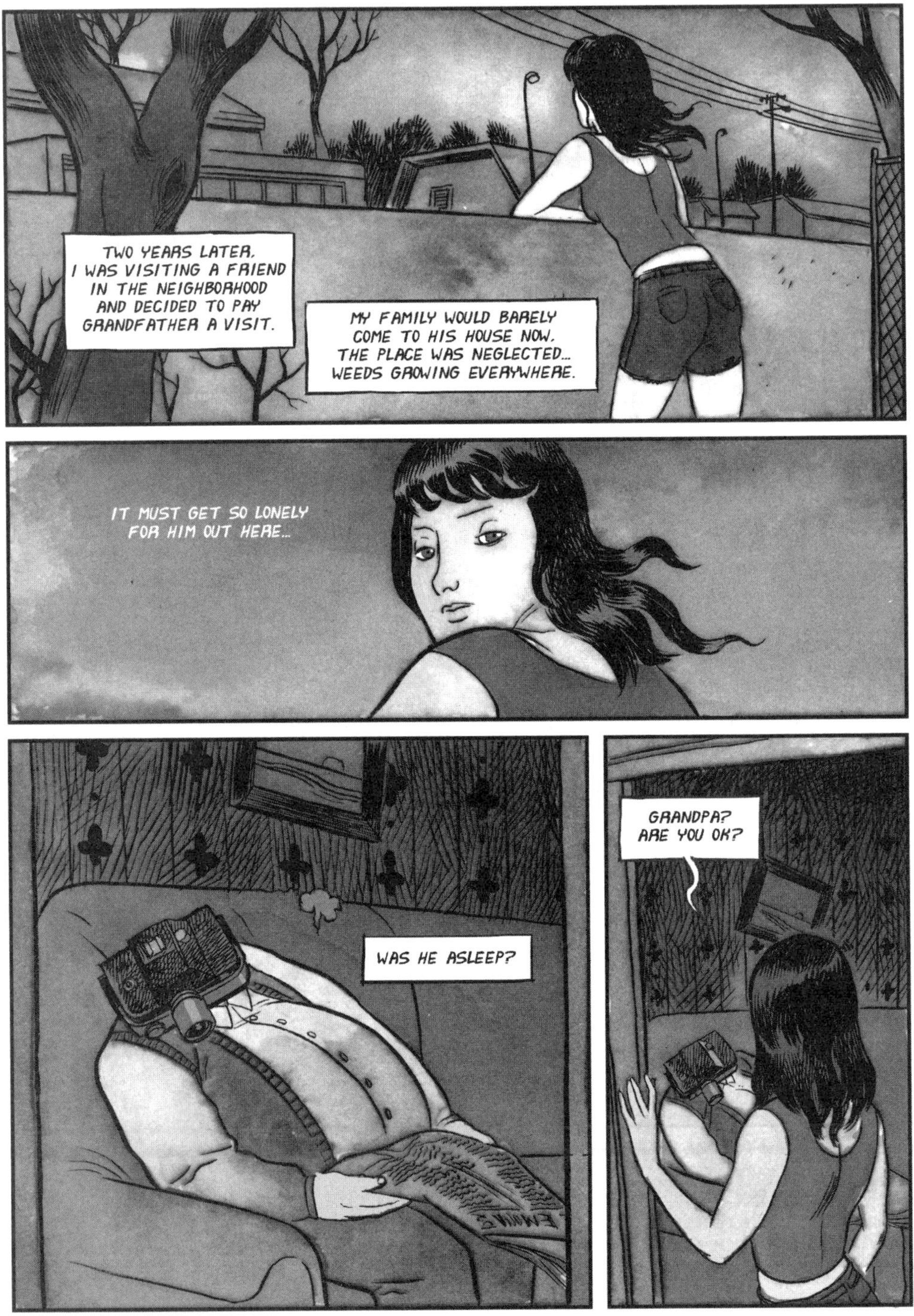
TWO YEARS LATER, I WAS VISITING A FRIEND IN THE NEIGHBORHOOD AND DECIDED TO PAY GRANDFATHER A VISIT.
MY FAMILY WOULD BARELY COME TO HIS HOUSE NOW. THE PLACE WAS NEGLECTED... WEEDS GROWING EVERYWHERE.
IT MUST GET SO LONELY FOR HIM OUT HERE...
WAS HE ASLEEP?
GRANDPA? ARE YOU OK?

SOMETHING WAS WRONG. I COULD TELL. HIS BLOATED STOMACH WASN'T MOVING. HE WASN'T BREATHING.

I HAD TO TOUCH HIM

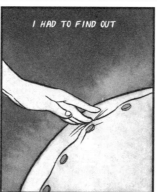

I HAD TO FIND OUT

AND THEN...

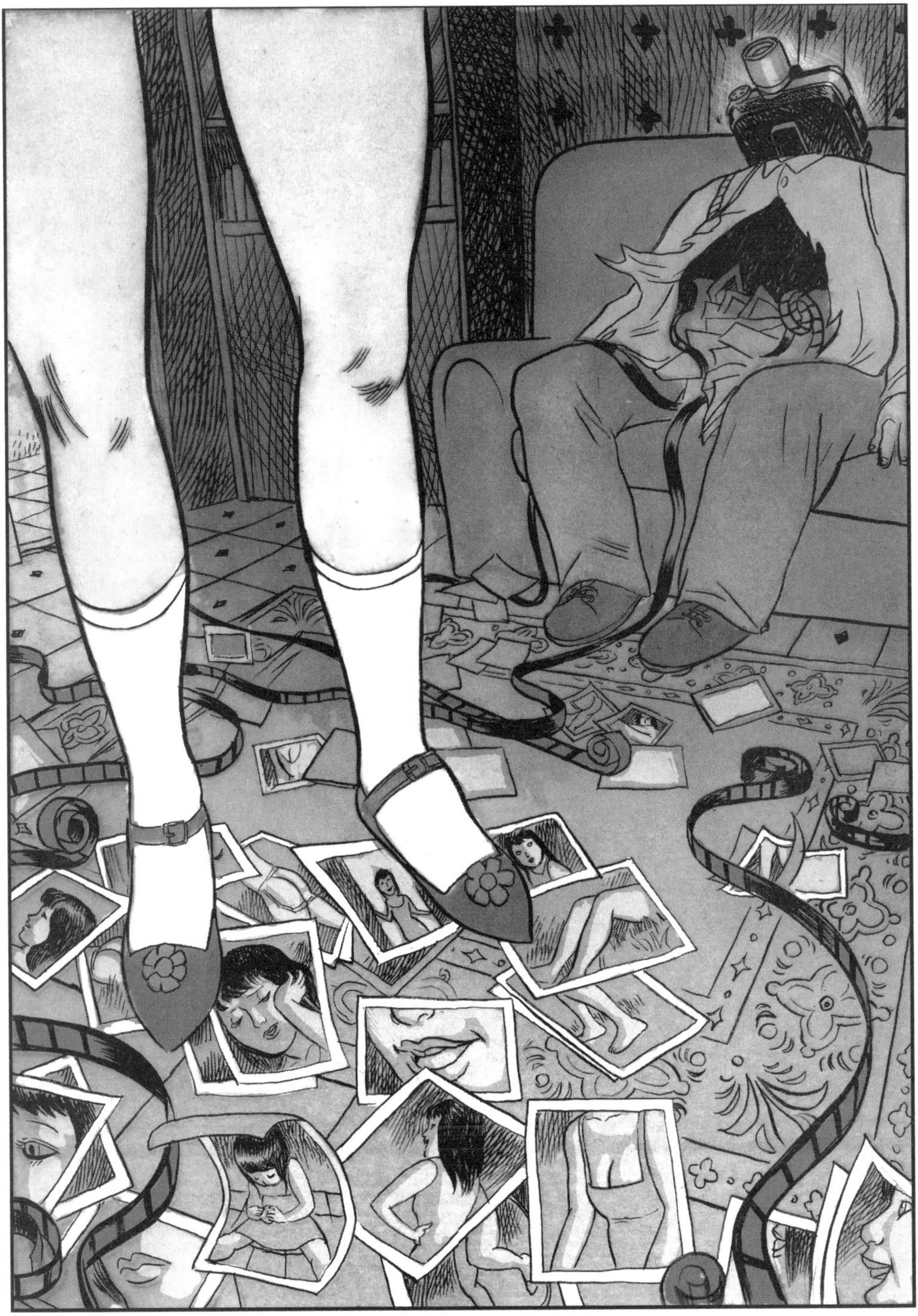

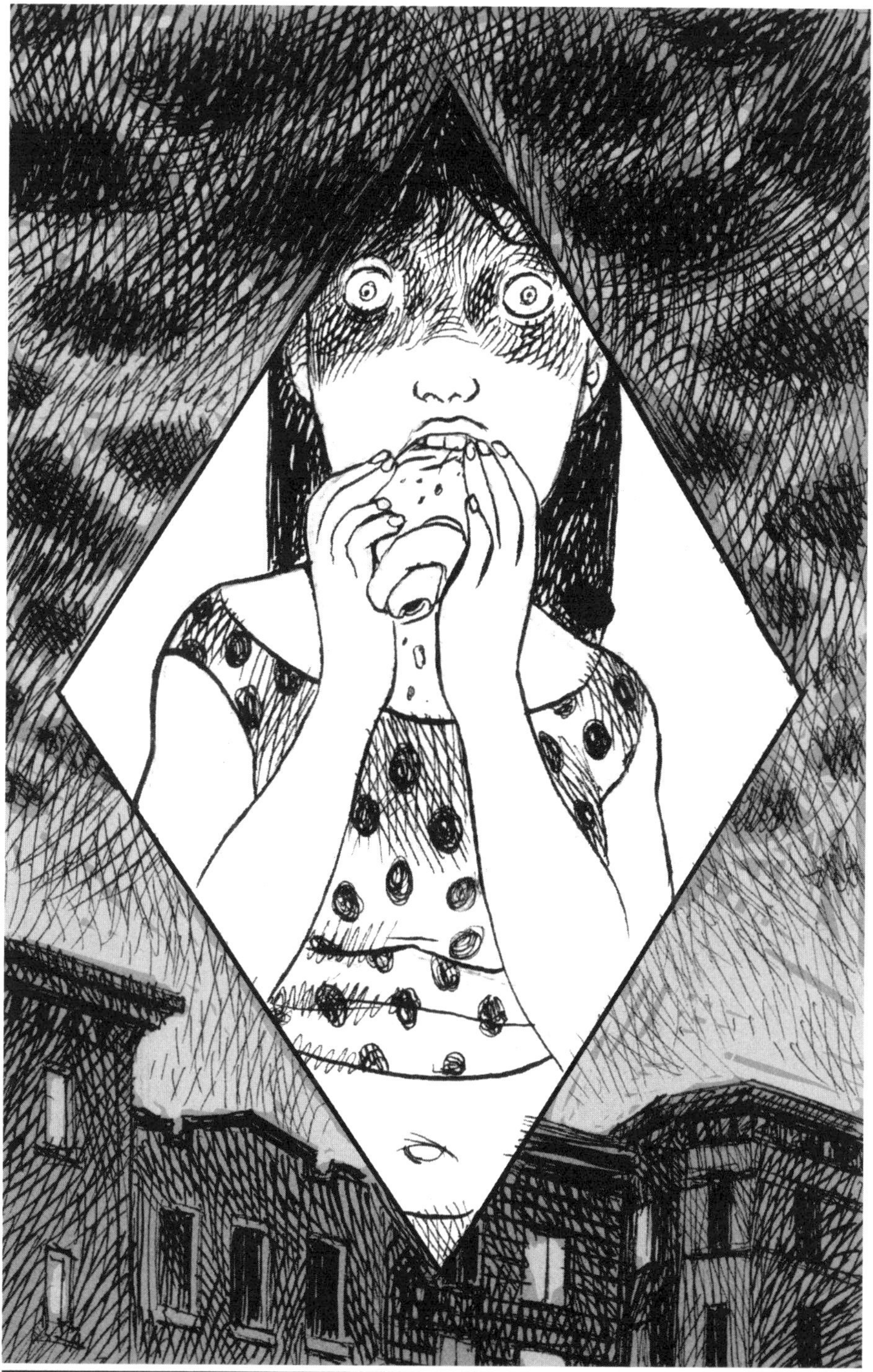

• PASTRY PARADISE •

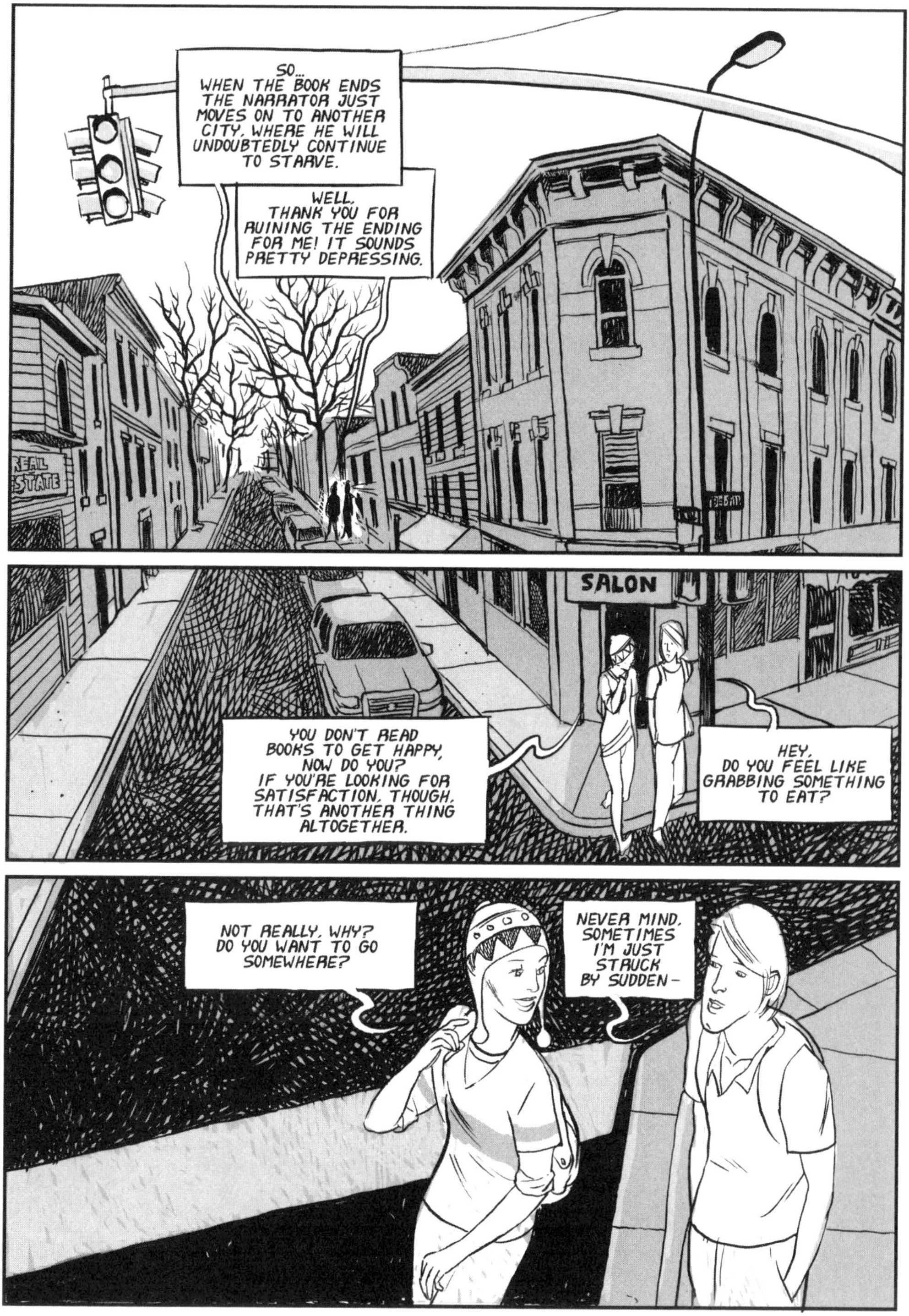
SO... WHEN THE BOOK ENDS THE NARRATOR JUST MOVES ON TO ANOTHER CITY, WHERE HE WILL UNDOUBTEDLY CONTINUE TO STARVE.
WELL, THANK YOU FOR RUINING THE ENDING FOR ME! IT SOUNDS PRETTY DEPRESSING.
REAL ESTATE
SALON
YOU DON'T READ BOOKS TO GET HAPPY, NOW DO YOU? IF YOU'RE LOOKING FOR SATISFACTION, THOUGH, THAT'S ANOTHER THING ALTOGETHER.
HEY, DO YOU FEEL LIKE GRABBING SOMETHING TO EAT?
NOT REALLY. WHY? DO YOU WANT TO GO SOMEWHERE?
NEVER MIND. SOMETIMES I'M JUST STRUCK BY SUDDEN-

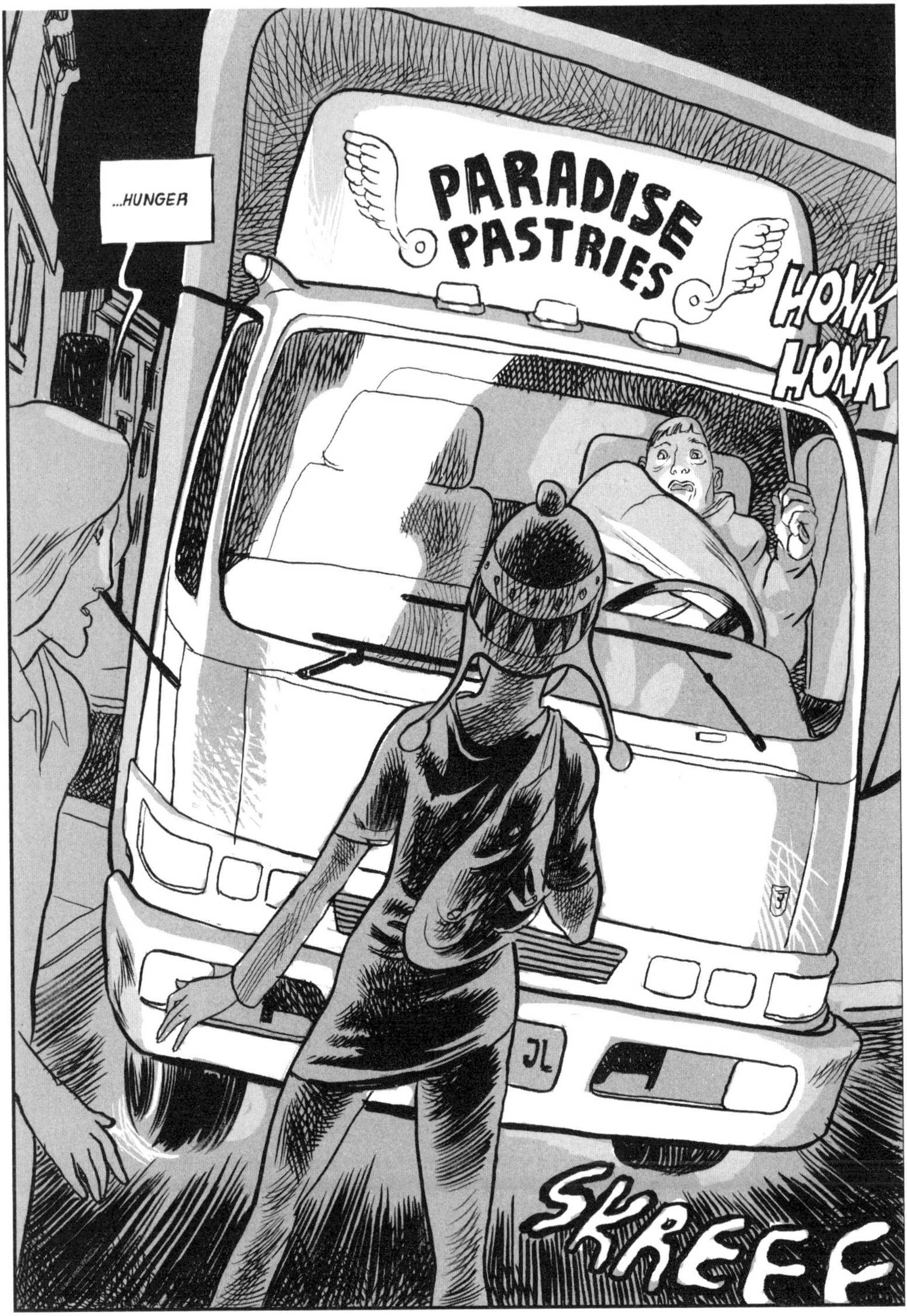
...HUNGER
PARADISE PASTRIES
HONK HONK
SKREEE

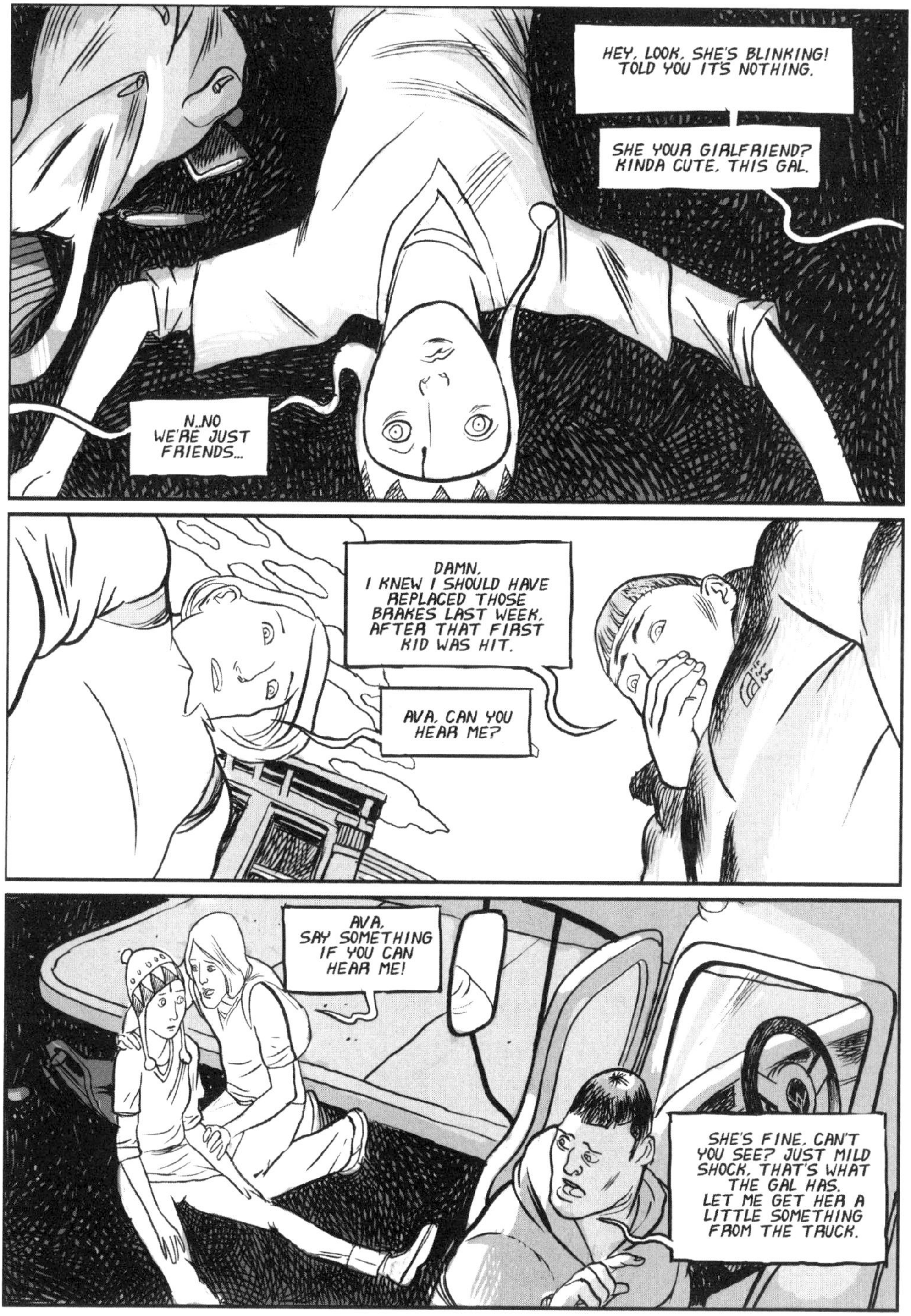
HEY, LOOK, SHE'S BLINKING! TOLD YOU IT'S NOTHING.
SHE YOUR GIRLFRIEND? KINDA CUTE, THIS GAL.
N..NO WE'RE JUST FRIENDS...
DAMN, I KNEW I SHOULD HAVE REPLACED THOSE BRAKES LAST WEEK, AFTER THAT FIRST KID WAS HIT.
AVA, CAN YOU HEAR ME?
AVA, SAY SOMETHING IF YOU CAN HEAR ME!
SHE'S FINE, CAN'T YOU SEE? JUST MILD SHOCK, THAT'S WHAT THE GAL HAS. LET ME GET HER A LITTLE SOMETHING FROM THE TRUCK.

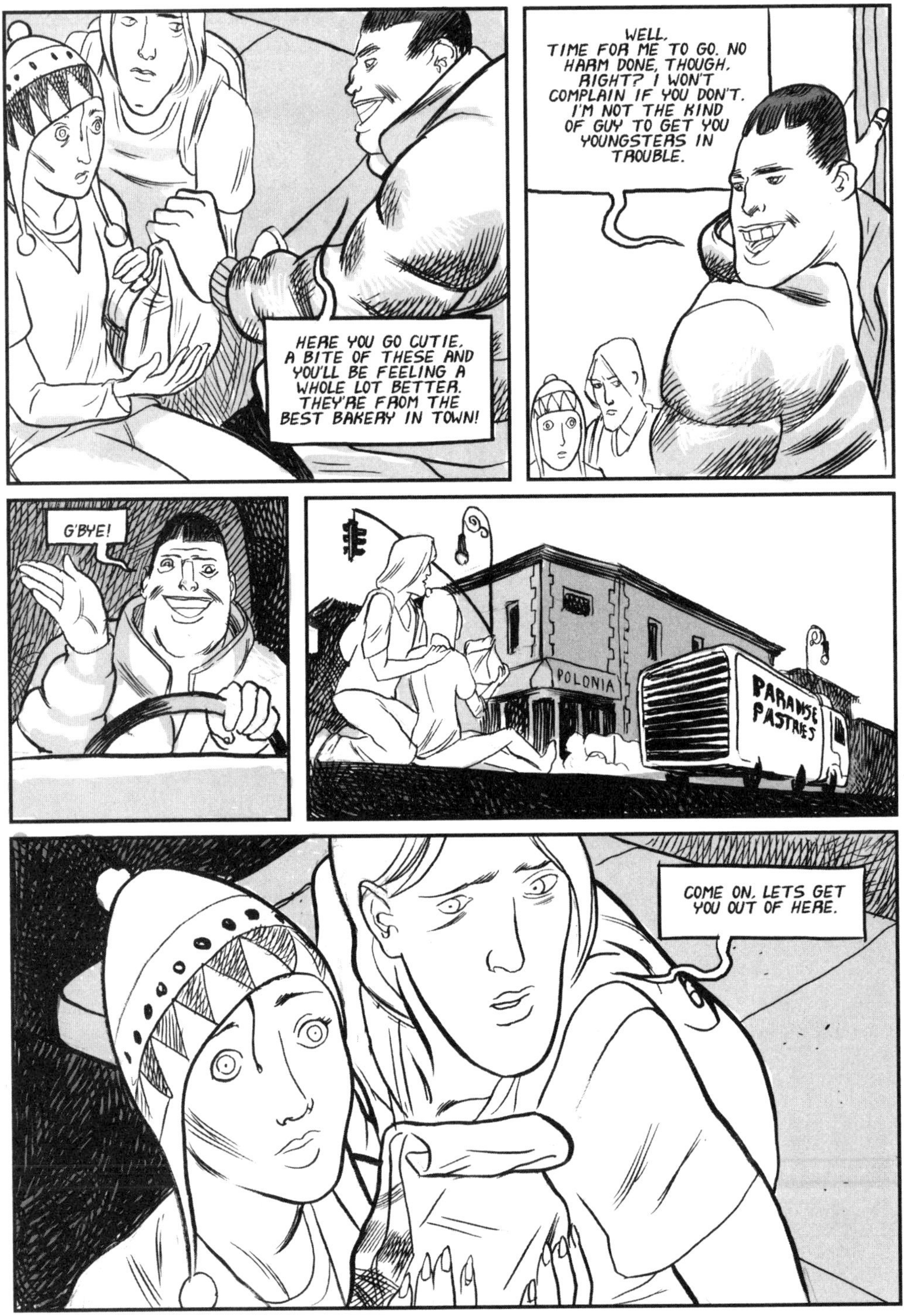
HERE YOU GO CUTIE, A BITE OF THESE AND YOU'LL BE FEELING A WHOLE LOT BETTER. THEY'RE FROM THE BEST BAKERY IN TOWN!
WELL, TIME FOR ME TO GO. NO HARM DONE, THOUGH, RIGHT? I WON'T COMPLAIN IF YOU DON'T. I'M NOT THE KIND OF GUY TO GET YOU YOUNGSTERS IN TROUBLE.
G'BYE!
POLONIA
PARADISE PASTRIES
COME ON. LETS GET YOU OUT OF HERE.

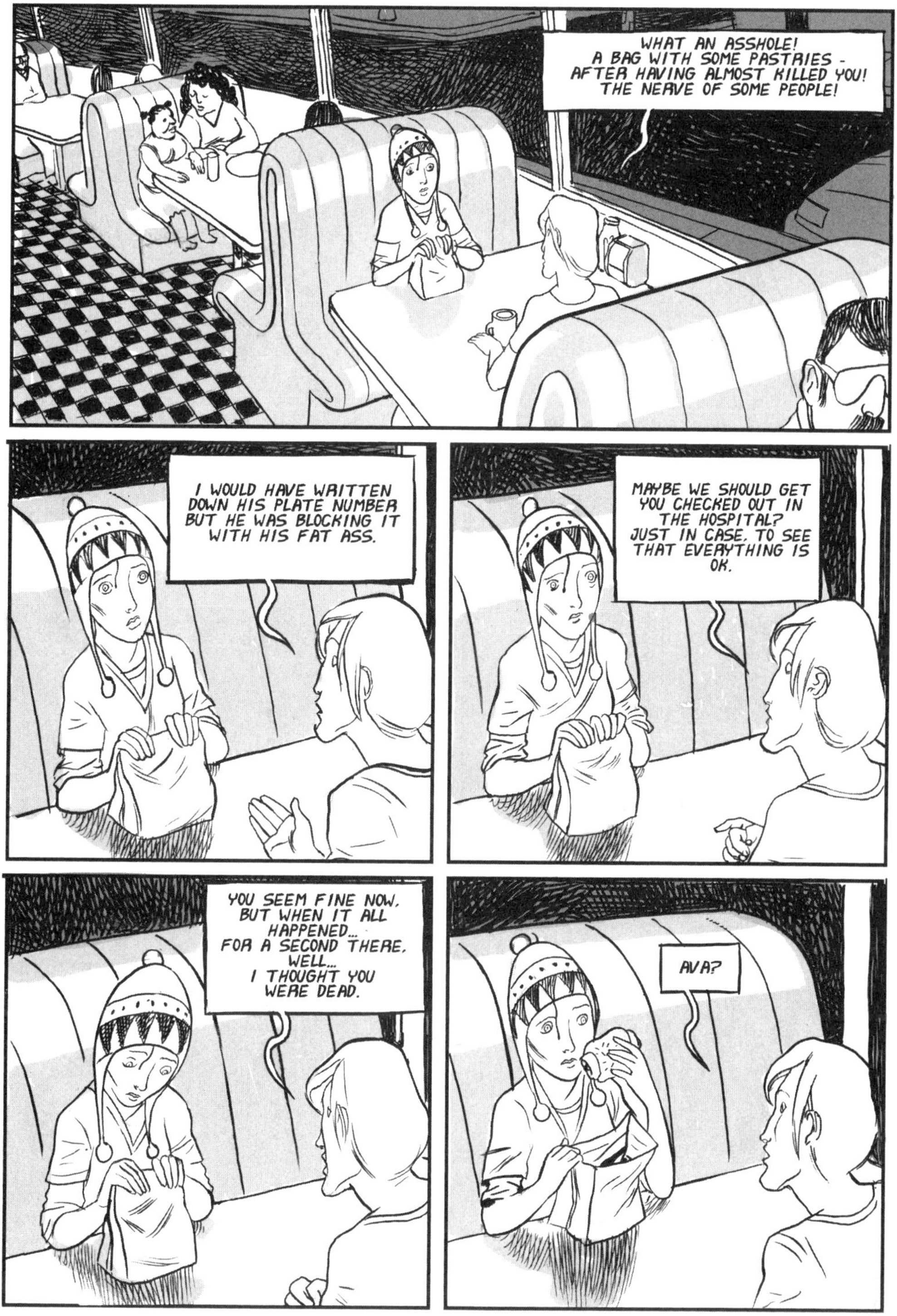
WHAT AN ASSHOLE! A BAG WITH SOME PASTRIES - AFTER HAVING ALMOST KILLED YOU! THE NERVE OF SOME PEOPLE!
I WOULD HAVE WRITTEN DOWN HIS PLATE NUMBER BUT HE WAS BLOCKING IT WITH HIS FAT ASS.
MAYBE WE SHOULD GET YOU CHECKED OUT IN THE HOSPITAL? JUST IN CASE, TO SEE THAT EVERYTHING IS OK.
YOU SEEM FINE NOW, BUT WHEN IT ALL HAPPENED... FOR A SECOND THERE, WELL... I THOUGHT YOU WERE DEAD.
AVA?

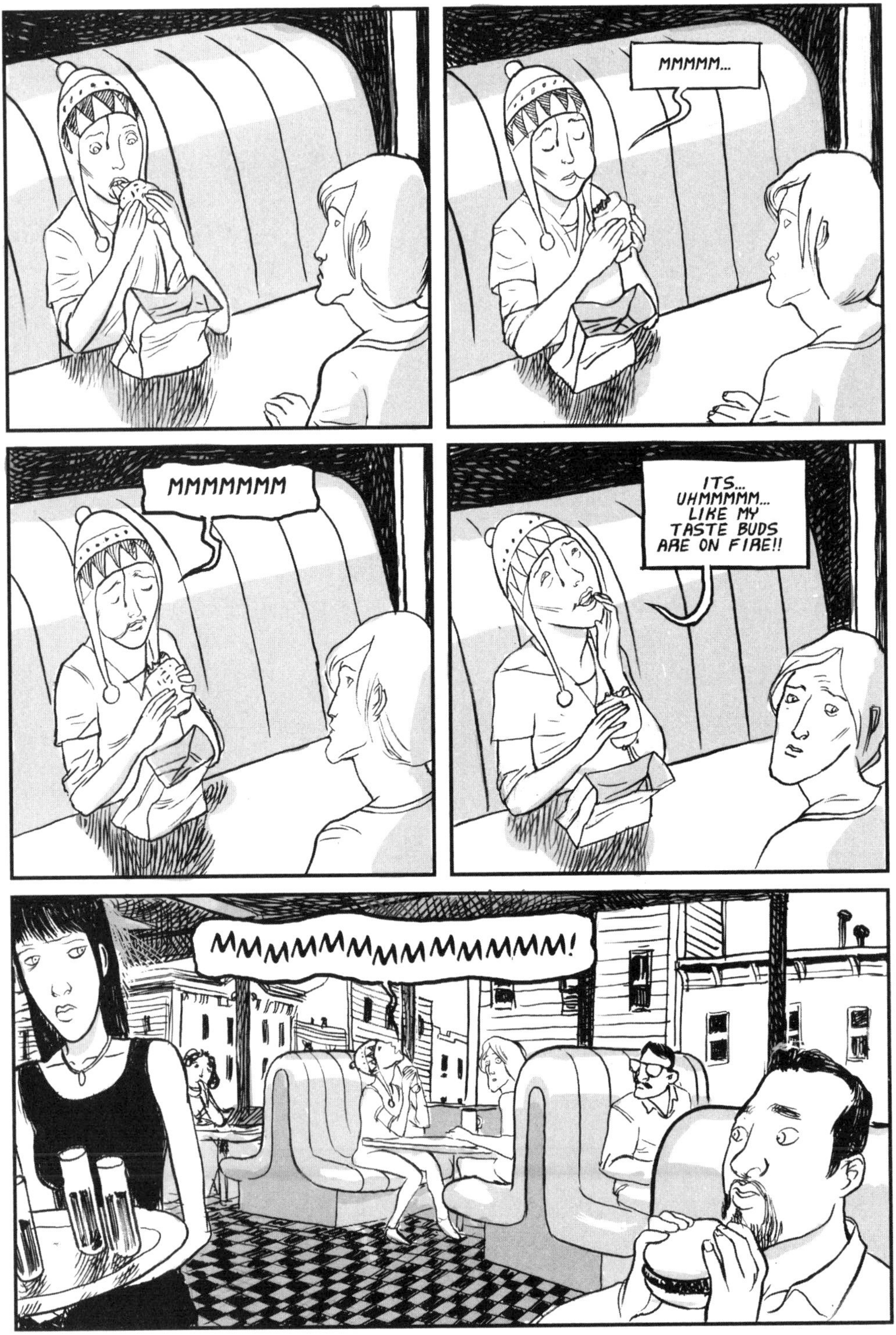
MMMMM...
MMMMMMM
ITS... UHMMMMM... LIKE MY TASTE BUDS ARE ON FIRE!!
MMMMMMMMMMMMMMM!

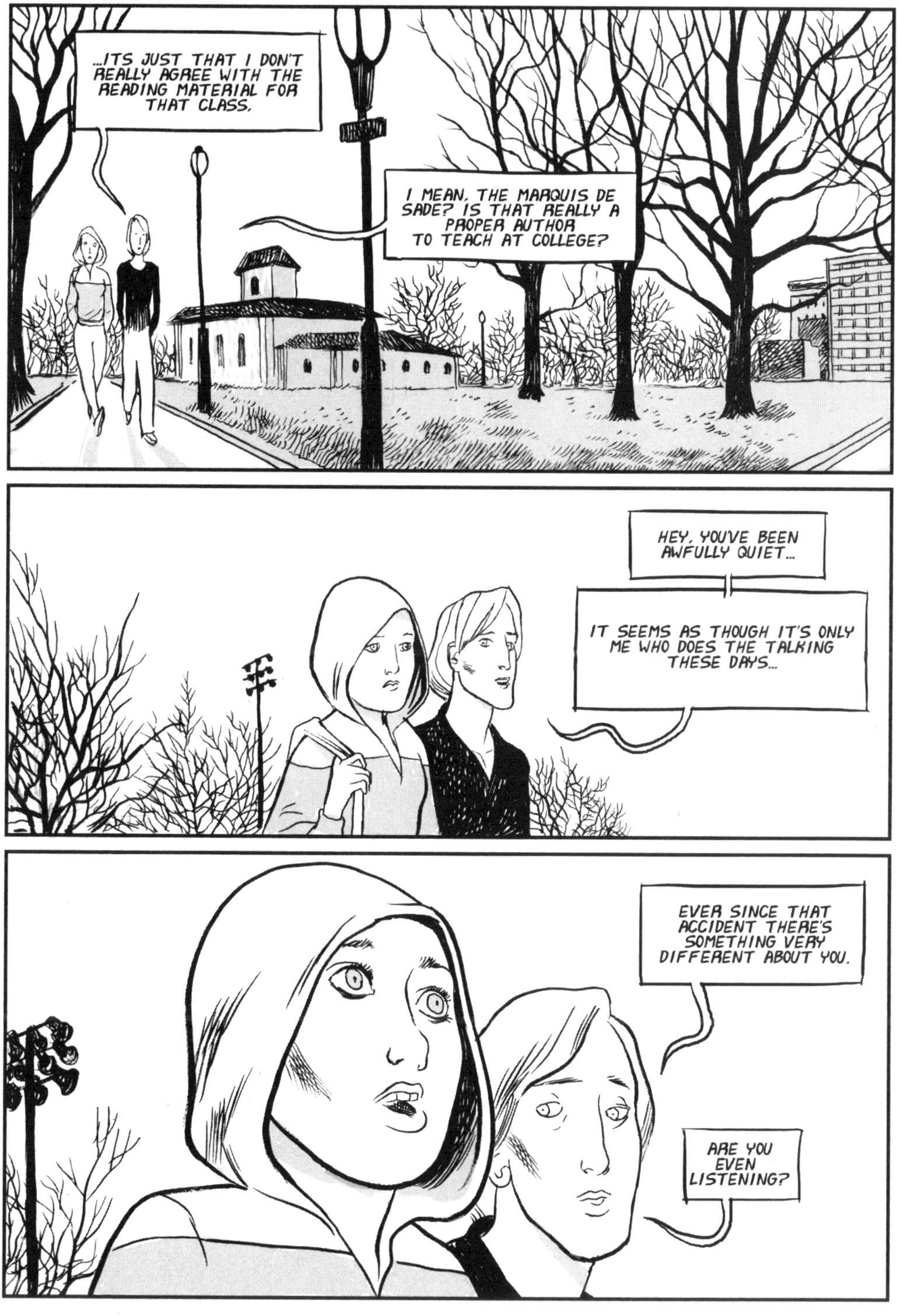
...ITS JUST THAT I DON'T REALLY AGREE WITH THE READING MATERIAL FOR THAT CLASS.
I MEAN, THE MARQUIS DE SADE? IS THAT REALLY A PROPER AUTHOR TO TEACH AT COLLEGE?
HEY, YOU'VE BEEN AWFULLY QUIET...
IT SEEMS AS THOUGH IT'S ONLY ME WHO DOES THE TALKING THESE DAYS...
EVER SINCE THAT ACCIDENT THERE'S SOMETHING VERY DIFFERENT ABOUT YOU.
ARE YOU EVEN LISTENING?

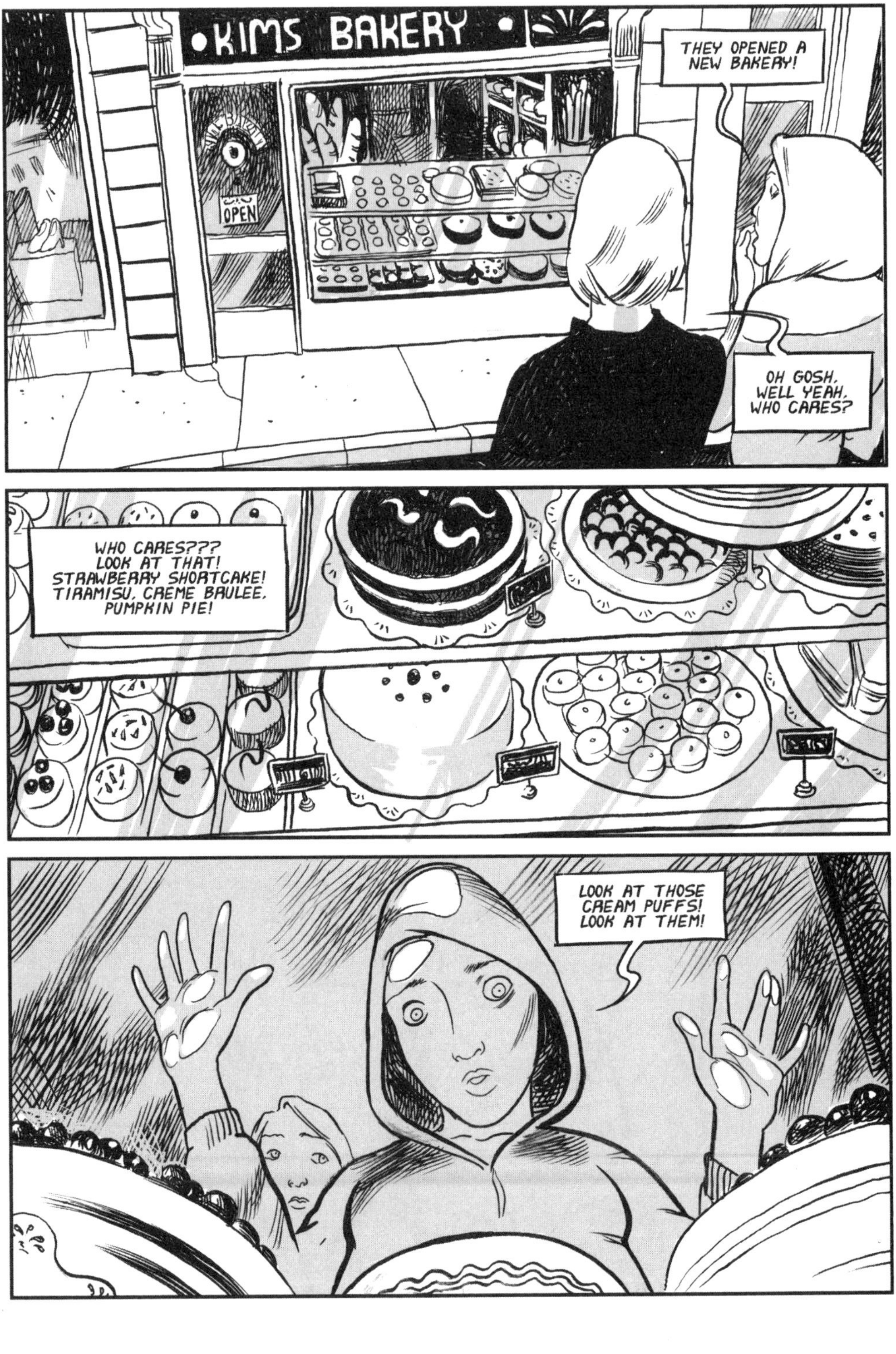
KIMS BAKERY
OPEN
THEY OPENED A NEW BAKERY!
OH GOSH. WELL YEAH. WHO CARES?
WHO CARES??? LOOK AT THAT! STRAWBERRY SHORTCAKE! TIRAMISU, CREME BRULEE, PUMPKIN PIE!
LOOK AT THOSE CREAM PUFFS! LOOK AT THEM!

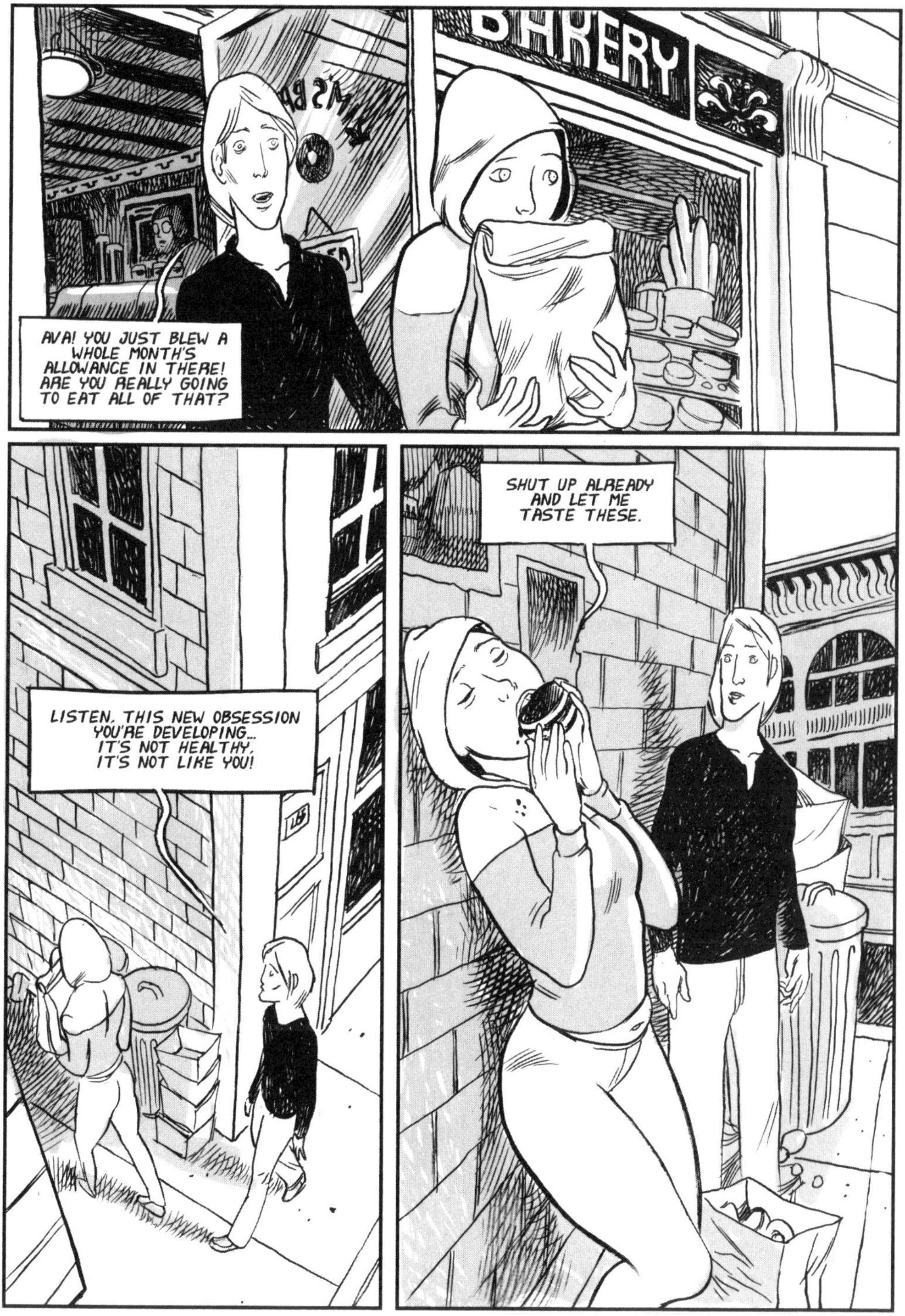
BAKERY
AVA! YOU JUST BLEW A WHOLE MONTH'S ALLOWANCE IN THERE! ARE YOU REALLY GOING TO EAT ALL OF THAT?
LISTEN, THIS NEW OBSESSION YOU'RE DEVELOPING... IT'S NOT HEALTHY. IT'S NOT LIKE YOU!
SHUT UP ALREADY AND LET ME TASTE THESE.

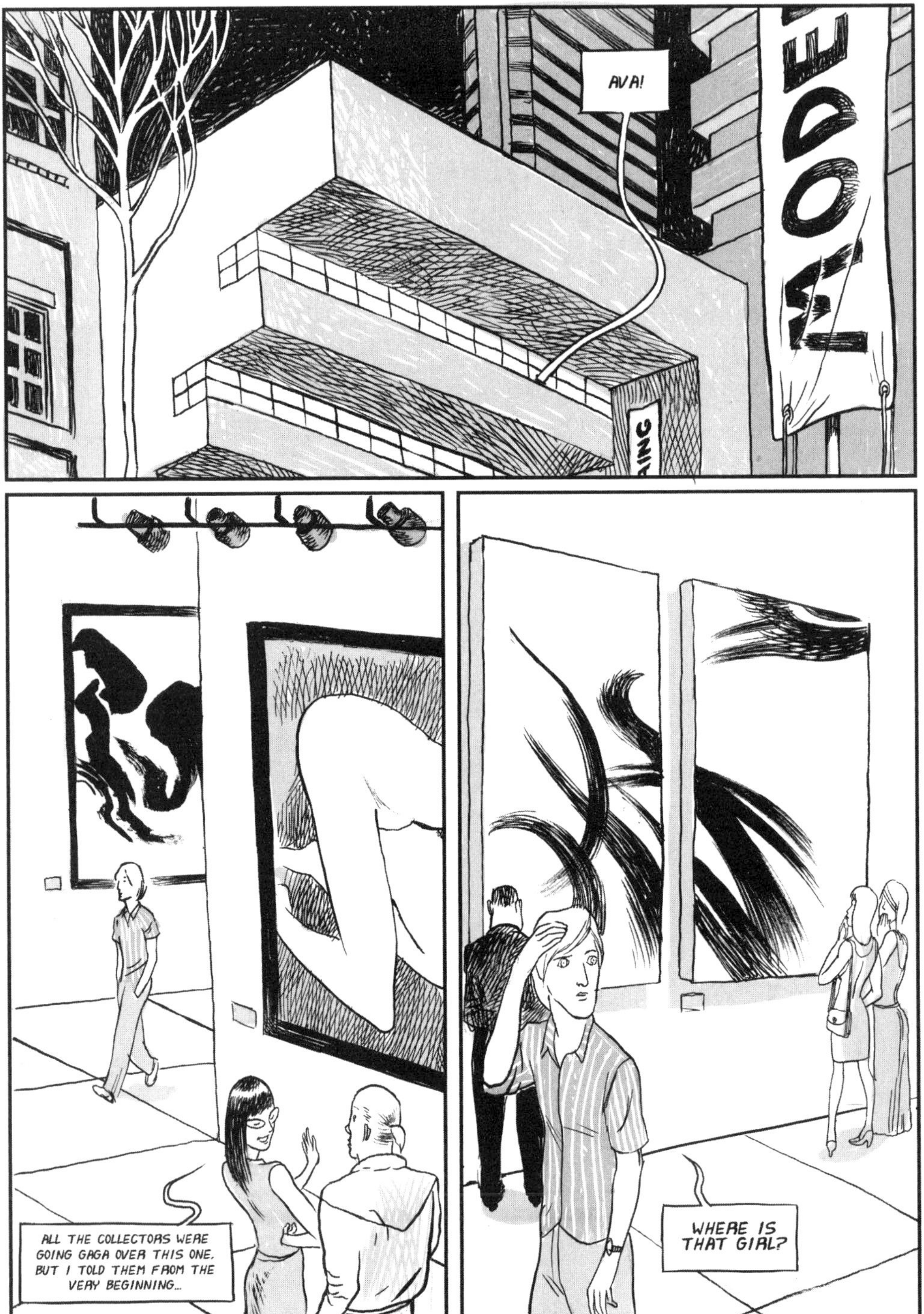
AVA!
ALL THE COLLECTORS WERE GOING GAGA OVER THIS ONE, BUT I TOLD THEM FROM THE VERY BEGINNING...
WHERE IS THAT GIRL?

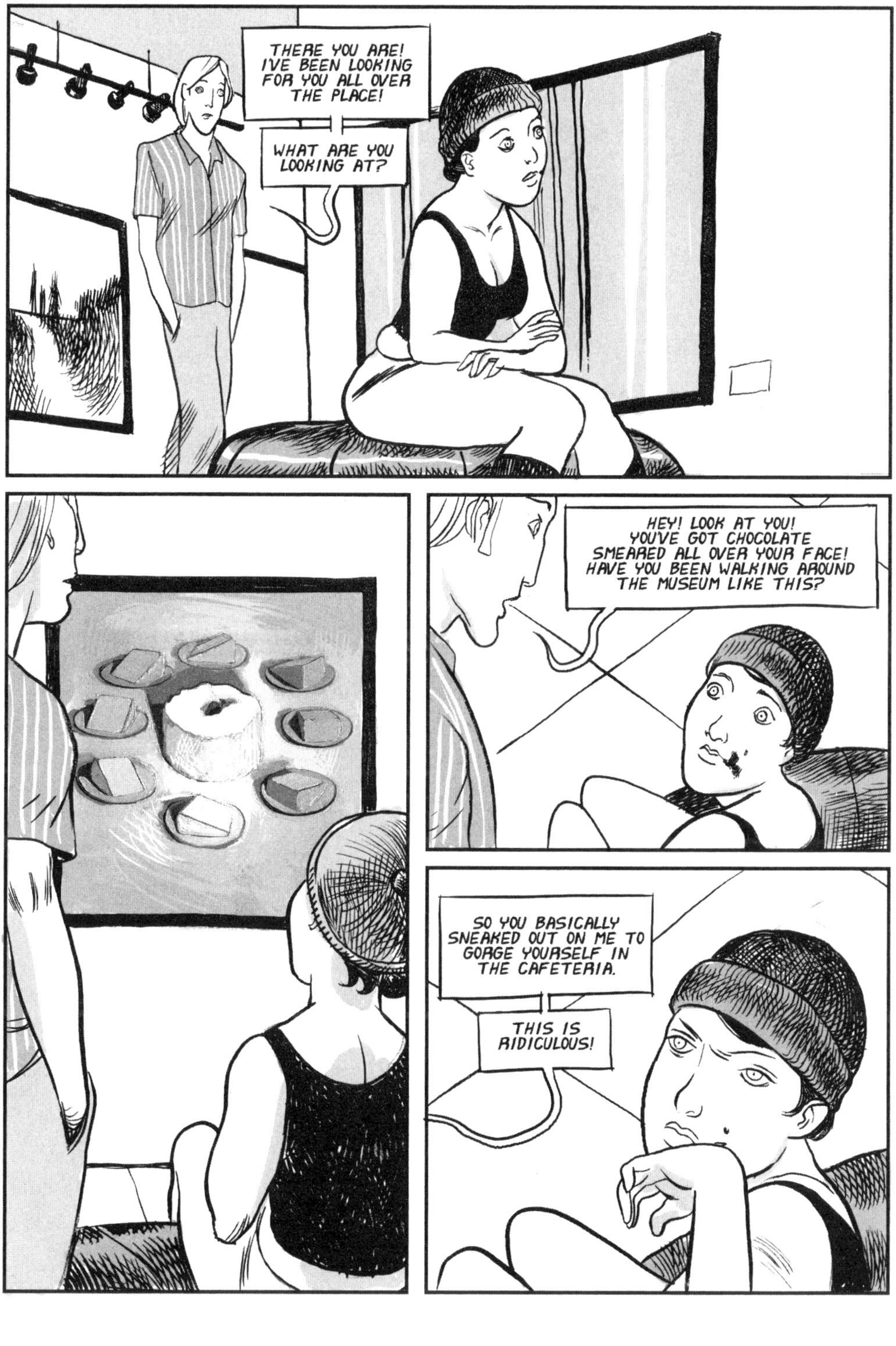
THERE YOU ARE! I'VE BEEN LOOKING FOR YOU ALL OVER THE PLACE!
WHAT ARE YOU LOOKING AT?
HEY! LOOK AT YOU! YOU'VE GOT CHOCOLATE SMEARED ALL OVER YOUR FACE! HAVE YOU BEEN WALKING AROUND THE MUSEUM LIKE THIS?
SO YOU BASICALLY SNEAKED OUT ON ME TO GORGE YOURSELF IN THE CAFETERIA.
THIS IS RIDICULOUS!

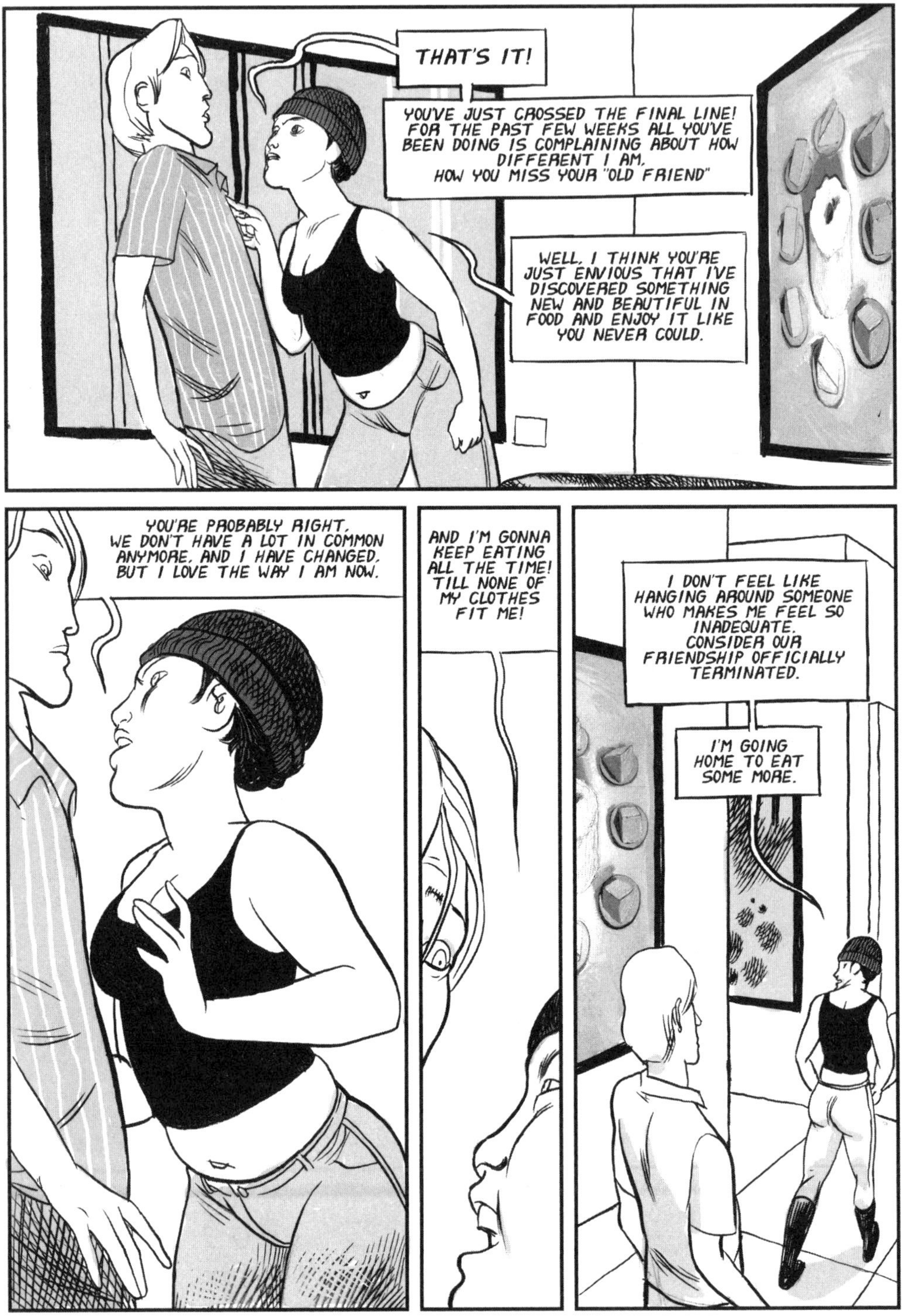
THAT'S IT!
YOU'VE JUST CROSSED THE FINAL LINE! FOR THE PAST FEW WEEKS ALL YOU'VE BEEN DOING IS COMPLAINING ABOUT HOW DIFFERENT I AM, HOW YOU MISS YOUR "OLD FRIEND"
WELL, I THINK YOU'RE JUST ENVIOUS THAT I'VE DISCOVERED SOMETHING NEW AND BEAUTIFUL IN FOOD AND ENJOY IT LIKE YOU NEVER COULD.
YOU'RE PROBABLY RIGHT, WE DON'T HAVE A LOT IN COMMON ANYMORE, AND I HAVE CHANGED, BUT I LOVE THE WAY I AM NOW.
AND I'M GONNA KEEP EATING ALL THE TIME! TILL NONE OF MY CLOTHES FIT ME!
I DON'T FEEL LIKE HANGING AROUND SOMEONE WHO MAKES ME FEEL SO INADEQUATE. CONSIDER OUR FRIENDSHIP OFFICIALLY TERMINATED.
I'M GOING HOME TO EAT SOME MORE.

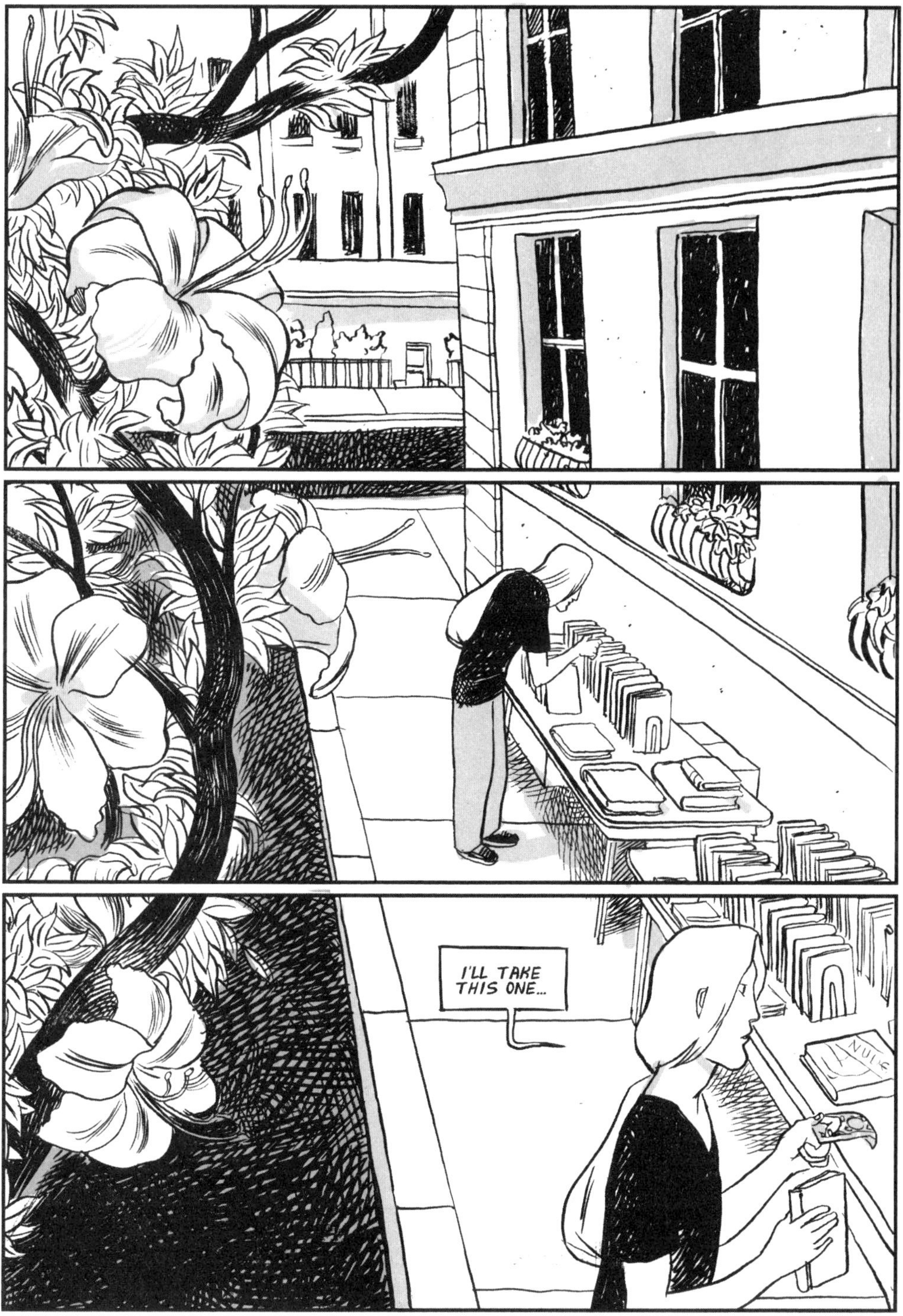
I'LL TAKE THIS ONE...

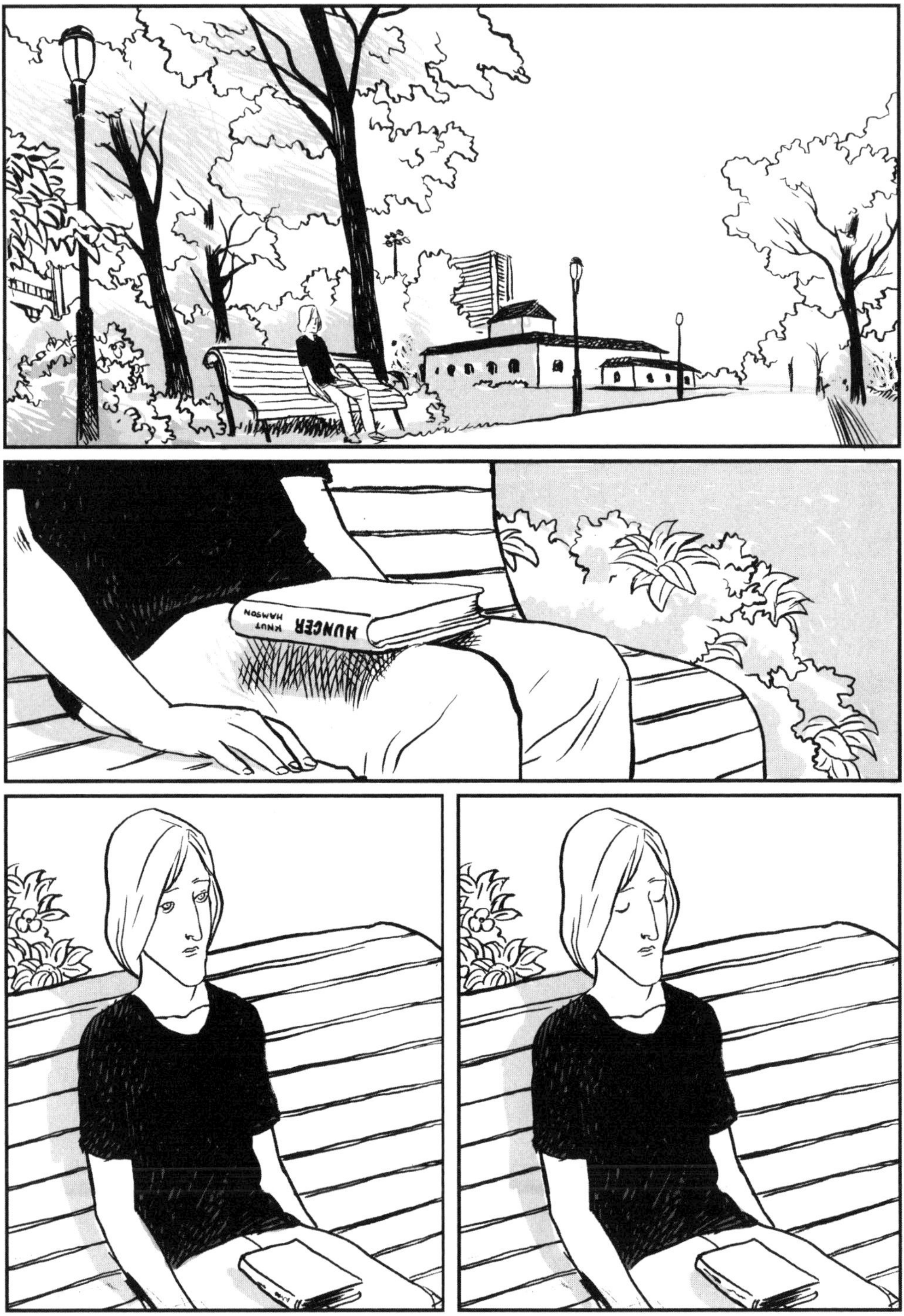
HUNGER
KNUT HAMSUN

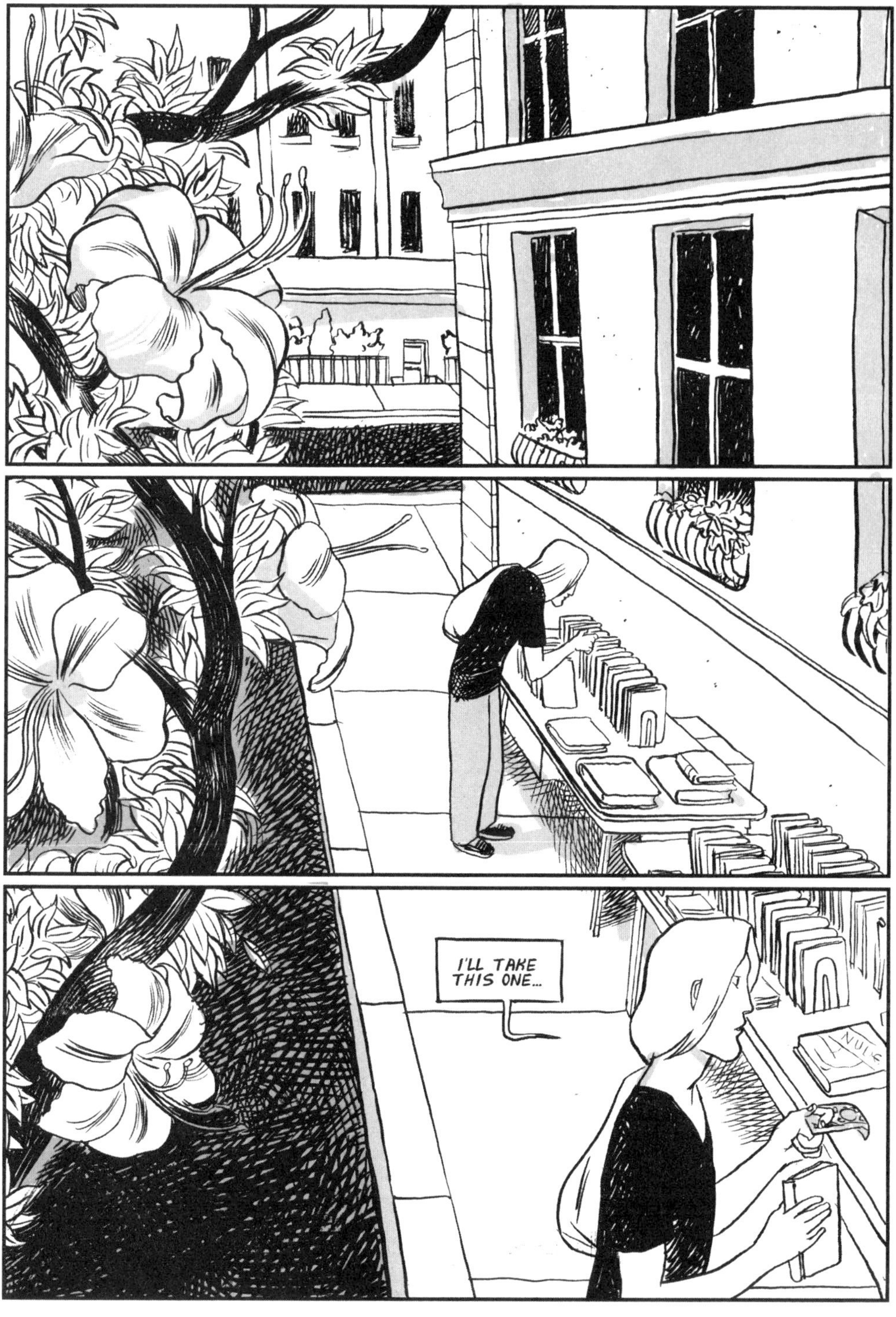
I'LL TAKE THIS ONE...

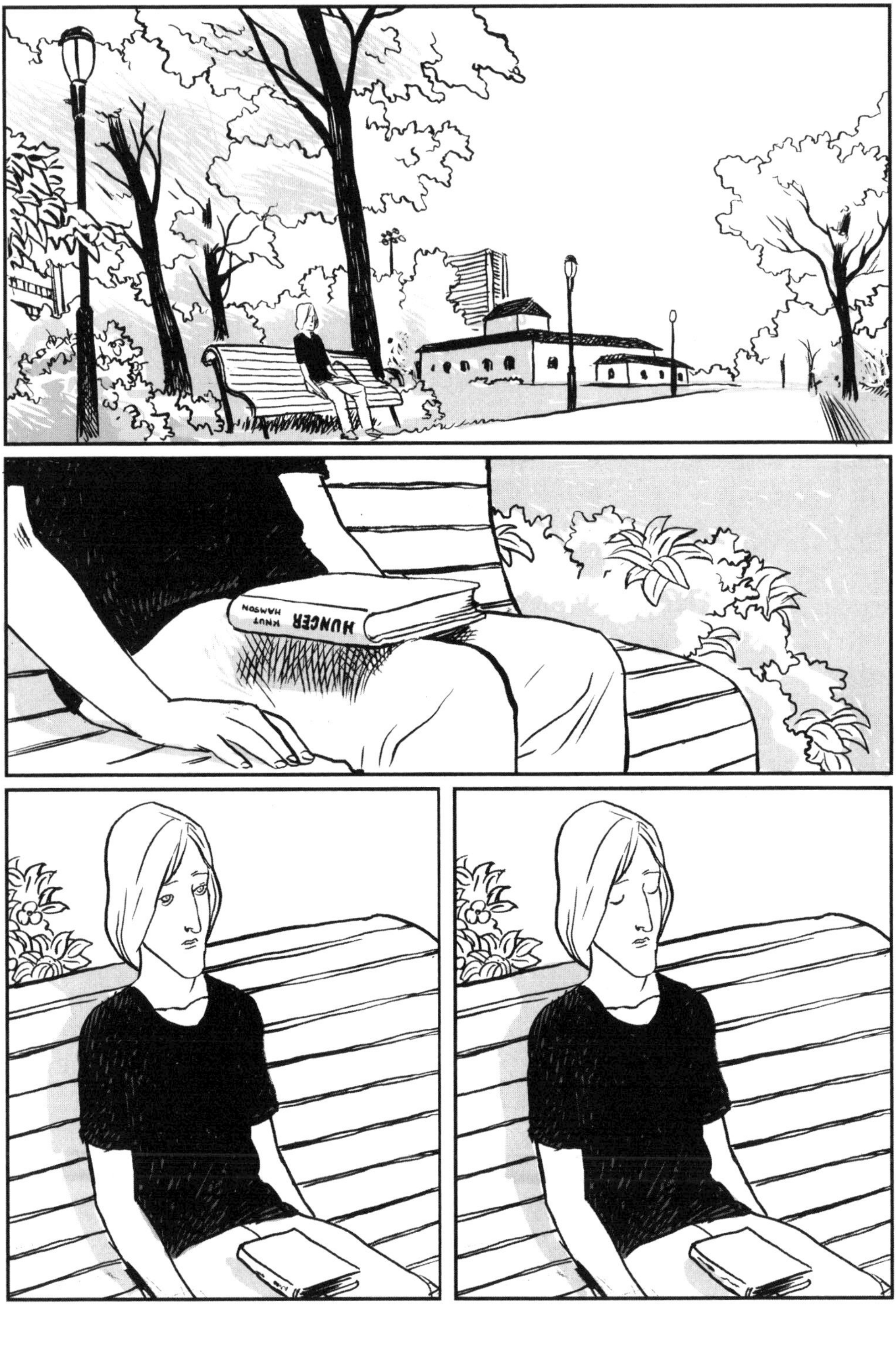
HUNGER
KNUT
HAMSON

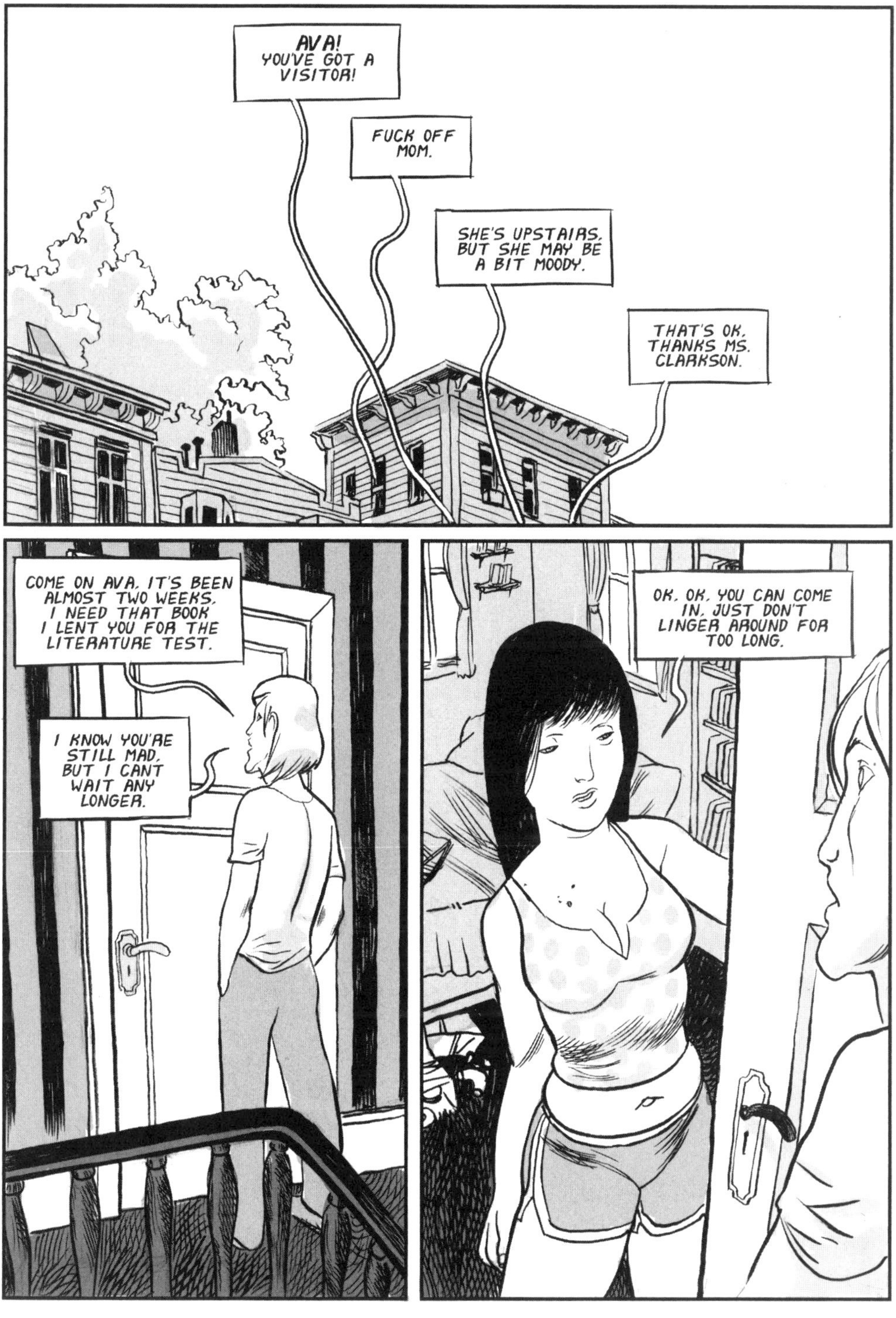
AVA! YOU'VE GOT A VISITOR!
FUCK OFF MOM.
SHE'S UPSTAIRS, BUT SHE MAY BE A BIT MOODY.
THAT'S OK, THANKS MS. CLARKSON.
COME ON AVA, IT'S BEEN ALMOST TWO WEEKS, I NEED THAT BOOK I LENT YOU FOR THE LITERATURE TEST.
I KNOW YOU'RE STILL MAD, BUT I CANT WAIT ANY LONGER.
OK, OK, YOU CAN COME IN, JUST DON'T LINGER AROUND FOR TOO LONG.

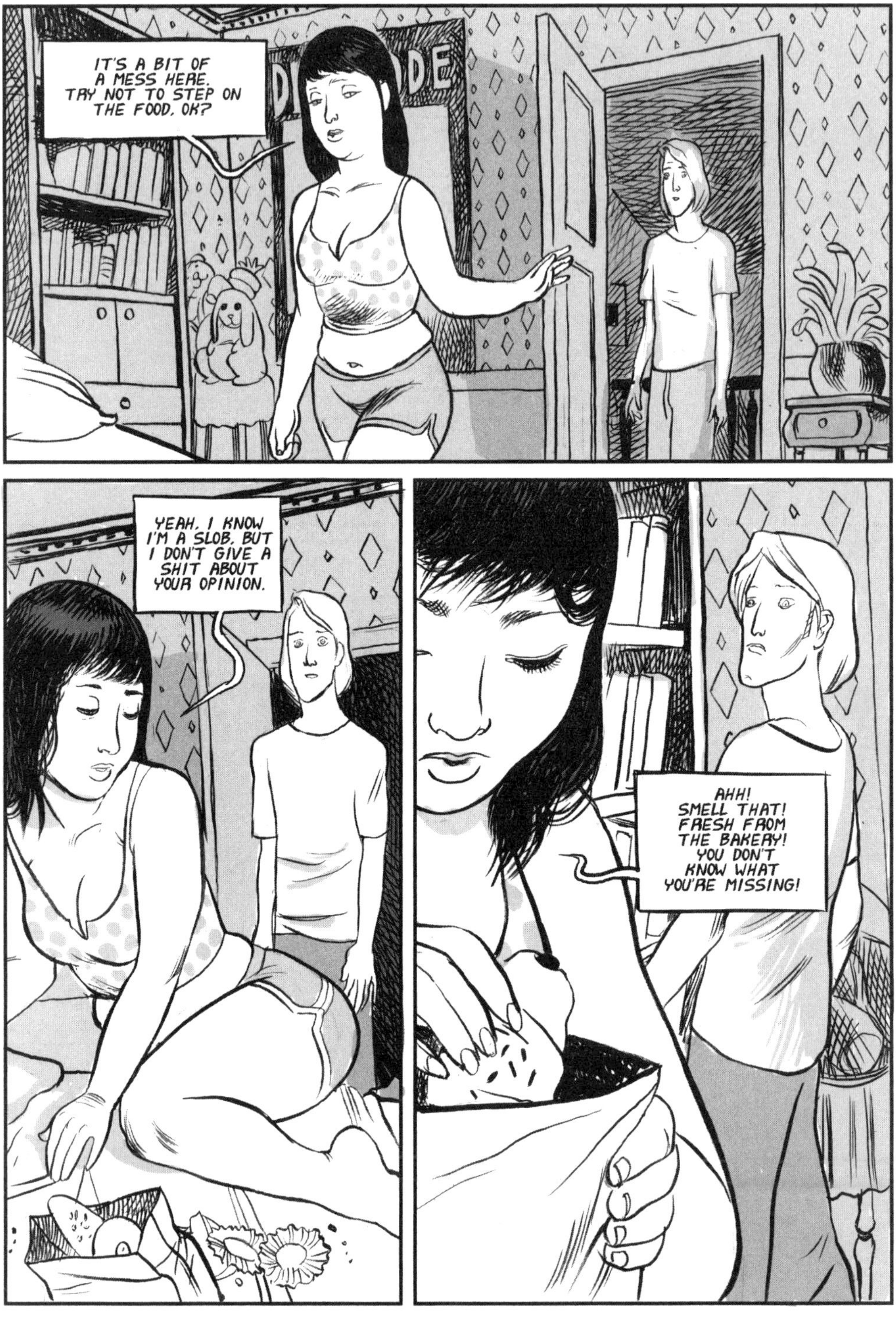
IT'S A BIT OF A MESS HERE. TRY NOT TO STEP ON THE FOOD, OK?
YEAH, I KNOW I'M A SLOB, BUT I DON'T GIVE A SHIT ABOUT YOUR OPINION.
AHH! SMELL THAT! FRESH FROM THE BAKERY! YOU DON'T KNOW WHAT YOU'RE MISSING!

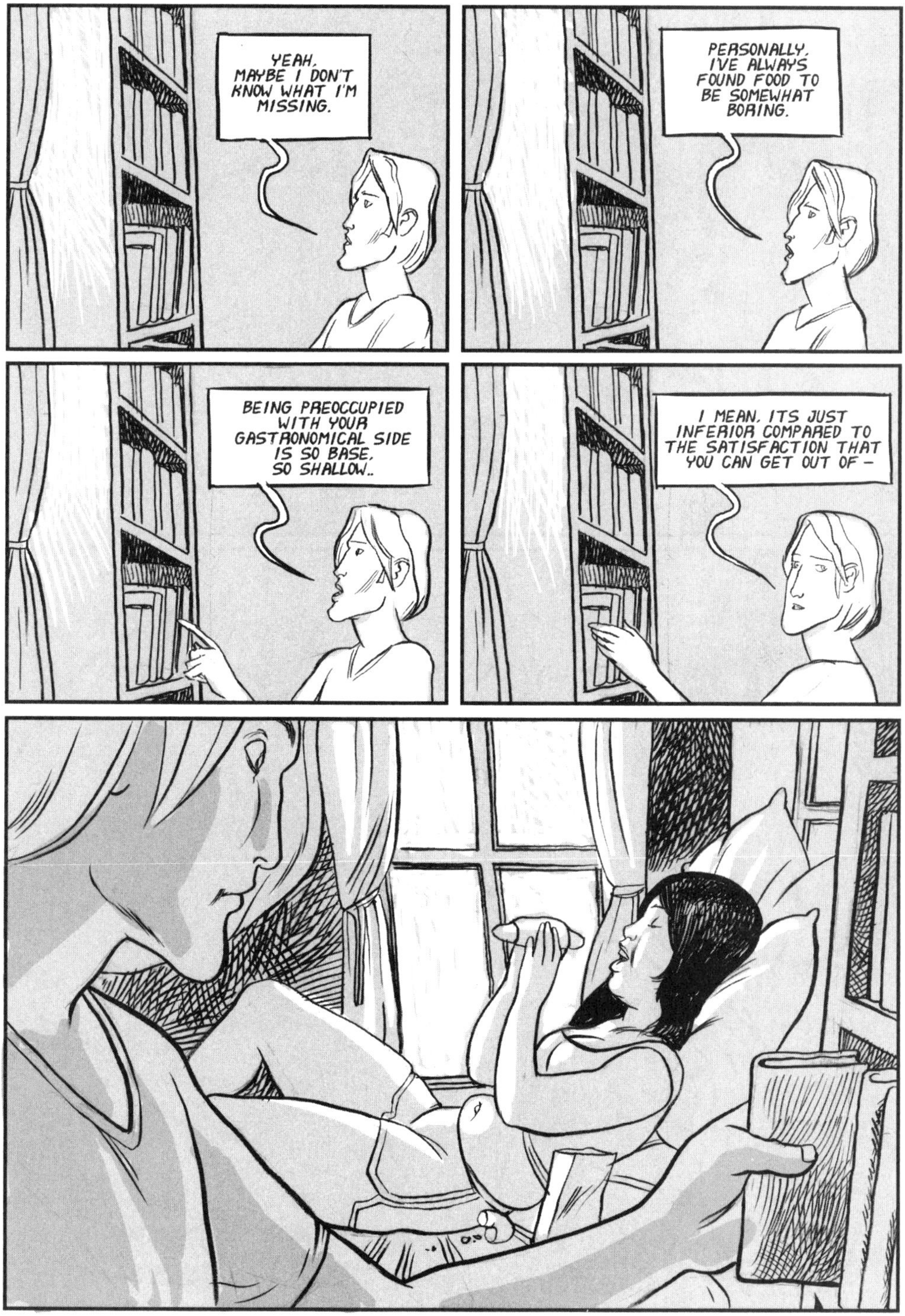
YEAH, MAYBE I DON'T KNOW WHAT I'M MISSING.
PERSONALLY, I'VE ALWAYS FOUND FOOD TO BE SOMEWHAT BORING.
BEING PREOCCUPIED WITH YOUR GASTRONOMICAL SIDE IS SO BASE, SO SHALLOW..
I MEAN, ITS JUST INFERIOR COMPARED TO THE SATISFACTION THAT YOU CAN GET OUT OF -

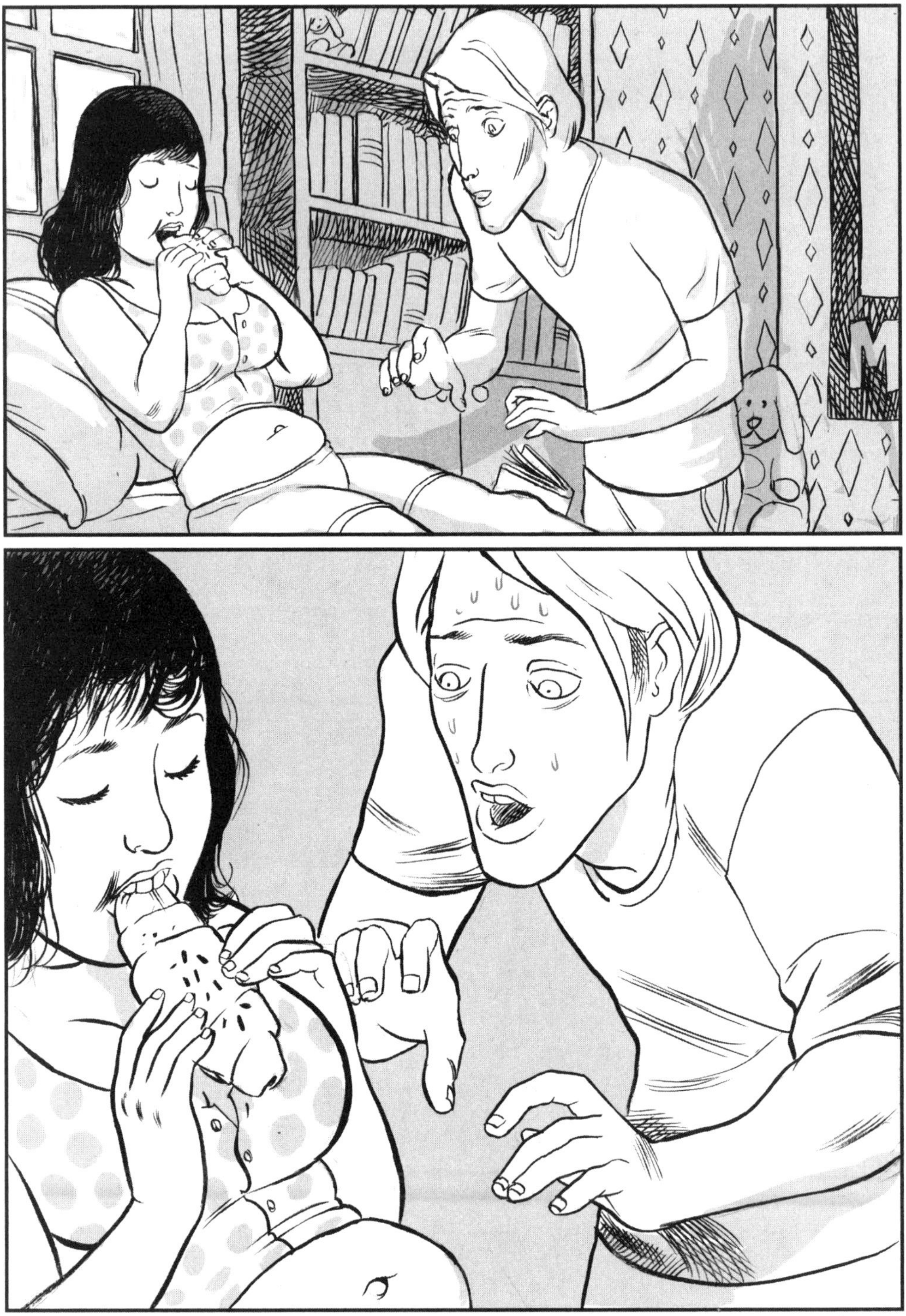

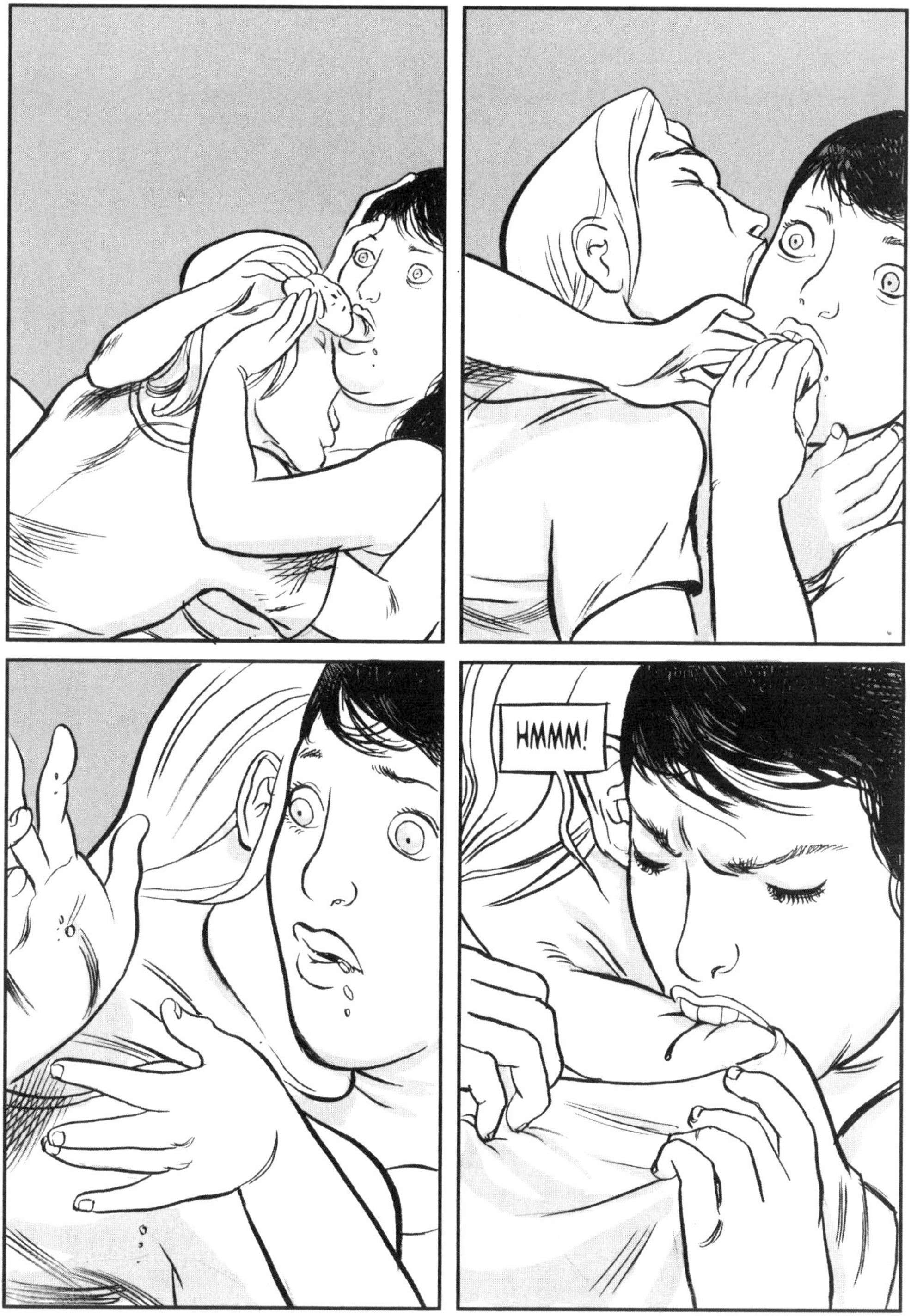
HMMM!

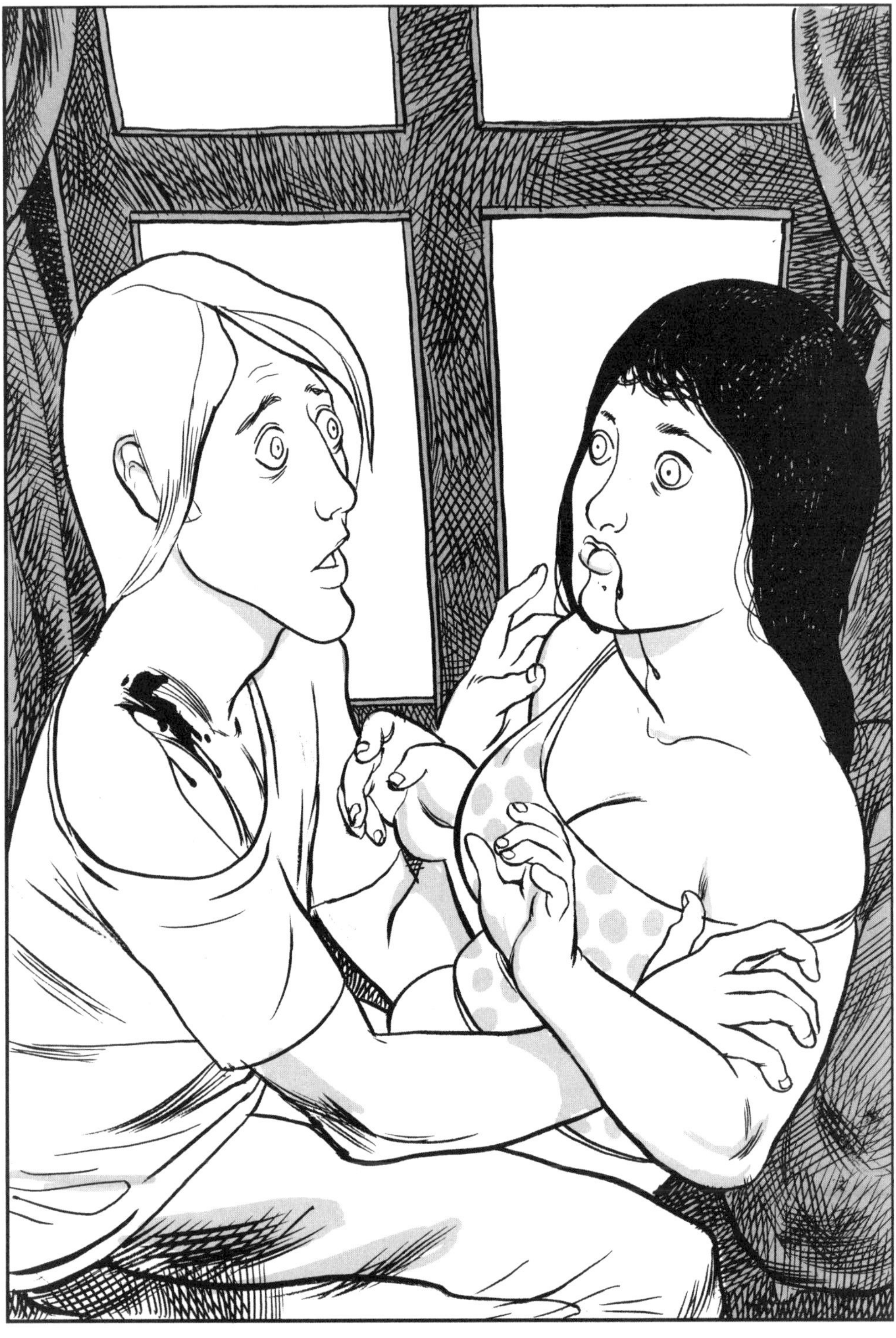

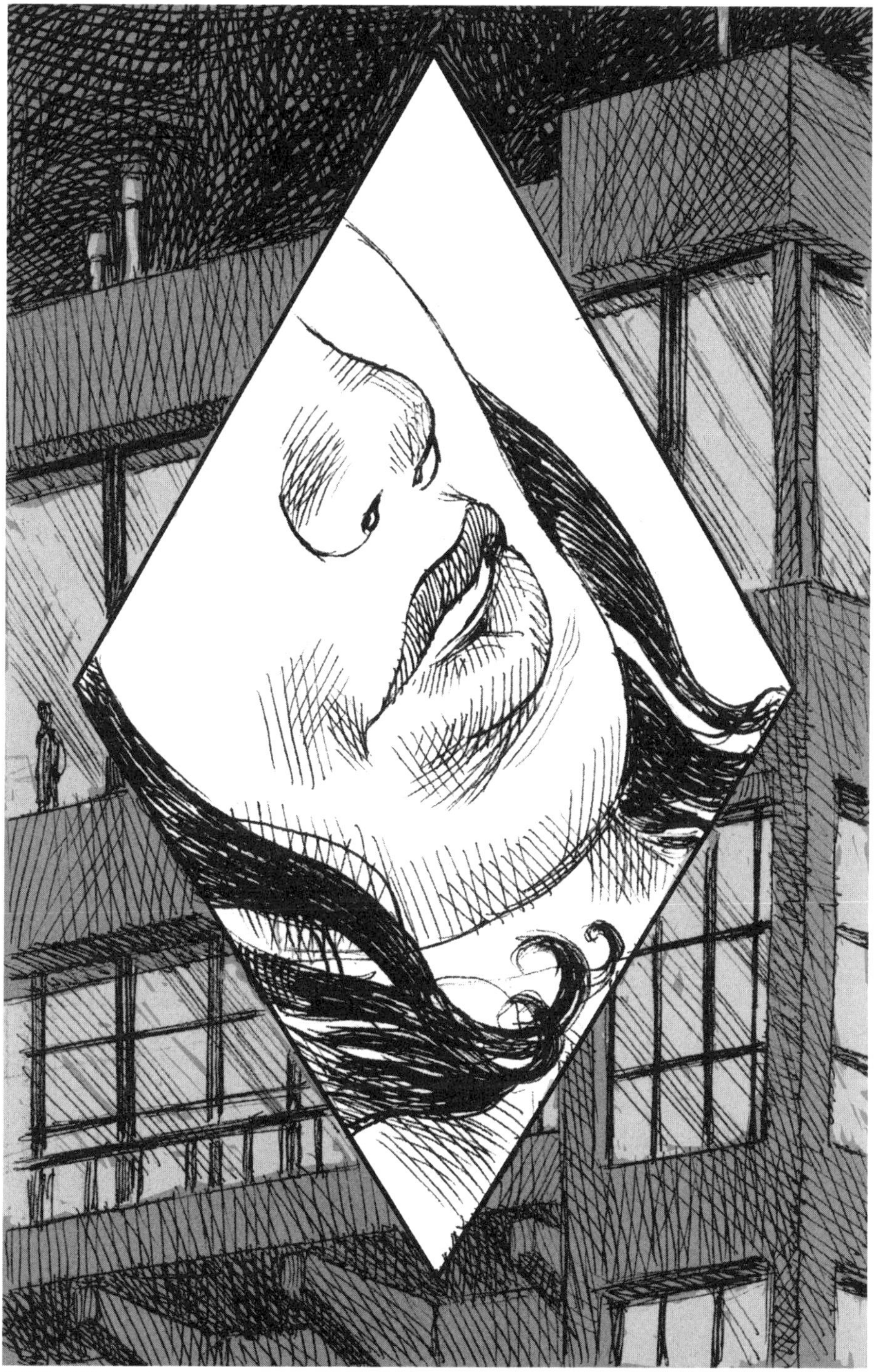

·CRUELTY·

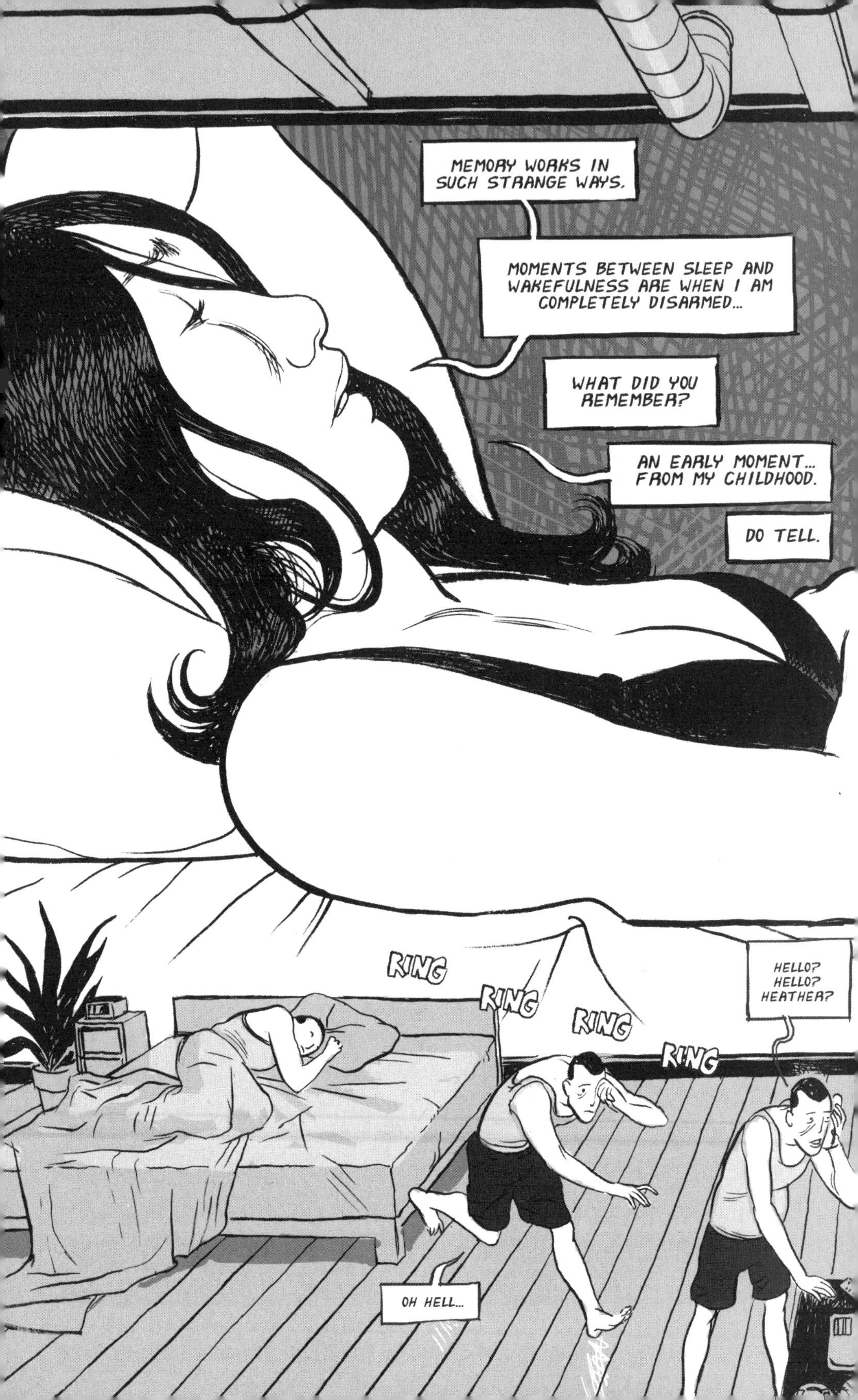
MEMORY WORKS IN SUCH STRANGE WAYS.
MOMENTS BETWEEN SLEEP AND WAKEFULNESS ARE WHEN I AM COMPLETELY DISARMED...
WHAT DID YOU REMEMBER?
AN EARLY MOMENT... FROM MY CHILDHOOD.
DO TELL.
RING
RING
RING
RING
OH HELL...
HELLO? HELLO? HEATHER?

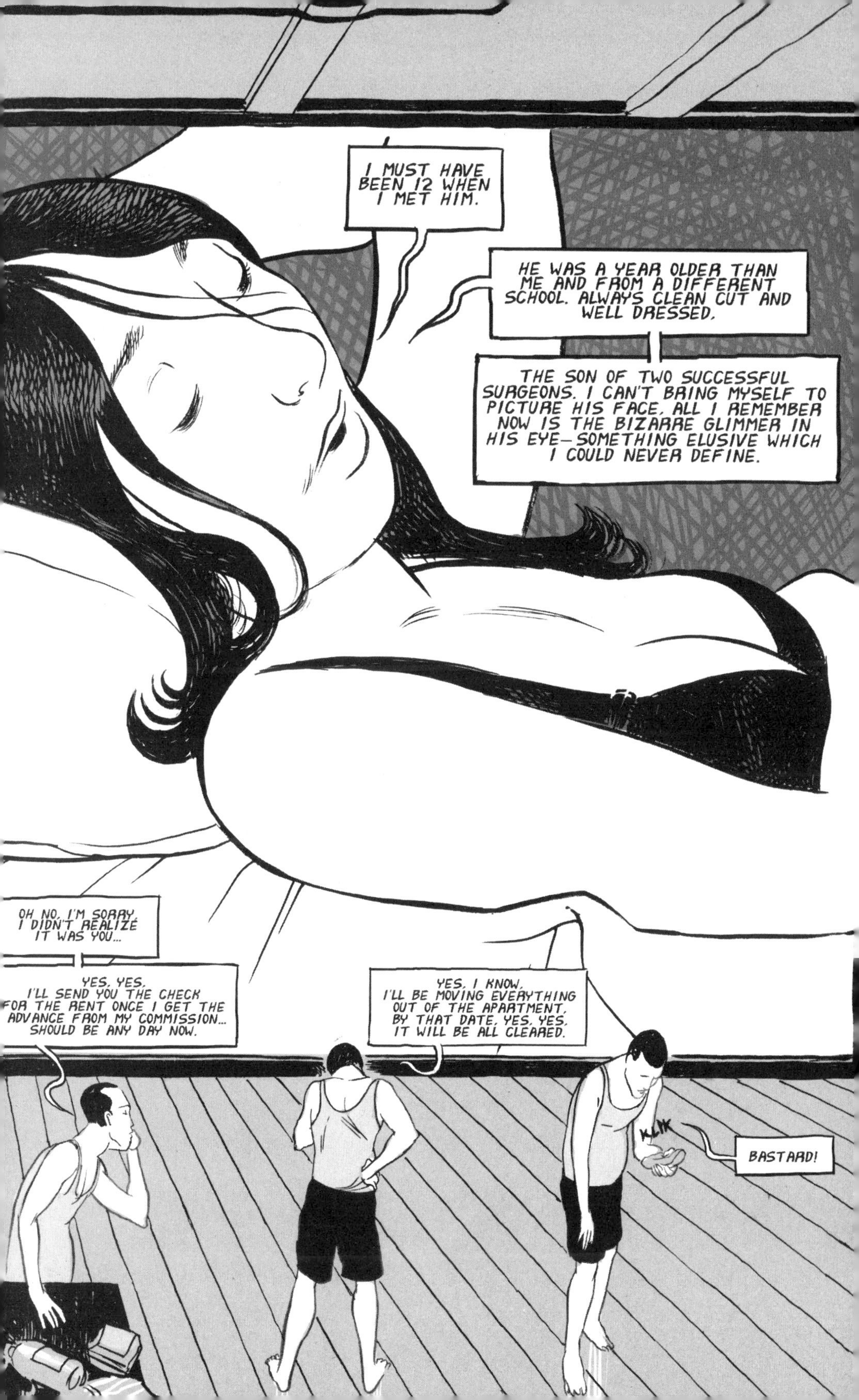
I MUST HAVE BEEN 12 WHEN I MET HIM.
HE WAS A YEAR OLDER THAN ME AND FROM A DIFFERENT SCHOOL. ALWAYS CLEAN CUT AND WELL DRESSED.
THE SON OF TWO SUCCESSFUL SURGEONS. I CAN'T BRING MYSELF TO PICTURE HIS FACE. ALL I REMEMBER NOW IS THE BIZARRE GLIMMER IN HIS EYE—SOMETHING ELUSIVE WHICH I COULD NEVER DEFINE.
OH NO, I'M SORRY, I DIDN'T REALIZE IT WAS YOU...
YES, YES. I'LL SEND YOU THE CHECK FOR THE RENT ONCE I GET THE ADVANCE FROM MY COMMISSION... SHOULD BE ANY DAY NOW.
YES, I KNOW. I'LL BE MOVING EVERYTHING OUT OF THE APARTMENT BY THAT DATE. YES, YES. IT WILL BE ALL CLEARED.
KLIK
BASTARD!

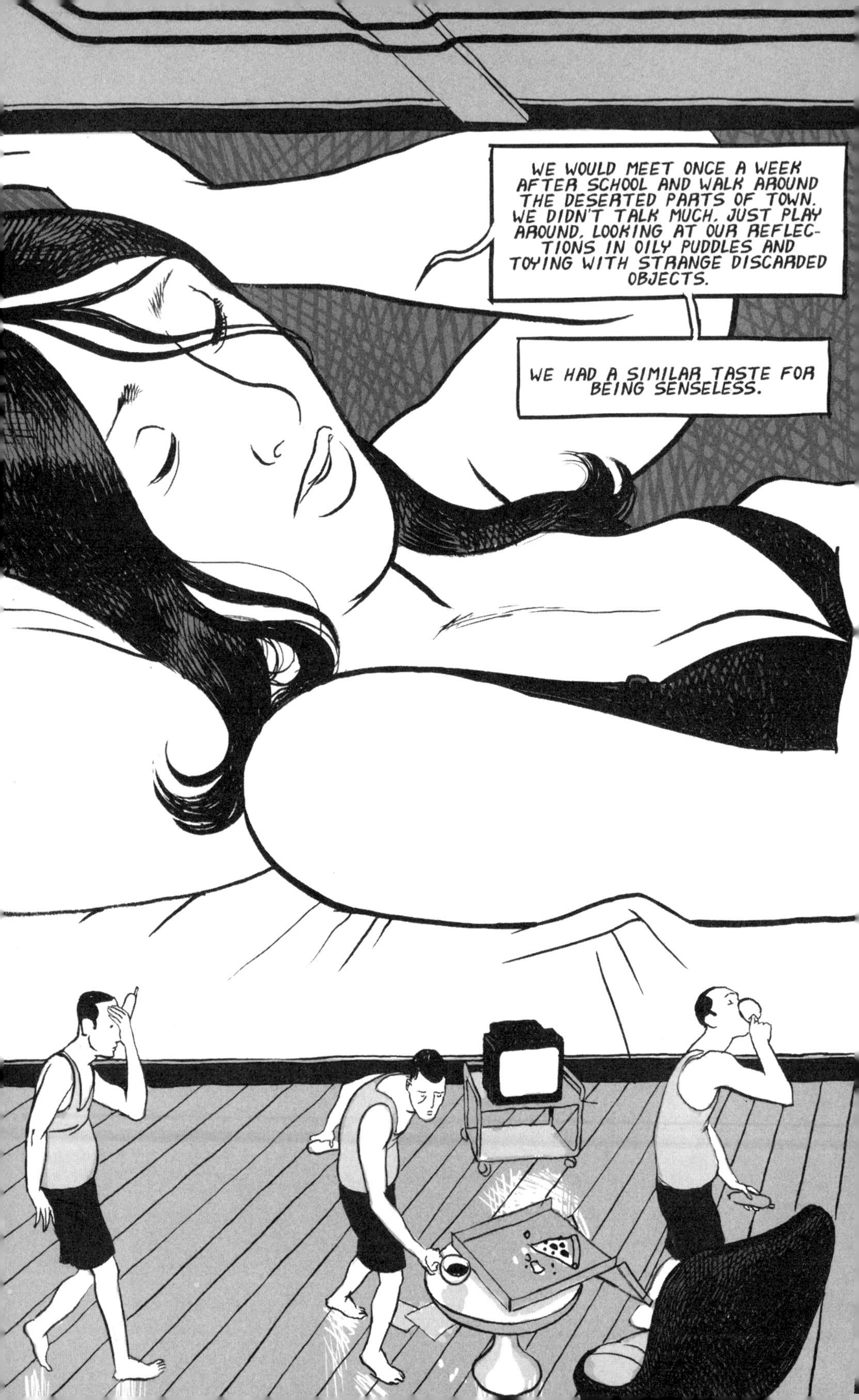
WE WOULD MEET ONCE A WEEK AFTER SCHOOL AND WALK AROUND THE DESERTED PARTS OF TOWN. WE DIDN'T TALK MUCH, JUST PLAY AROUND, LOOKING AT OUR REFLECTIONS IN OILY PUDDLES AND TOYING WITH STRANGE DISCARDED OBJECTS.
WE HAD A SIMILAR TASTE FOR BEING SENSELESS.

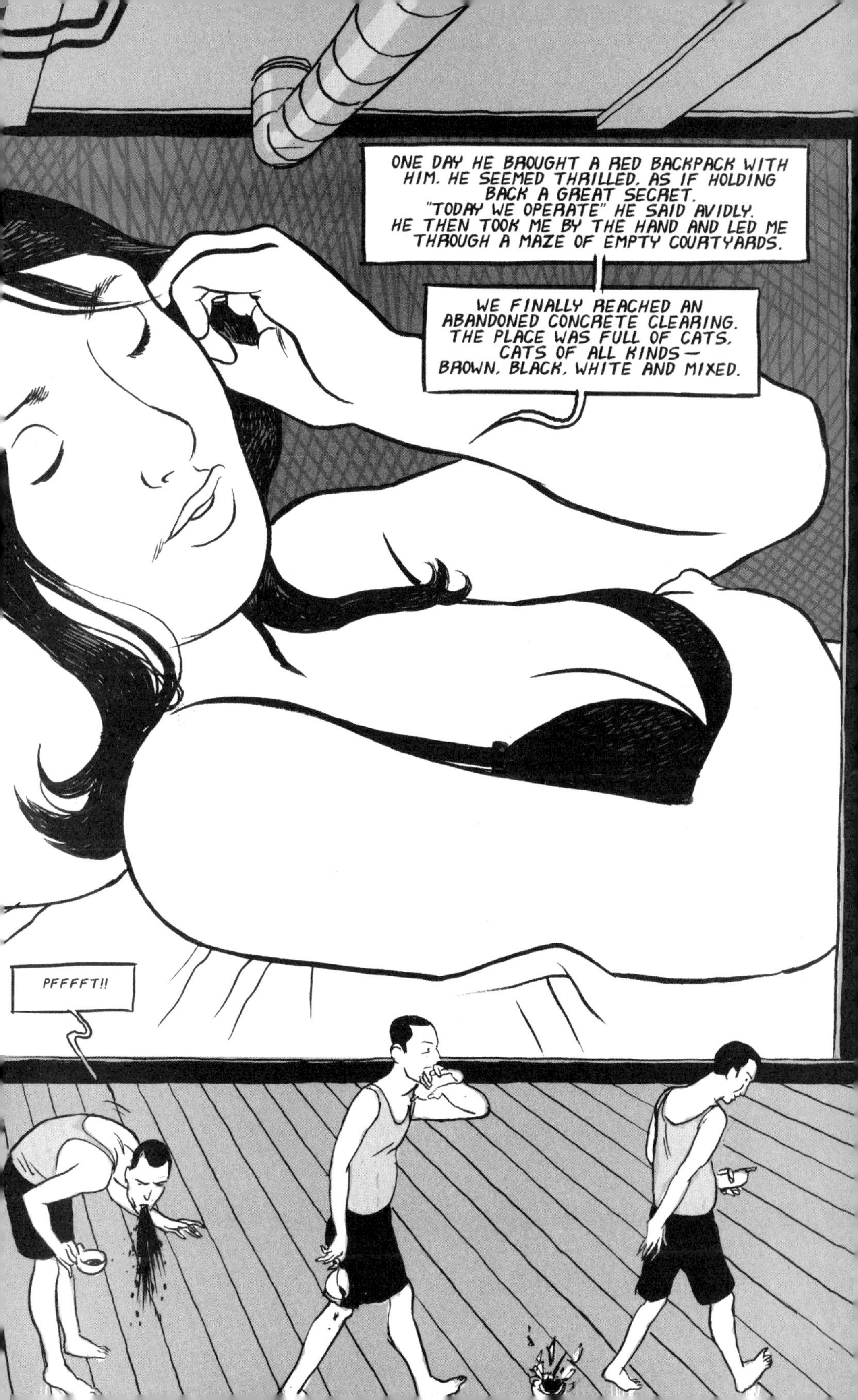
ONE DAY HE BROUGHT A RED BACKPACK WITH HIM. HE SEEMED THRILLED, AS IF HOLDING BACK A GREAT SECRET. "TODAY WE OPERATE" HE SAID AVIDLY. HE THEN TOOK ME BY THE HAND AND LED ME THROUGH A MAZE OF EMPTY COURTYARDS.
WE FINALLY REACHED AN ABANDONED CONCRETE CLEARING. THE PLACE WAS FULL OF CATS, CATS OF ALL KINDS— BROWN, BLACK, WHITE AND MIXED.
PFFFFT!!

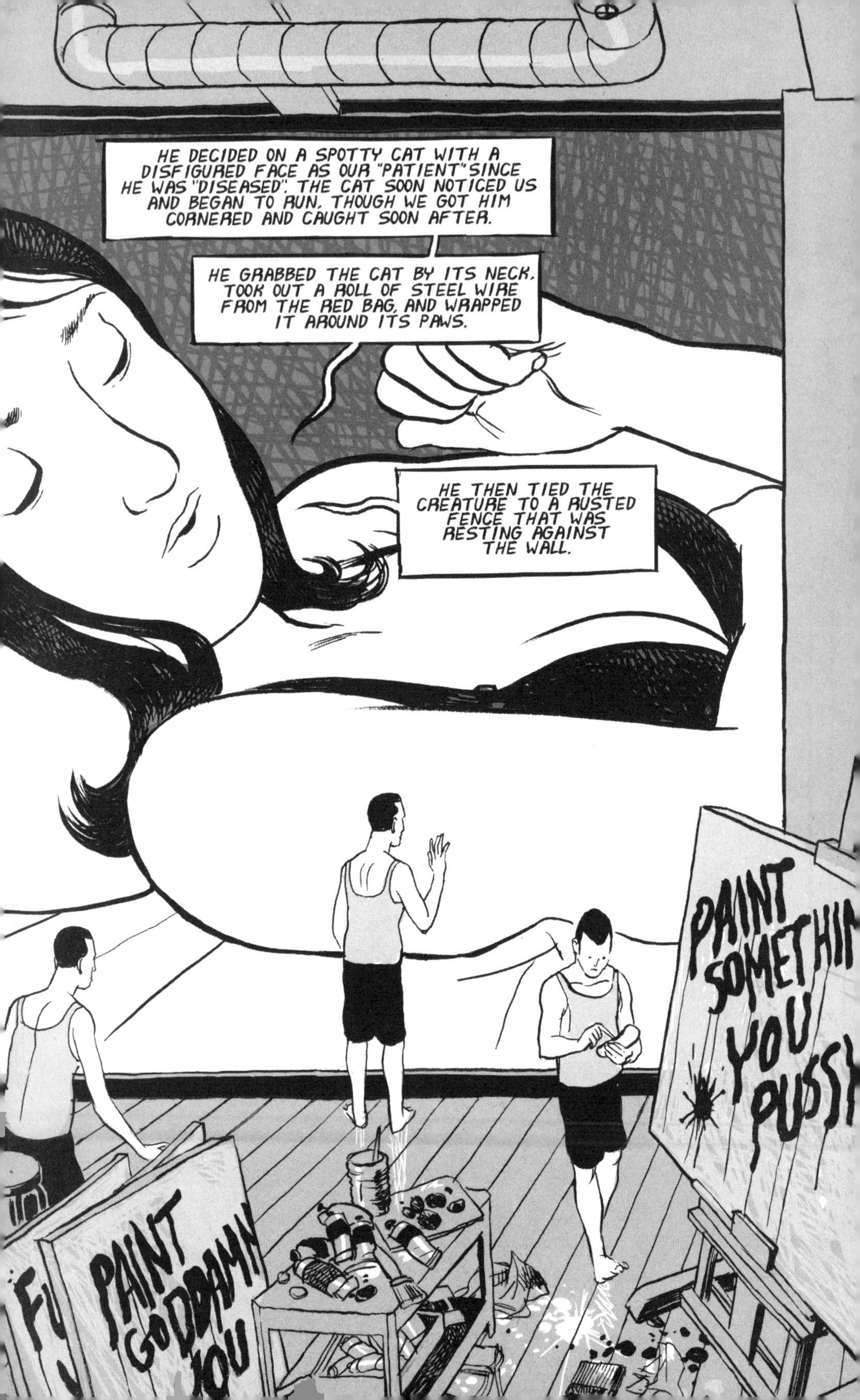
HE DECIDED ON A SPOTTY CAT WITH A DISFIGURED FACE AS OUR "PATIENT" SINCE HE WAS "DISEASED". THE CAT SOON NOTICED US AND BEGAN TO RUN, THOUGH WE GOT HIM CORNERED AND CAUGHT SOON AFTER.
HE GRABBED THE CAT BY ITS NECK, TOOK OUT A ROLL OF STEEL WIRE FROM THE RED BAG, AND WRAPPED IT AROUND ITS PAWS.
HE THEN TIED THE CREATURE TO A RUSTED FENCE THAT WAS RESTING AGAINST THE WALL.
PAINT SOMETHI
YOU
PUSS
PAINT GODDAMN YOU

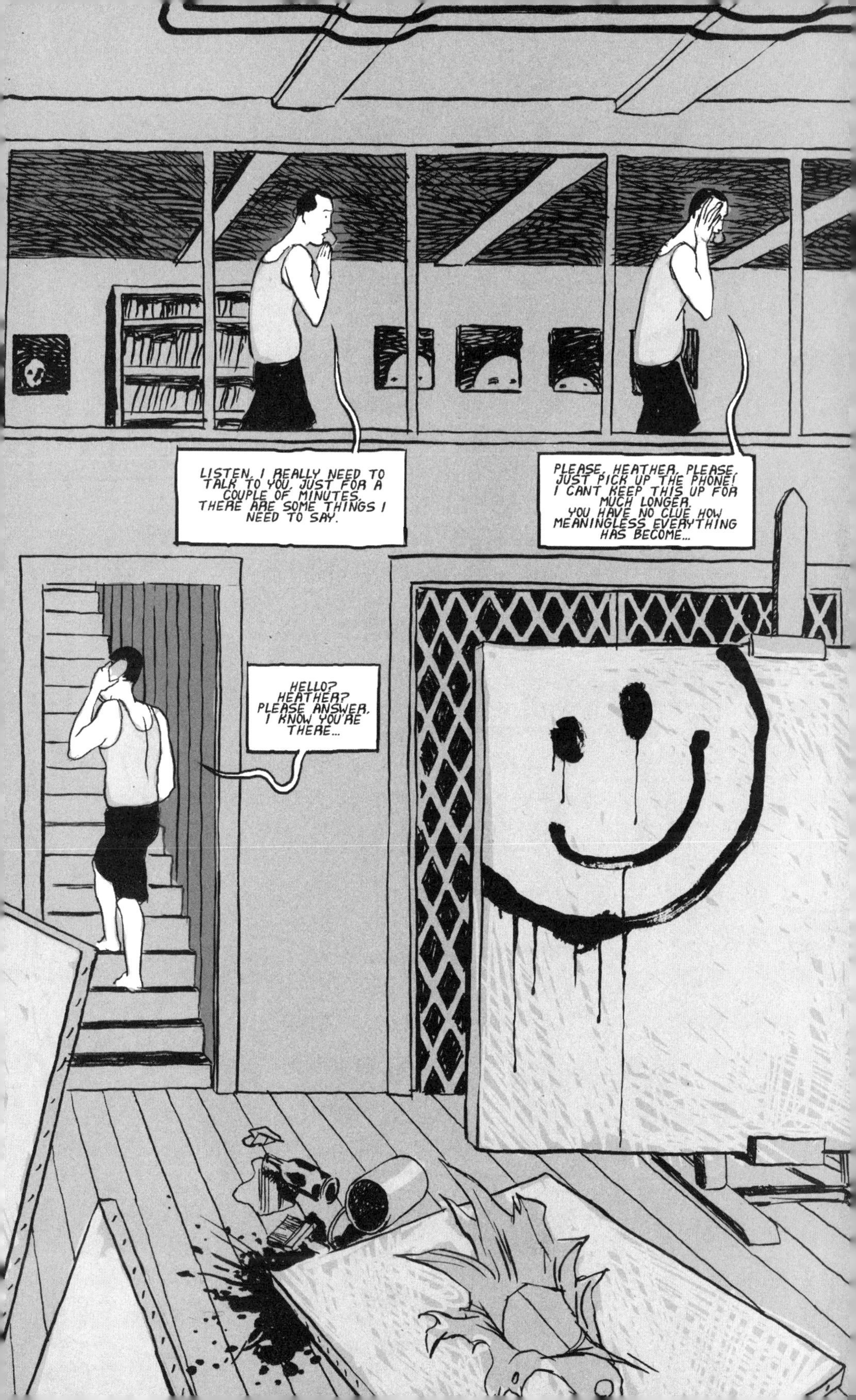
LISTEN, I REALLY NEED TO TALK TO YOU, JUST FOR A COUPLE OF MINUTES. THERE ARE SOME THINGS I NEED TO SAY.
PLEASE, HEATHER, PLEASE, JUST PICK UP THE PHONE! I CANT KEEP THIS UP FOR MUCH LONGER. YOU HAVE NO CLUE HOW MEANINGLESS EVERYTHING HAS BECOME...
HELLO? HEATHER? PLEASE ANSWER, I KNOW YOU'RE THERE...

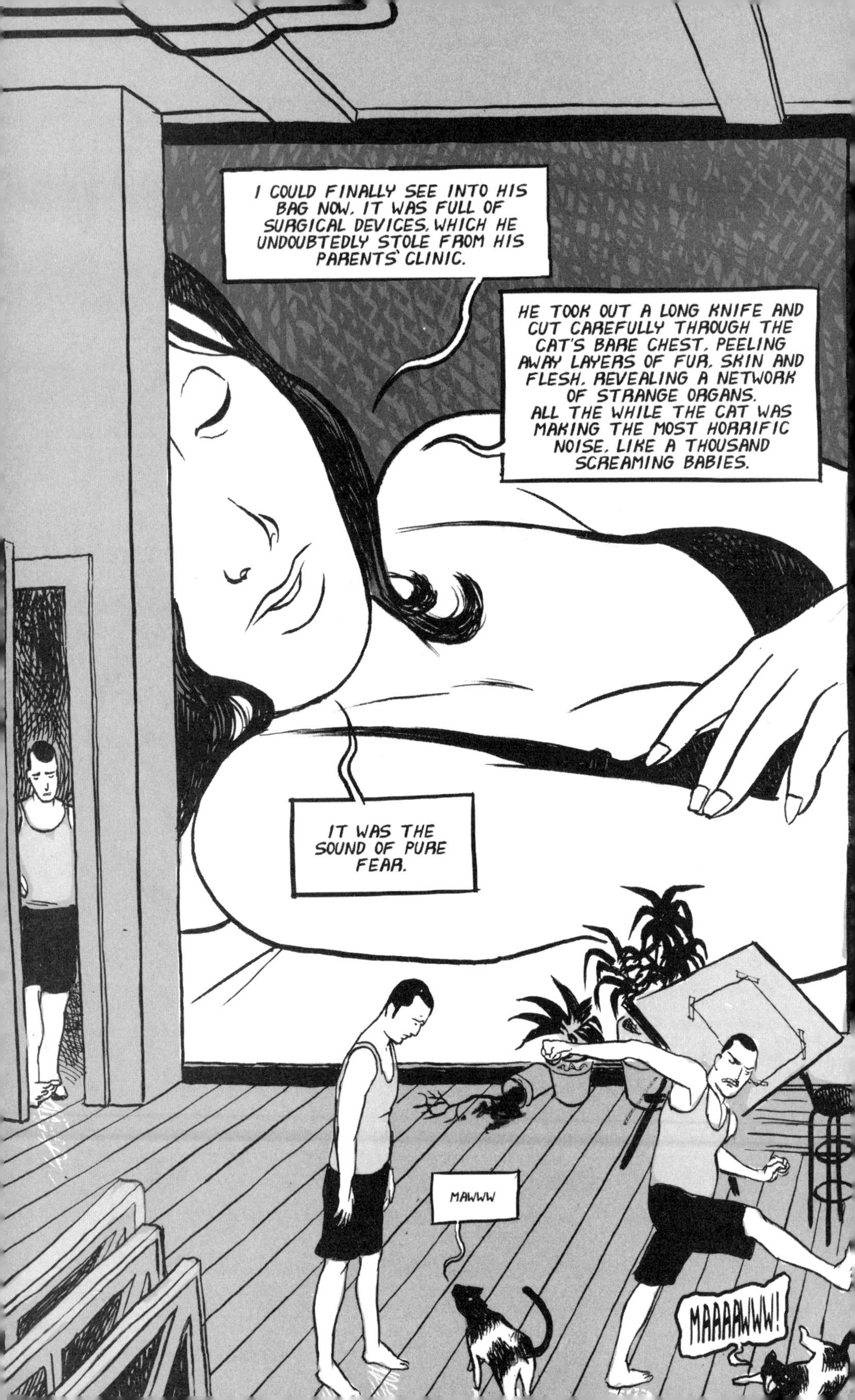
I COULD FINALLY SEE INTO HIS BAG NOW. IT WAS FULL OF SURGICAL DEVICES, WHICH HE UNDOUBTEDLY STOLE FROM HIS PARENTS' CLINIC.
HE TOOK OUT A LONG KNIFE AND CUT CAREFULLY THROUGH THE CAT'S BARE CHEST, PEELING AWAY LAYERS OF FUR, SKIN AND FLESH, REVEALING A NETWORK OF STRANGE ORGANS. ALL THE WHILE THE CAT WAS MAKING THE MOST HORRIFIC NOISE, LIKE A THOUSAND SCREAMING BABIES.
IT WAS THE SOUND OF PURE FEAR.
MAWWW
MAAAAWWW!

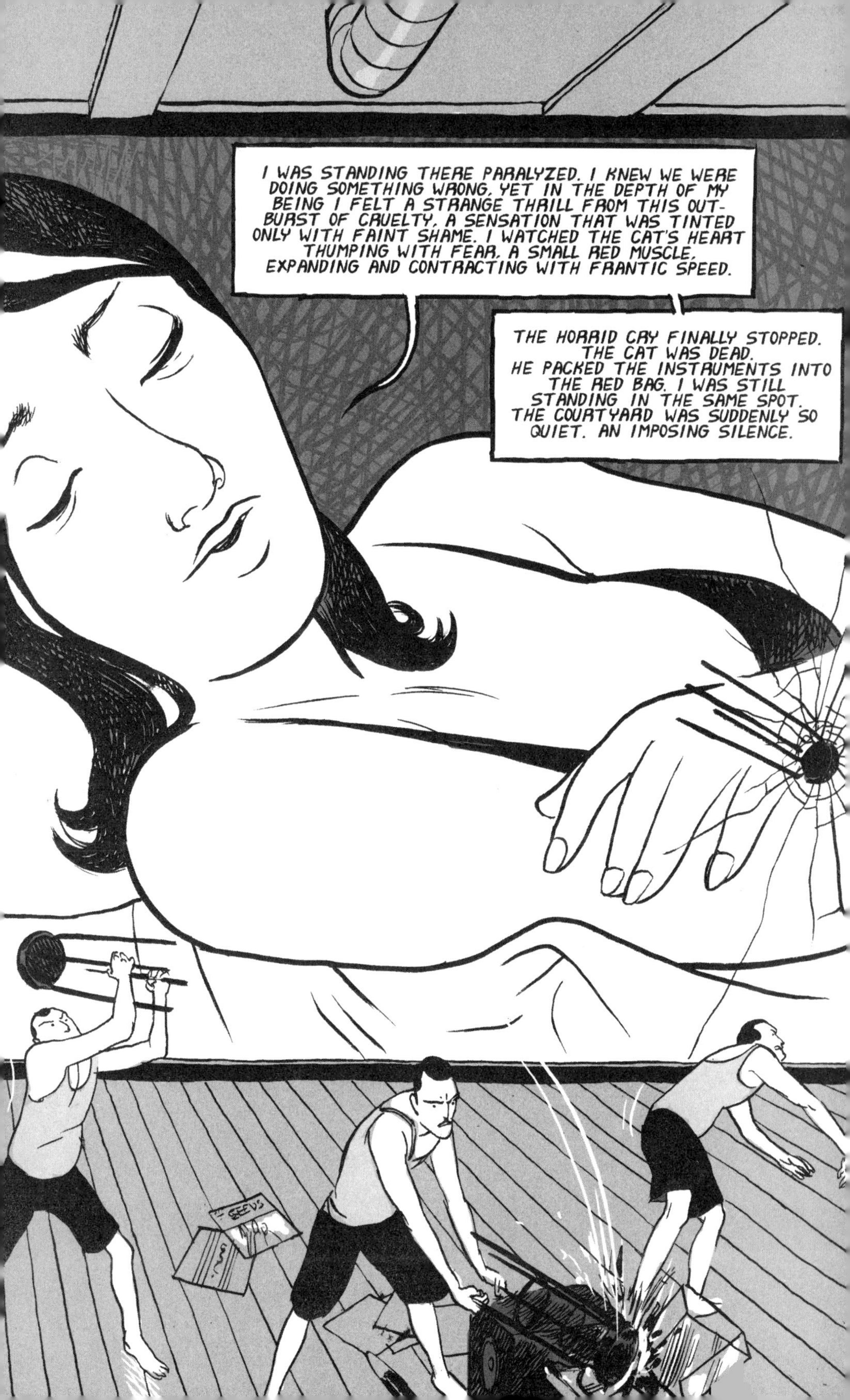
I WAS STANDING THERE PARALYZED. I KNEW WE WERE DOING SOMETHING WRONG. YET IN THE DEPTH OF MY BEING I FELT A STRANGE THRILL FROM THIS OUTBURST OF CRUELTY, A SENSATION THAT WAS TINTED ONLY WITH FAINT SHAME. I WATCHED THE CAT'S HEART THUMPING WITH FEAR, A SMALL RED MUSCLE, EXPANDING AND CONTRACTING WITH FRANTIC SPEED.
THE HORRID CRY FINALLY STOPPED. THE CAT WAS DEAD. HE PACKED THE INSTRUMENTS INTO THE RED BAG. I WAS STILL STANDING IN THE SAME SPOT. THE COURTYARD WAS SUDDENLY SO QUIET. AN IMPOSING SILENCE.

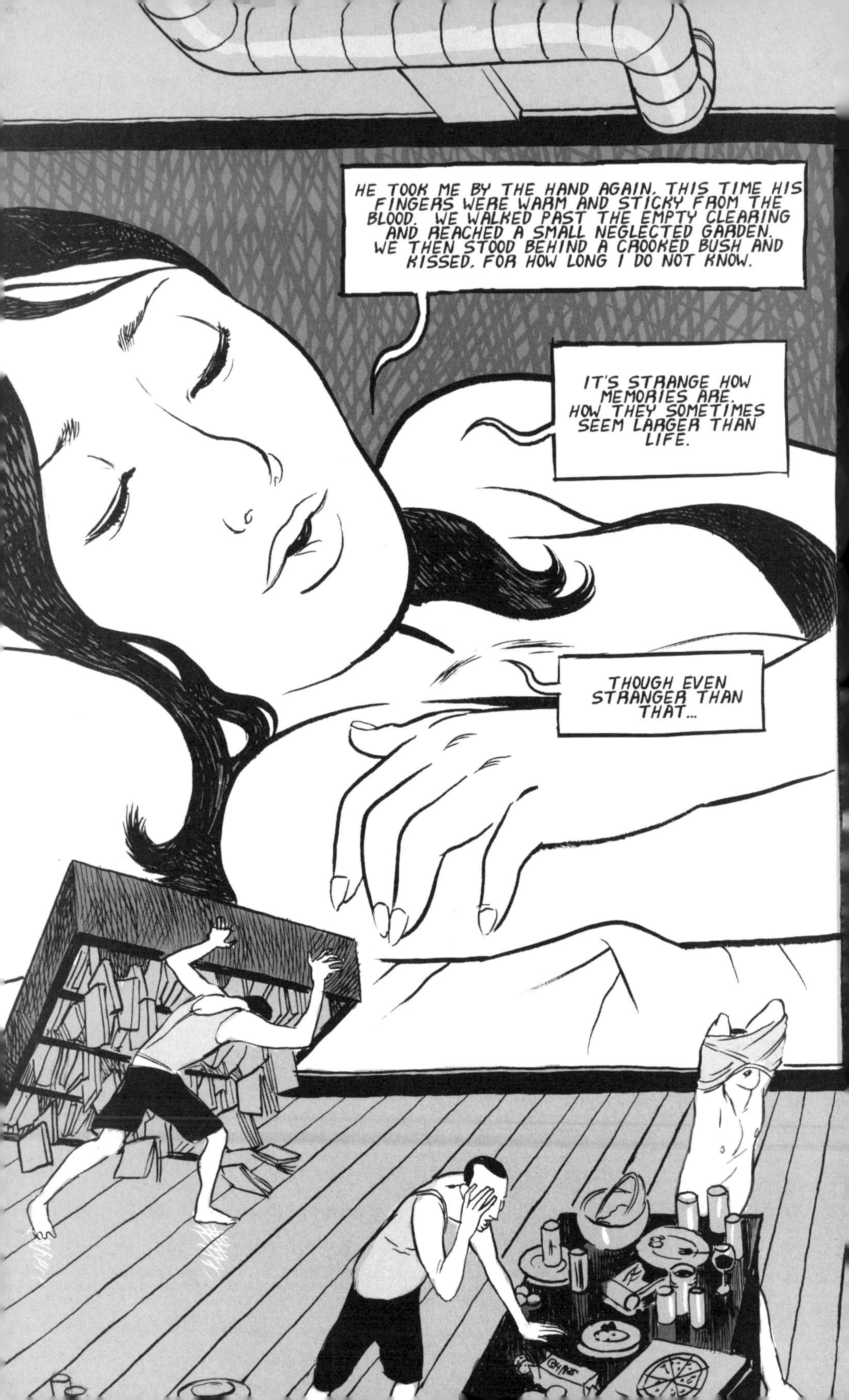
HE TOOK ME BY THE HAND AGAIN. THIS TIME HIS FINGERS WERE WARM AND STICKY FROM THE BLOOD. WE WALKED PAST THE EMPTY CLEARING AND REACHED A SMALL NEGLECTED GARDEN. WE THEN STOOD BEHIND A CROOKED BUSH AND KISSED, FOR HOW LONG I DO NOT KNOW.
IT'S STRANGE HOW MEMORIES ARE. HOW THEY SOMETIMES SEEM LARGER THAN LIFE.
THOUGH EVEN STRANGER THAN THAT...

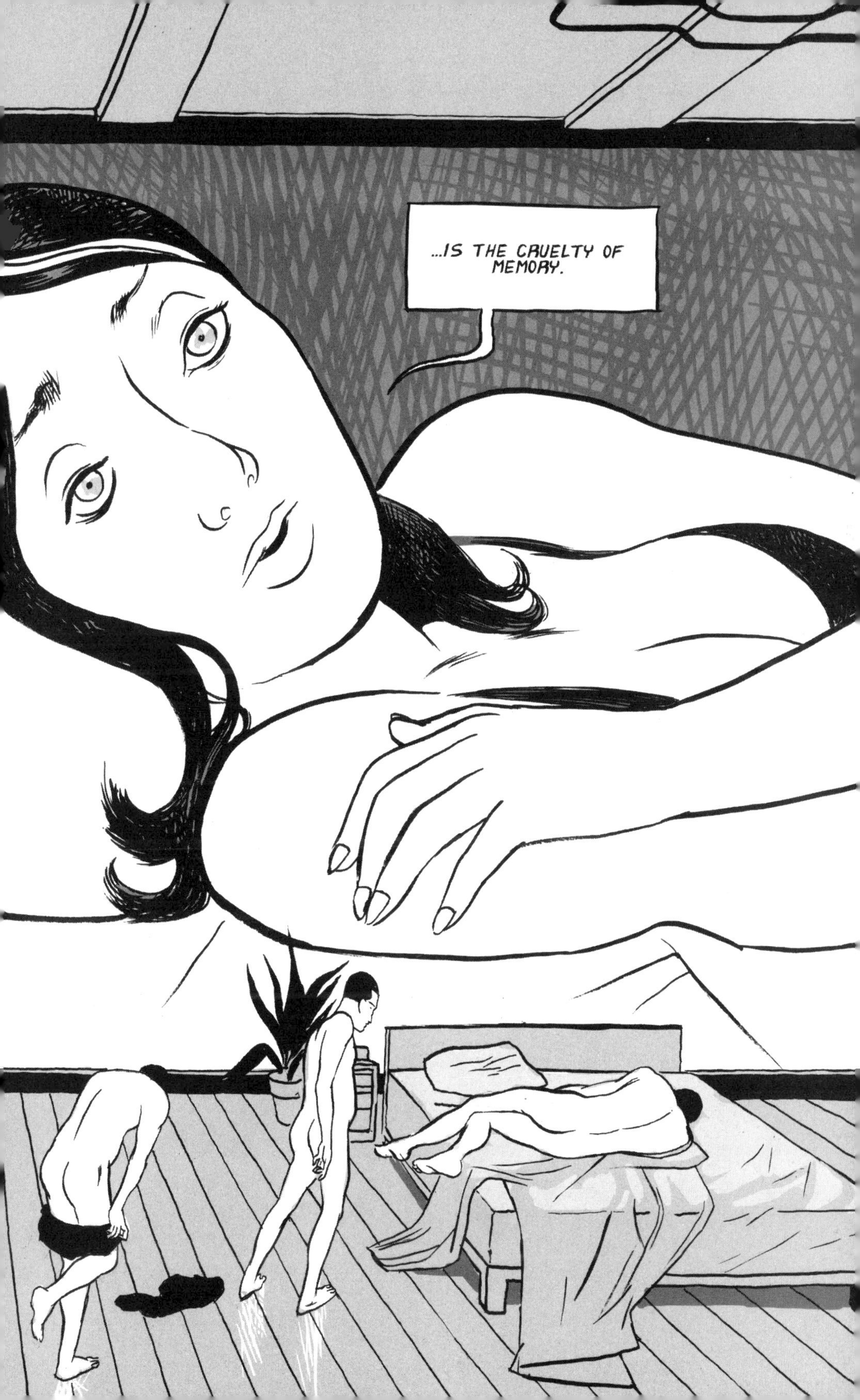
...IS THE CRUELTY OF MEMORY.

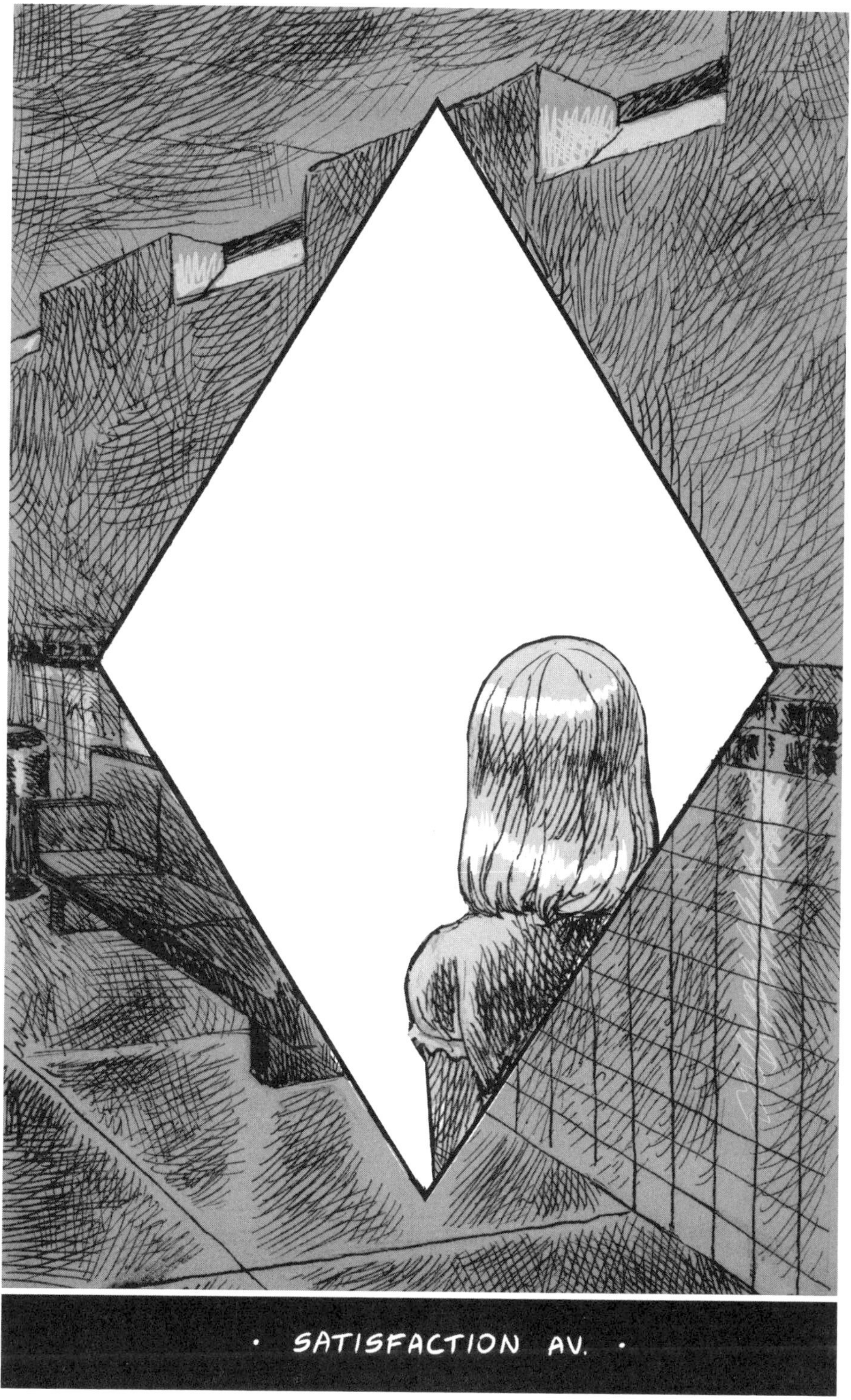
· SATISFACTION AV. ·

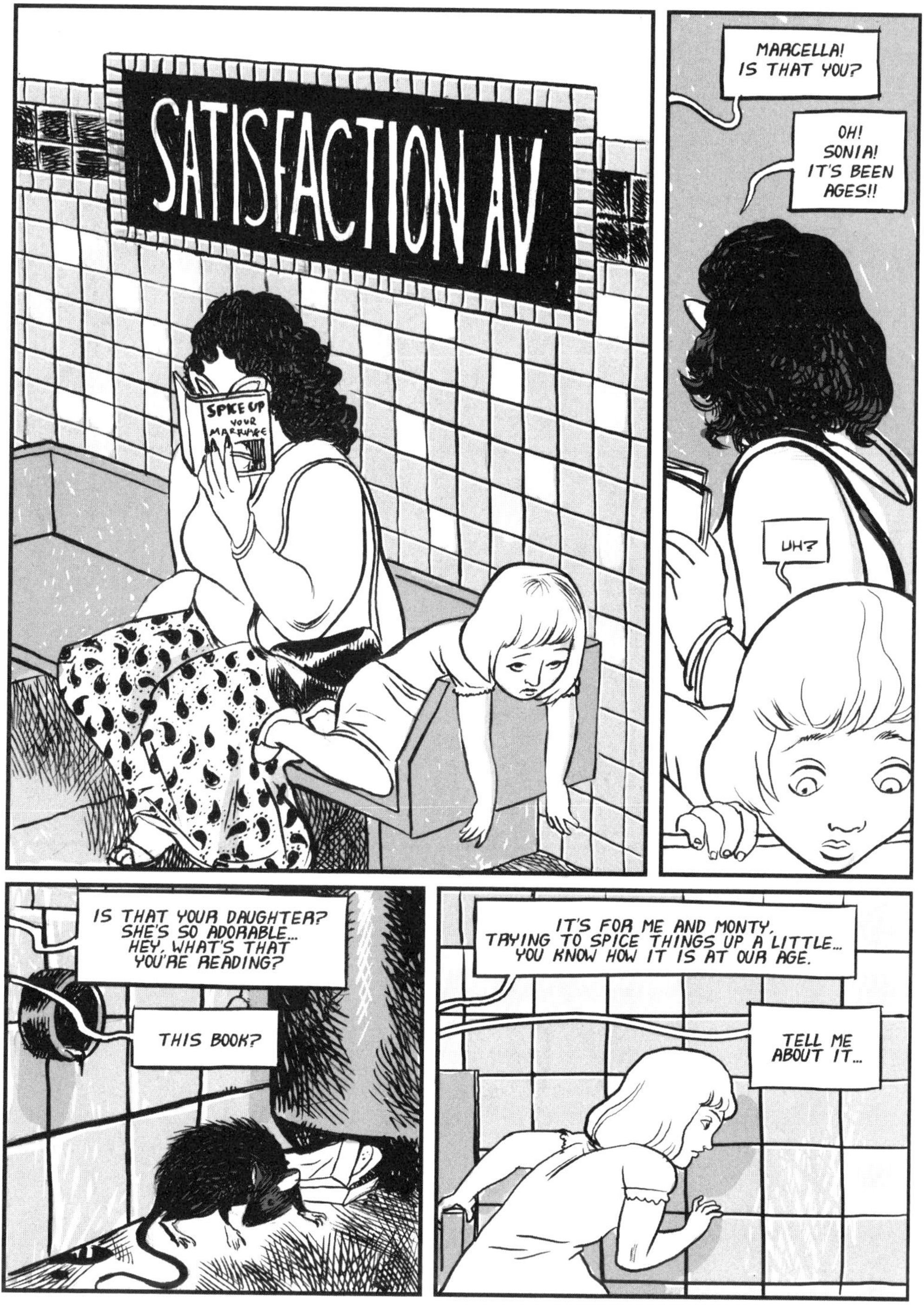
SATISFACTION AV
SPICE UP YOUR MARRIAGE
MARCELLA! IS THAT YOU?
OH! SONIA! IT'S BEEN AGES!!
UH?
IS THAT YOUR DAUGHTER? SHE'S SO ADORABLE... HEY, WHAT'S THAT YOU'RE READING?
THIS BOOK?
IT'S FOR ME AND MONTY, TRYING TO SPICE THINGS UP A LITTLE... YOU KNOW HOW IT IS AT OUR AGE.
TELL ME ABOUT IT...

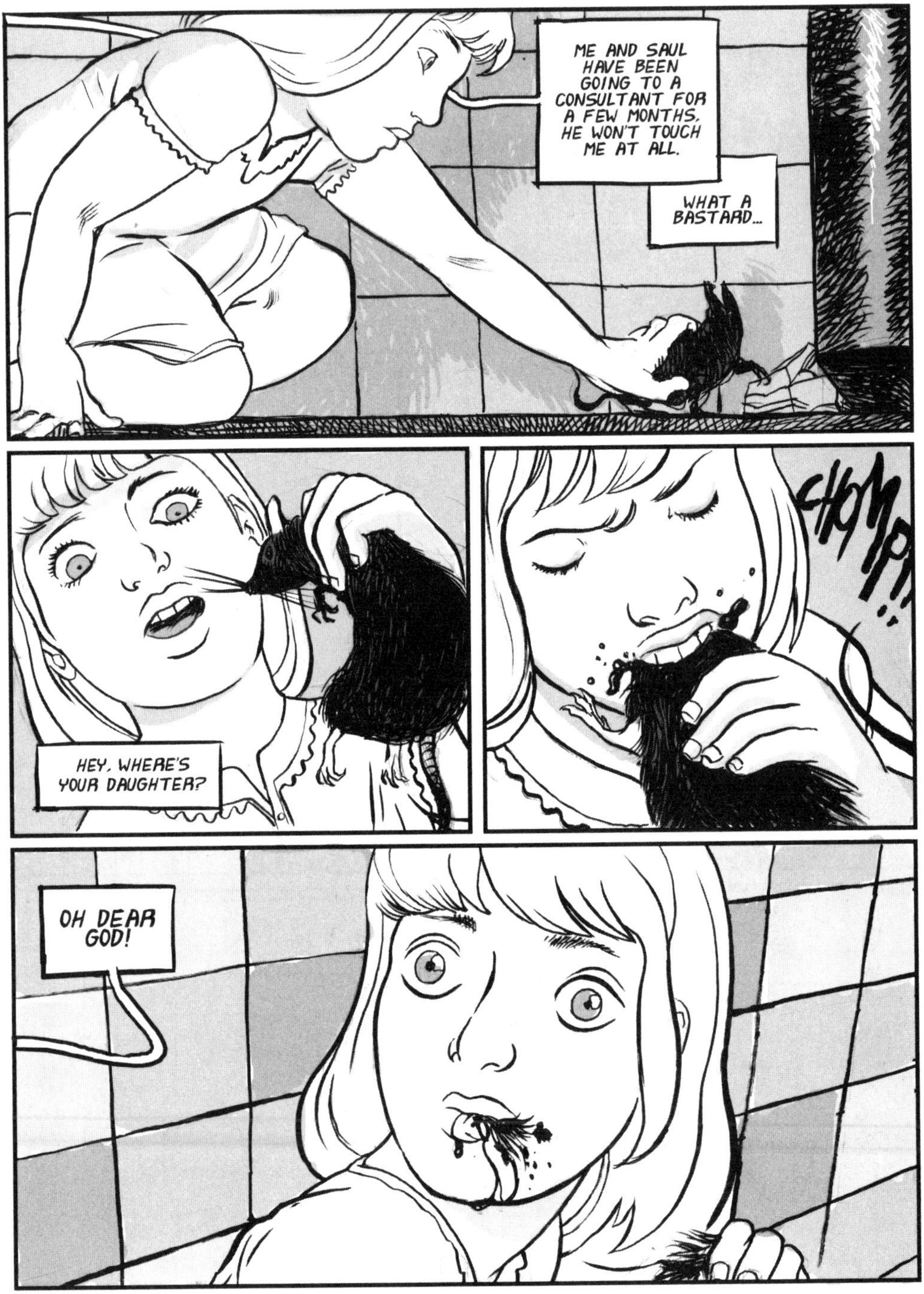
ME AND SAUL HAVE BEEN GOING TO A CONSULTANT FOR A FEW MONTHS. HE WON'T TOUCH ME AT ALL.
WHAT A BASTARD...
HEY, WHERE'S YOUR DAUGHTER?
CHOMP!!
OH DEAR GOD!

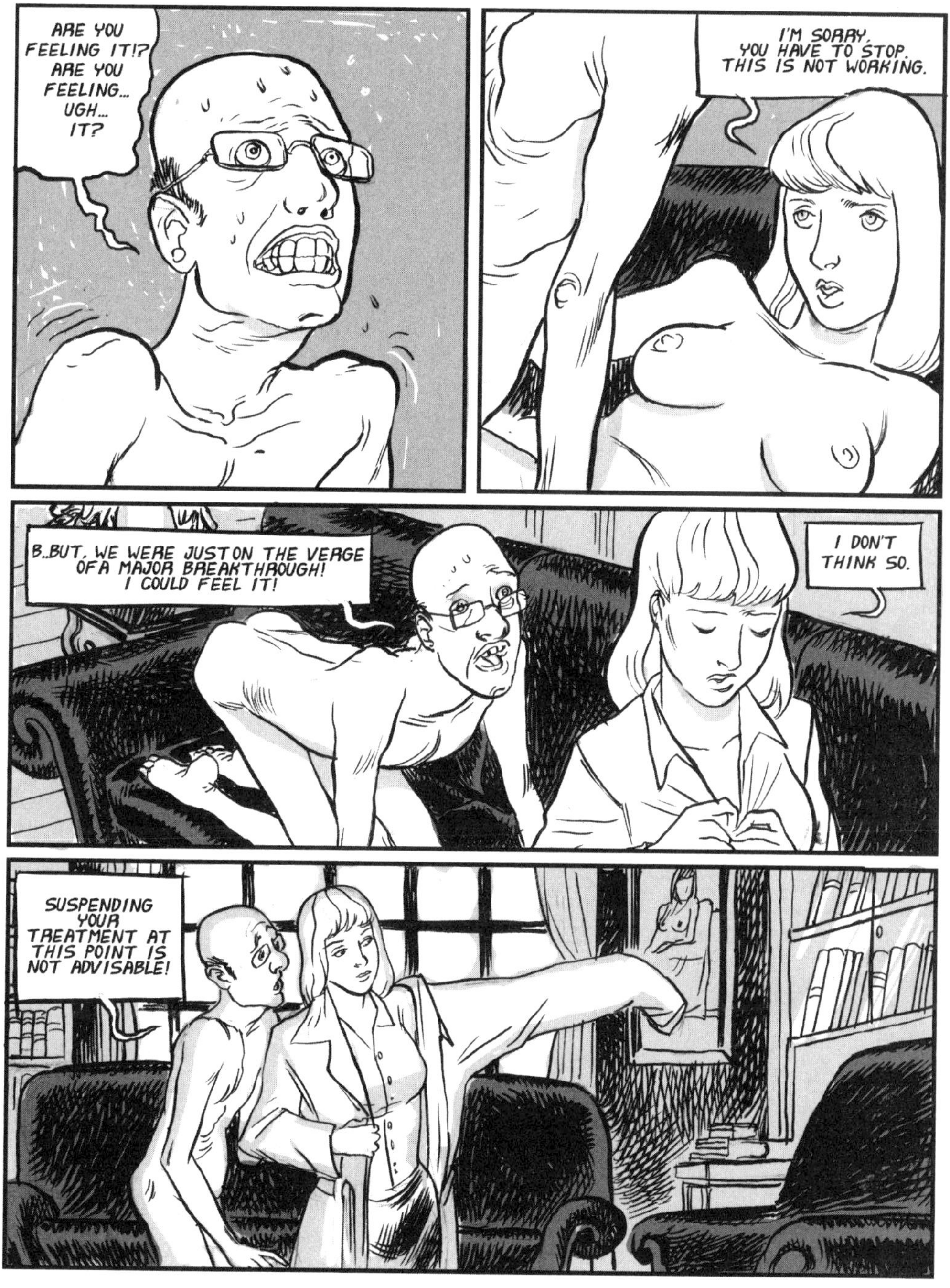
ARE YOU FEELING IT!? ARE YOU FEELING... UGH... IT?
I'M SORRY. YOU HAVE TO STOP. THIS IS NOT WORKING.
B..BUT, WE WERE JUST ON THE VERGE OF A MAJOR BREAKTHROUGH! I COULD FEEL IT!
I DON'T THINK SO.
SUSPENDING YOUR TREATMENT AT THIS POINT IS NOT ADVISABLE!

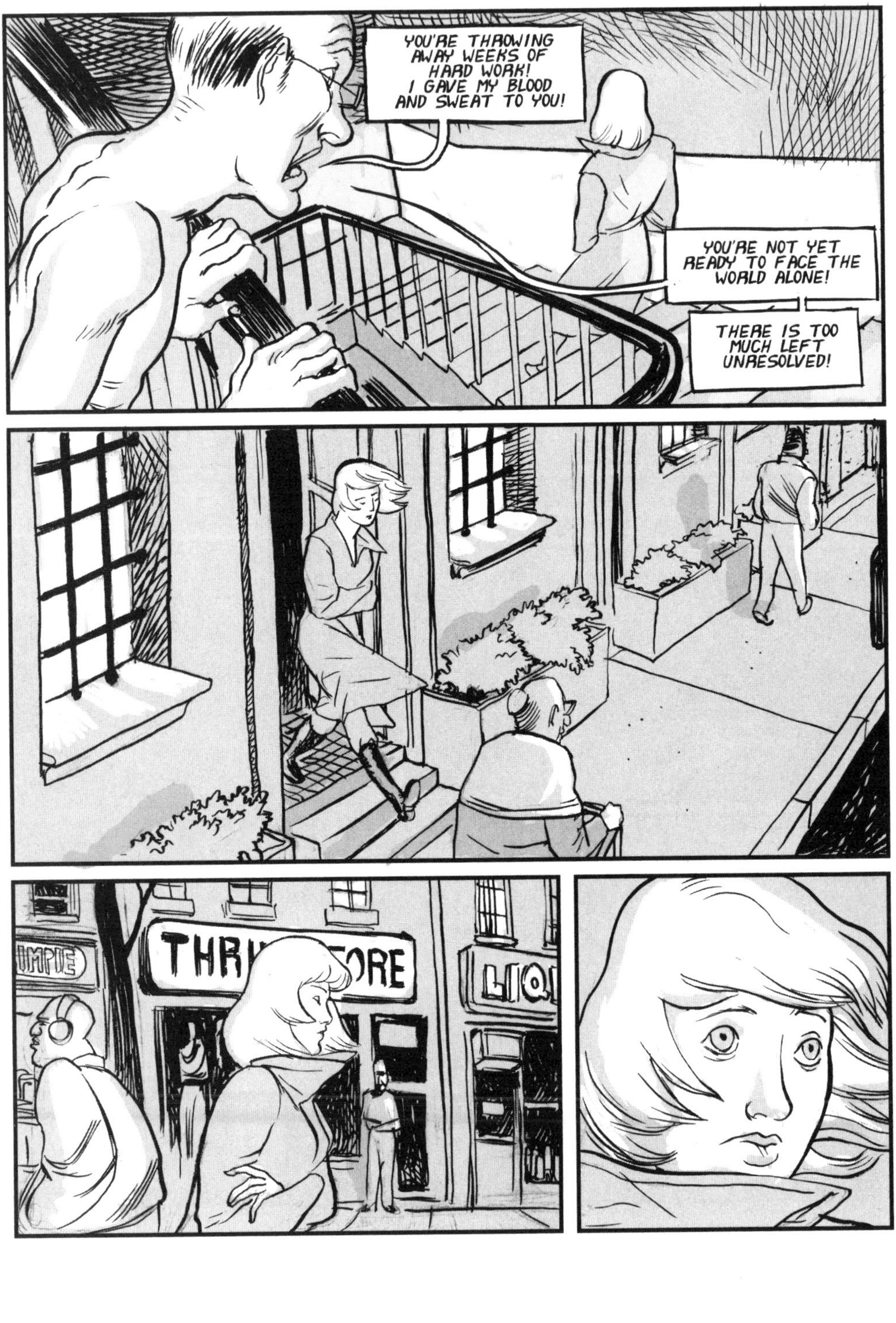
YOU'RE THROWING AWAY WEEKS OF HARD WORK! I GAVE MY BLOOD AND SWEAT TO YOU!
YOU'RE NOT YET READY TO FACE THE WORLD ALONE!
THERE IS TOO MUCH LEFT UNRESOLVED!
THRI ORE
LIQ

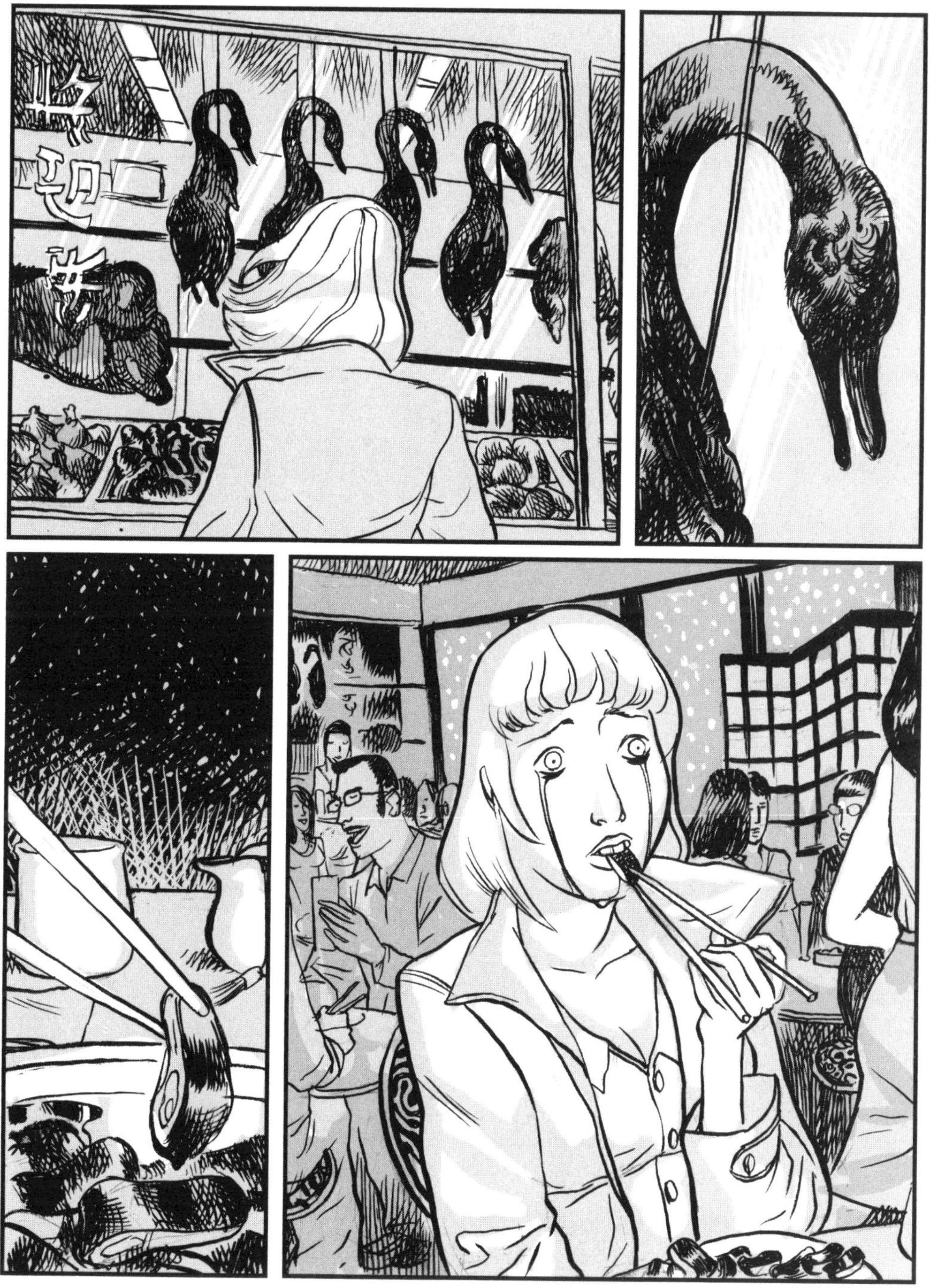

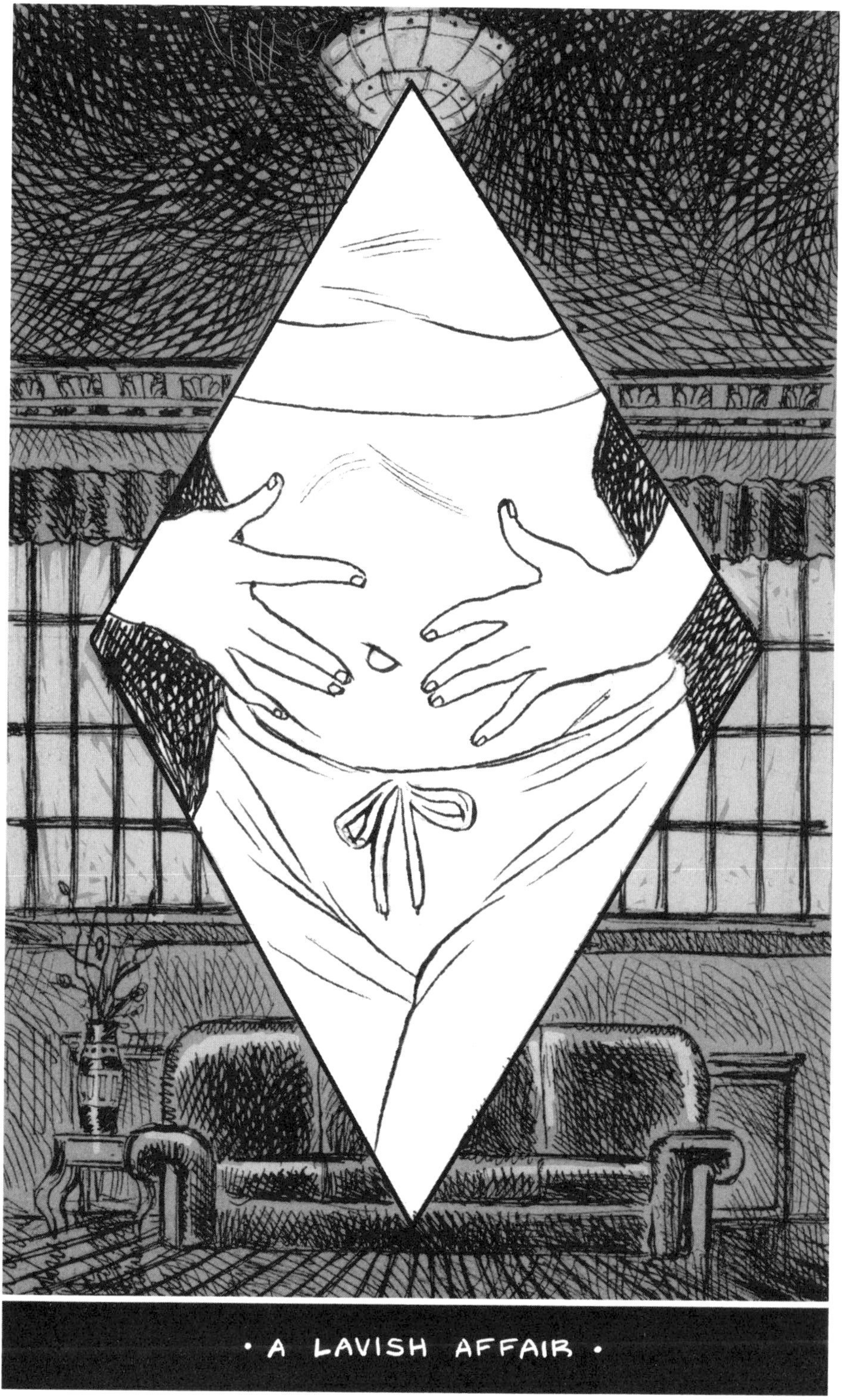

• A LAVISH AFFAIR •

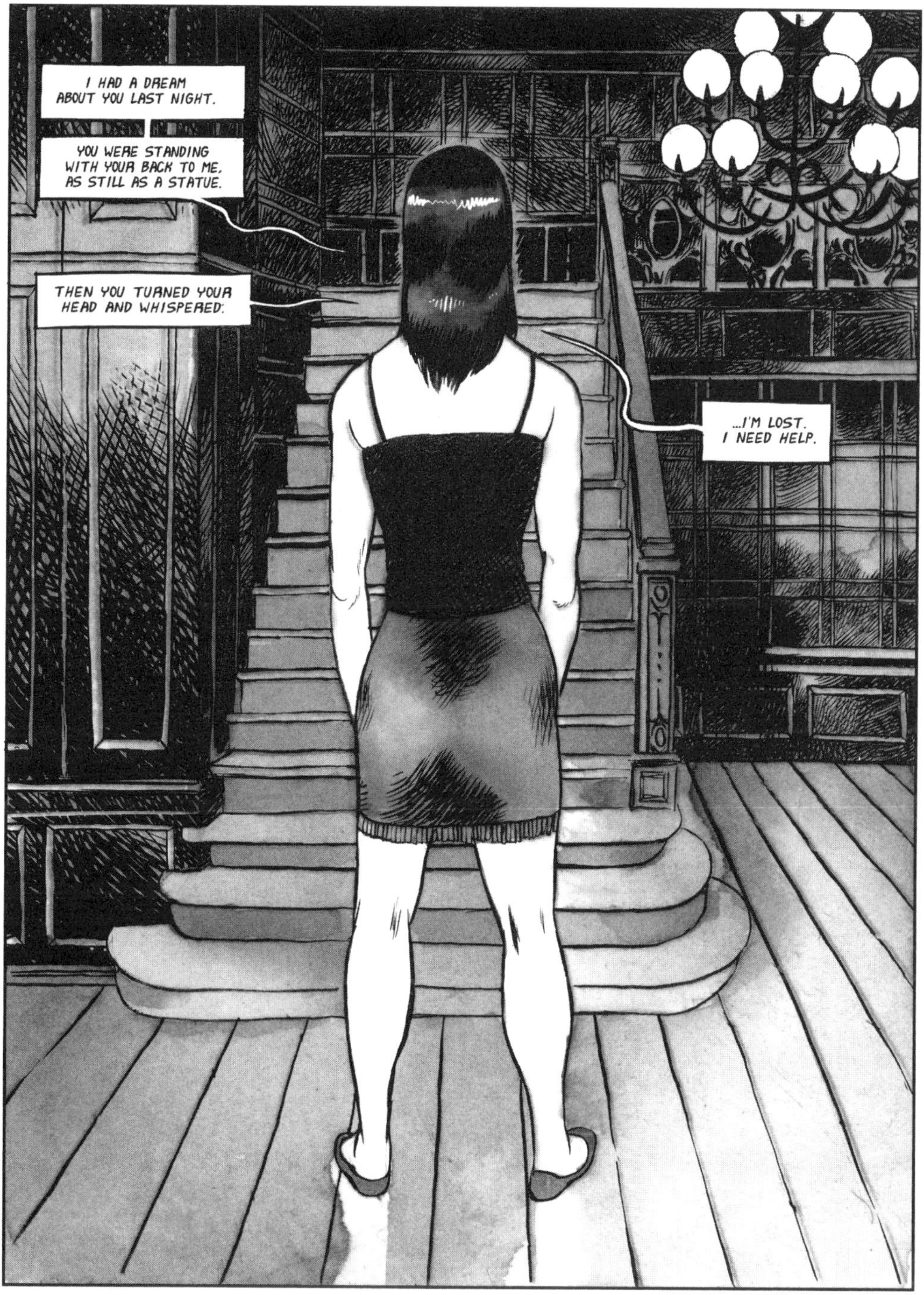
I HAD A DREAM ABOUT YOU LAST NIGHT.
YOU WERE STANDING WITH YOUR BACK TO ME, AS STILL AS A STATUE.
THEN YOU TURNED YOUR HEAD AND WHISPERED:
...I'M LOST. I NEED HELP.

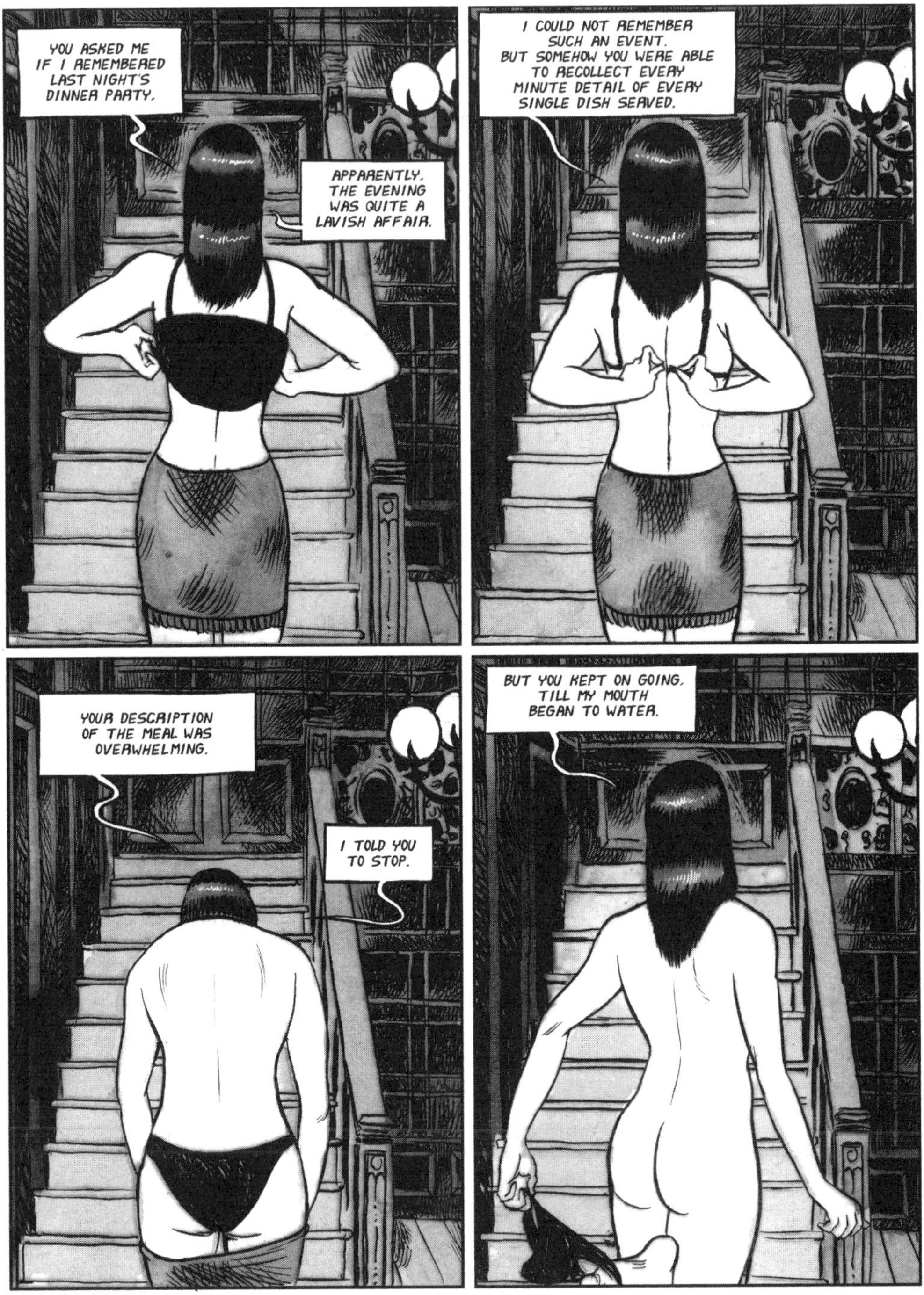
YOU ASKED ME IF I REMEMBERED LAST NIGHT'S DINNER PARTY.
APPARENTLY, THE EVENING WAS QUITE A LAVISH AFFAIR.
I COULD NOT REMEMBER SUCH AN EVENT. BUT SOMEHOW YOU WERE ABLE TO RECOLLECT EVERY MINUTE DETAIL OF EVERY SINGLE DISH SERVED.
YOUR DESCRIPTION OF THE MEAL WAS OVERWHELMING.
I TOLD YOU TO STOP.
BUT YOU KEPT ON GOING, TILL MY MOUTH BEGAN TO WATER.

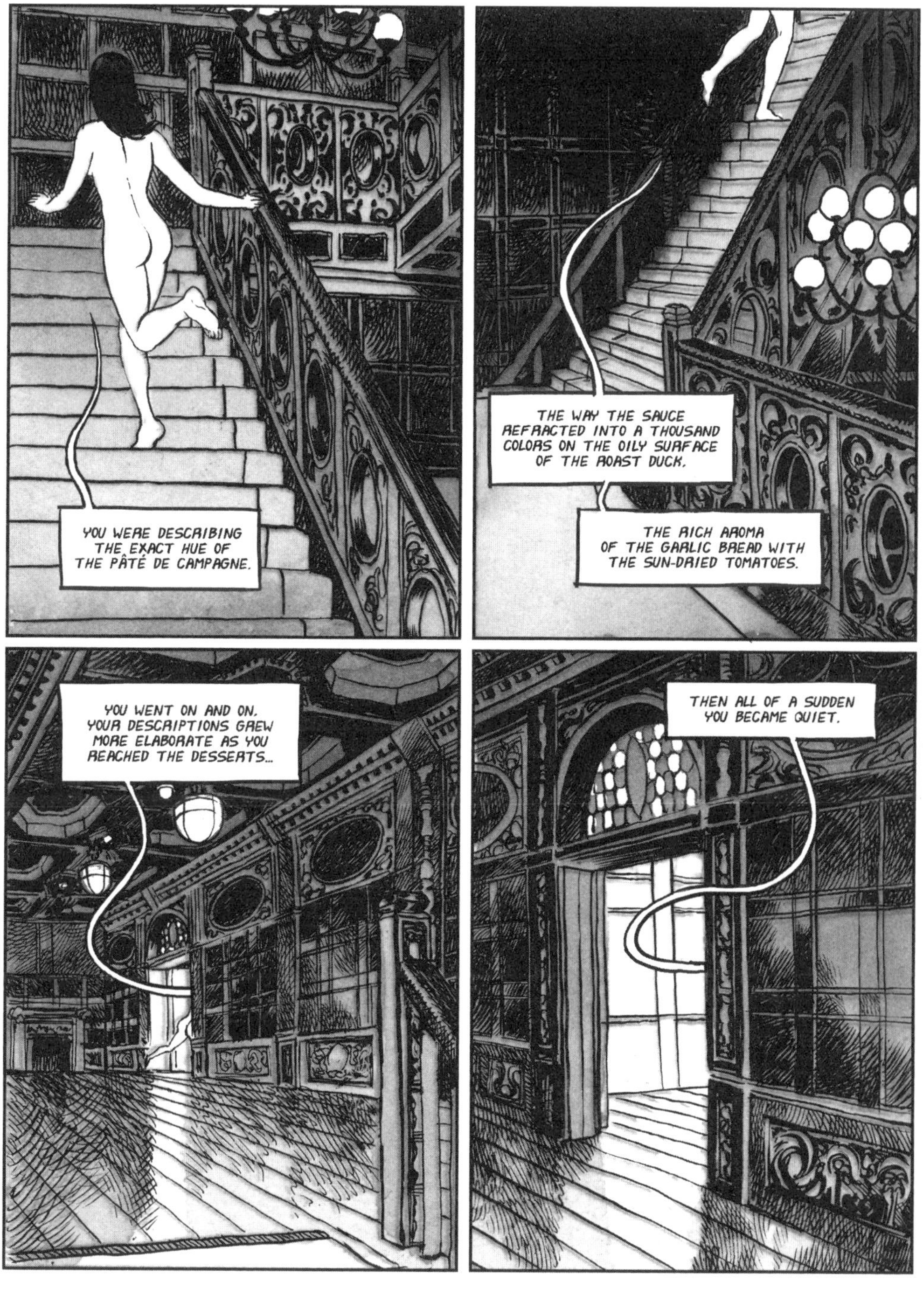

YOU WERE DESCRIBING THE EXACT HUE OF THE PÂTÉ DE CAMPAGNE.
THE WAY THE SAUCE REFRACTED INTO A THOUSAND COLORS ON THE OILY SURFACE OF THE ROAST DUCK.
THE RICH AROMA OF THE GARLIC BREAD WITH THE SUN-DRIED TOMATOES.
YOU WENT ON AND ON. YOUR DESCRIPTIONS GREW MORE ELABORATE AS YOU REACHED THE DESSERTS...
THEN ALL OF A SUDDEN YOU BECAME QUIET.

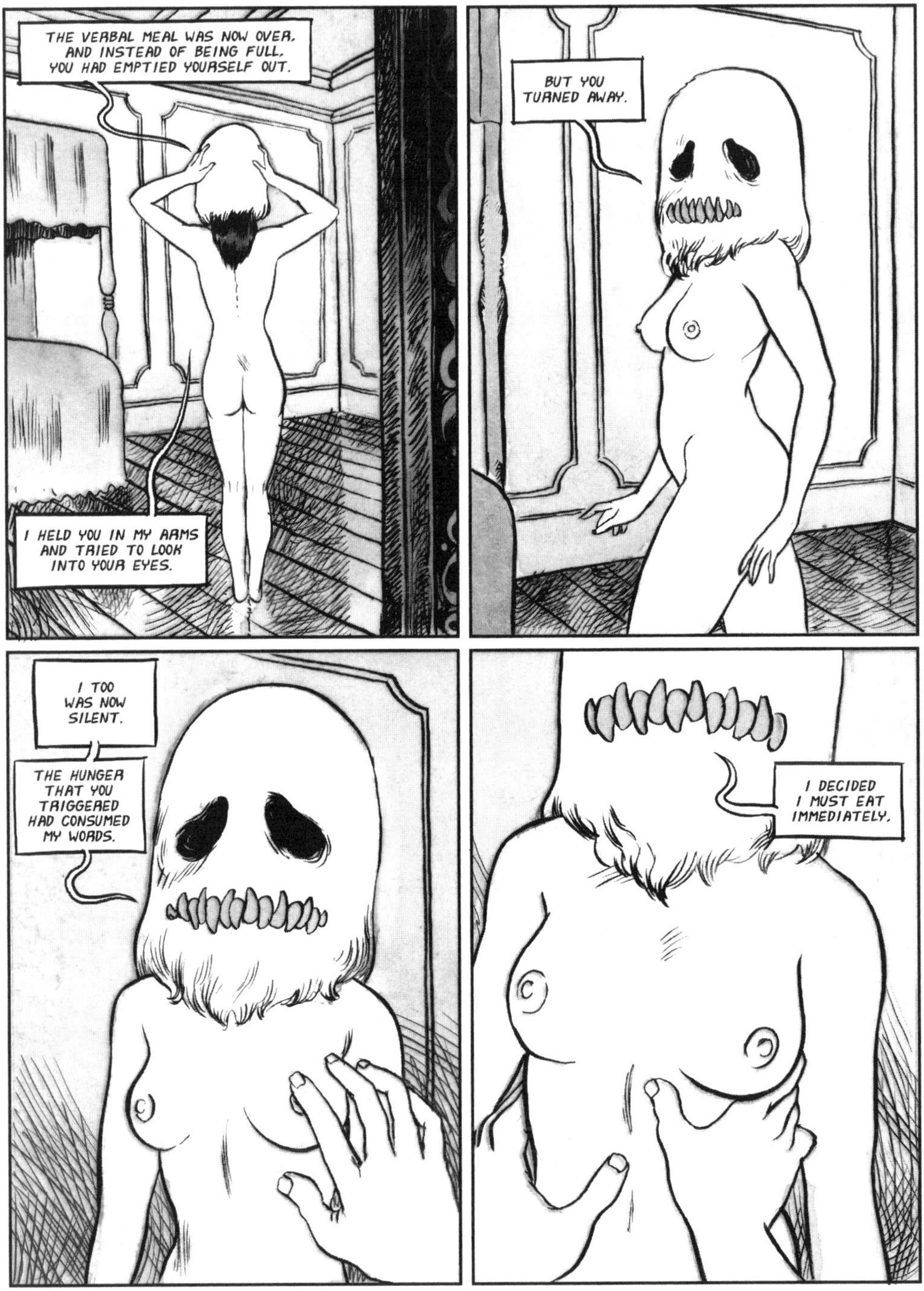
THE VERBAL MEAL WAS NOW OVER, AND INSTEAD OF BEING FULL, YOU HAD EMPTIED YOURSELF OUT.
I HELD YOU IN MY ARMS AND TRIED TO LOOK INTO YOUR EYES.
BUT YOU TURNED AWAY.
I TOO WAS NOW SILENT.
THE HUNGER THAT YOU TRIGGERED HAD CONSUMED MY WORDS.
I DECIDED I MUST EAT IMMEDIATELY.

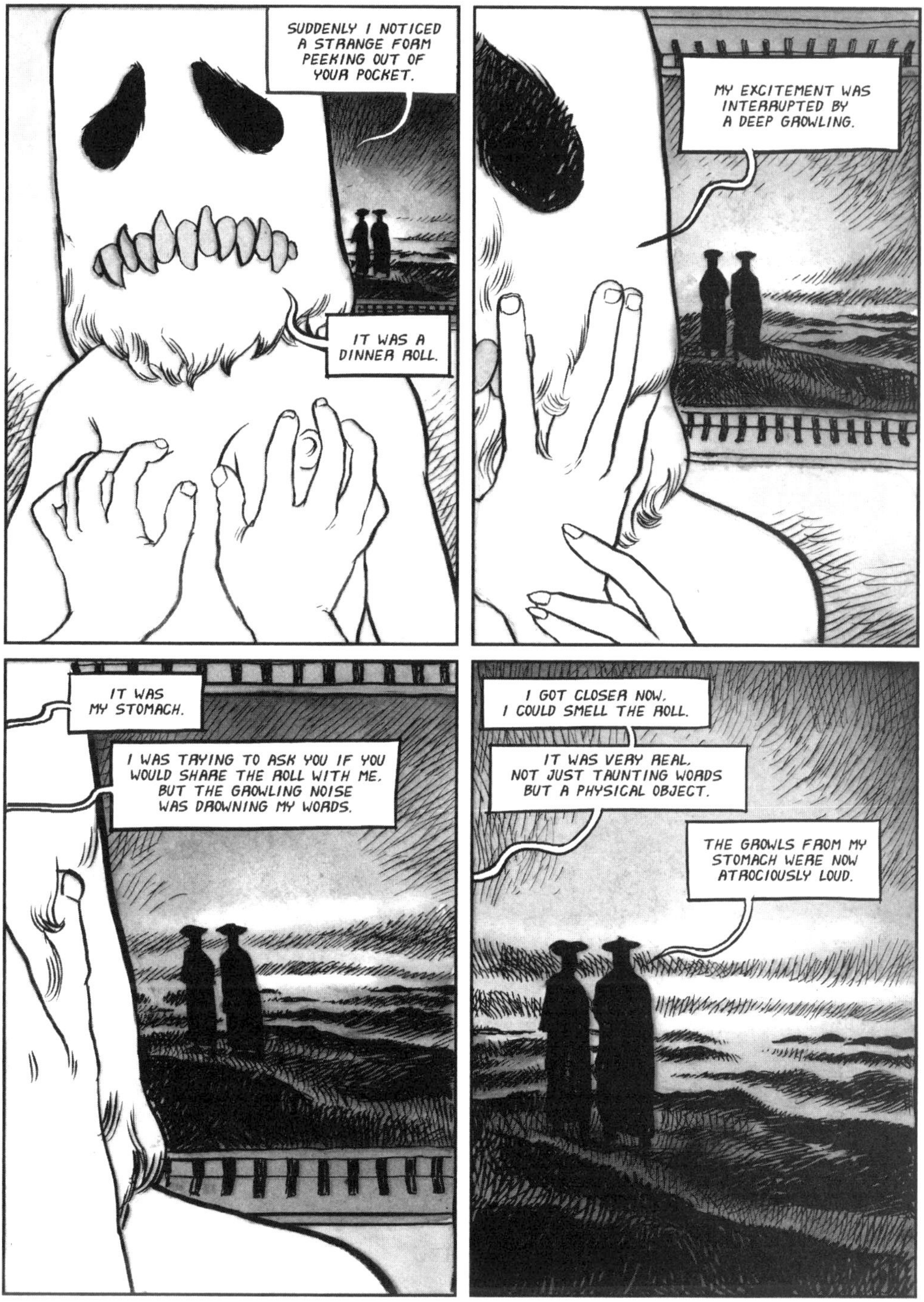
SUDDENLY I NOTICED A STRANGE FORM PEEKING OUT OF YOUR POCKET.
IT WAS A DINNER ROLL.
MY EXCITEMENT WAS INTERRUPTED BY A DEEP GROWLING.
IT WAS MY STOMACH.
I WAS TRYING TO ASK YOU IF YOU WOULD SHARE THE ROLL WITH ME, BUT THE GROWLING NOISE WAS DROWNING MY WORDS.
I GOT CLOSER NOW. I COULD SMELL THE ROLL.
IT WAS VERY REAL, NOT JUST TAUNTING WORDS BUT A PHYSICAL OBJECT.
THE GROWLS FROM MY STOMACH WERE NOW ATROCIOUSLY LOUD.

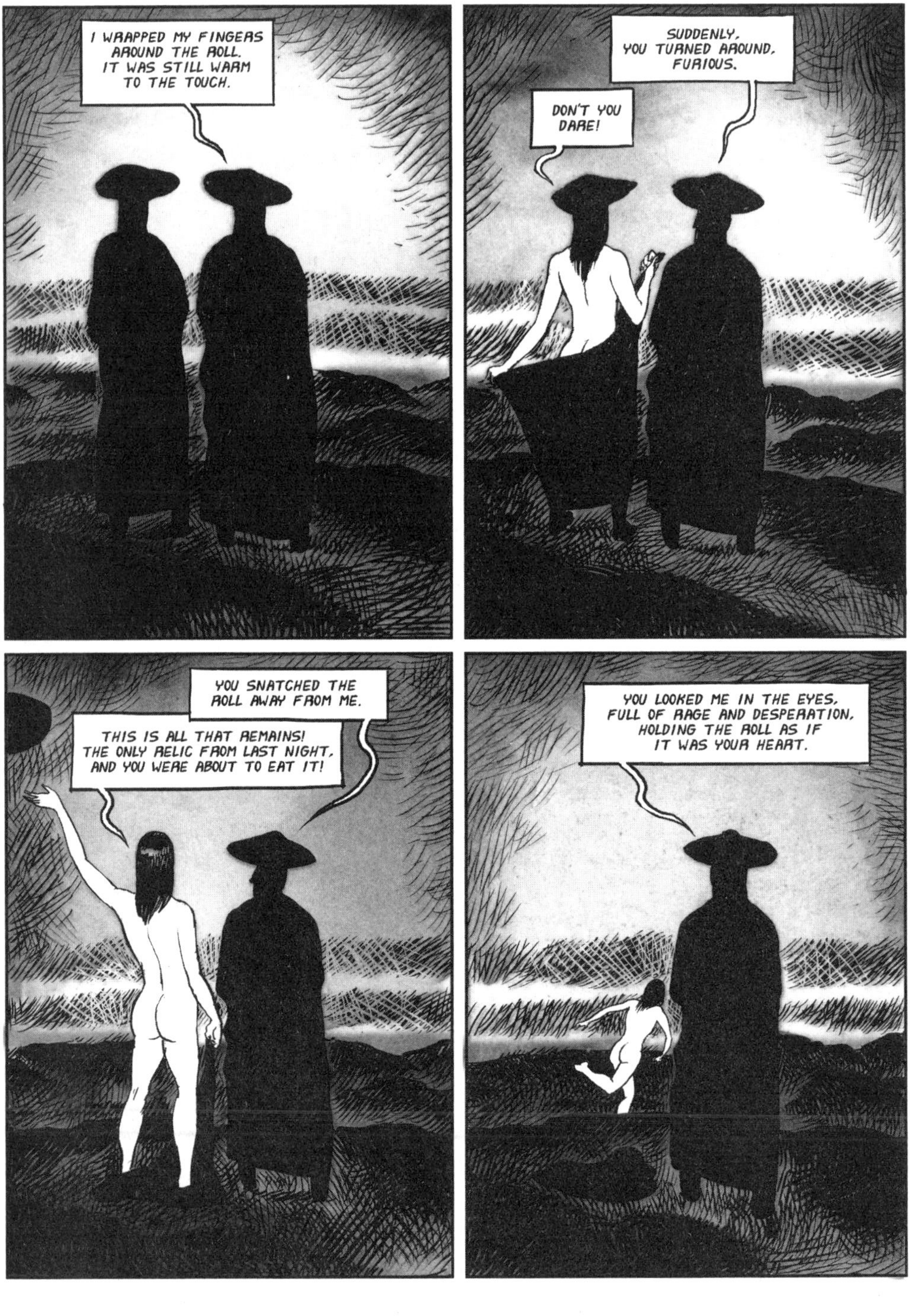
I WRAPPED MY FINGERS AROUND THE ROLL. IT WAS STILL WARM TO THE TOUCH.
SUDDENLY, YOU TURNED AROUND, FURIOUS.
DON'T YOU DARE!
YOU SNATCHED THE ROLL AWAY FROM ME.
THIS IS ALL THAT REMAINS! THE ONLY RELIC FROM LAST NIGHT, AND YOU WERE ABOUT TO EAT IT!
YOU LOOKED ME IN THE EYES, FULL OF RAGE AND DESPERATION, HOLDING THE ROLL AS IF IT WAS YOUR HEART.

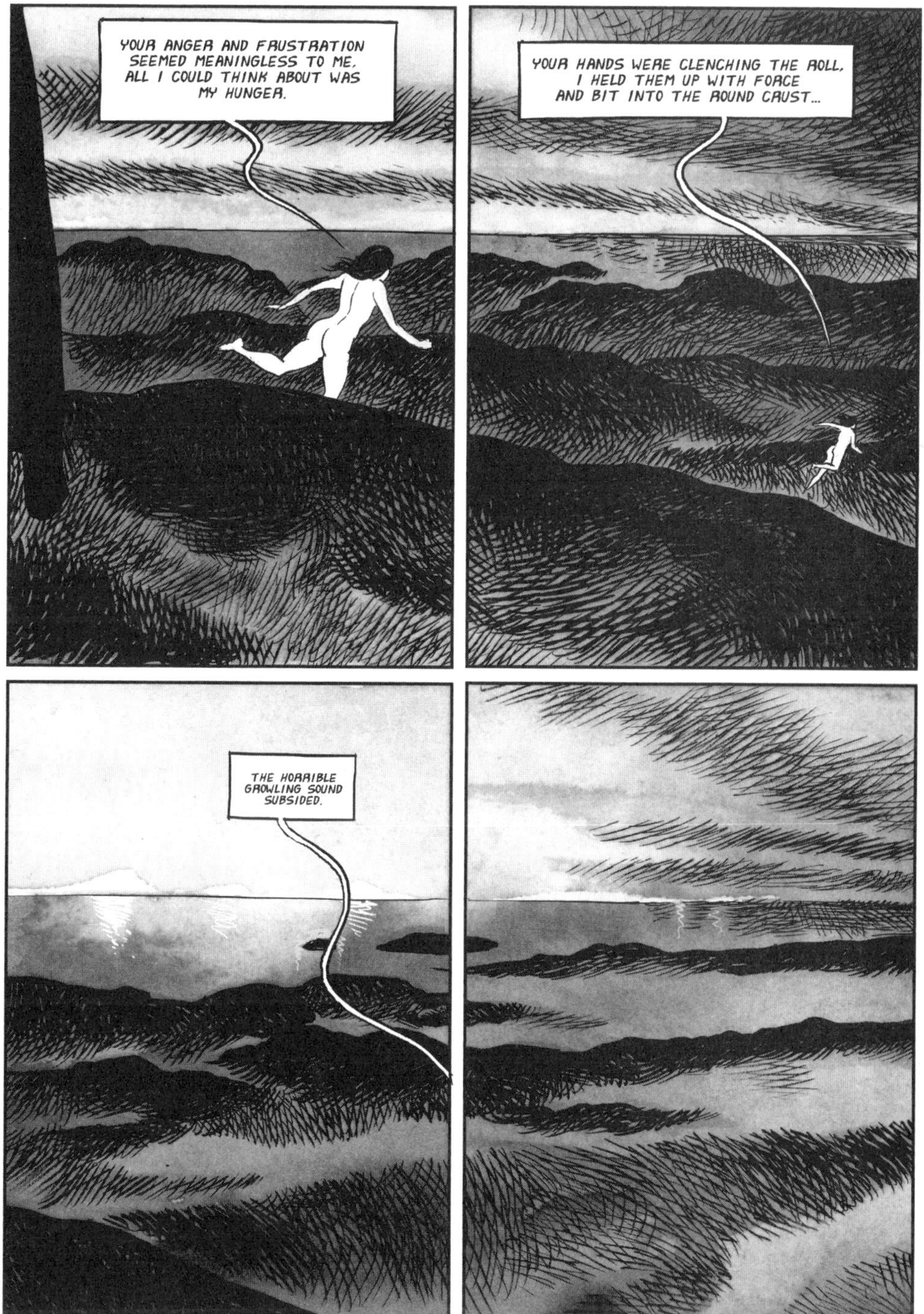
YOUR ANGER AND FRUSTRATION SEEMED MEANINGLESS TO ME. ALL I COULD THINK ABOUT WAS MY HUNGER.
YOUR HANDS WERE CLENCHING THE ROLL. I HELD THEM UP WITH FORCE AND BIT INTO THE ROUND CRUST...
THE HORRIBLE GROWLING SOUND SUBSIDED.

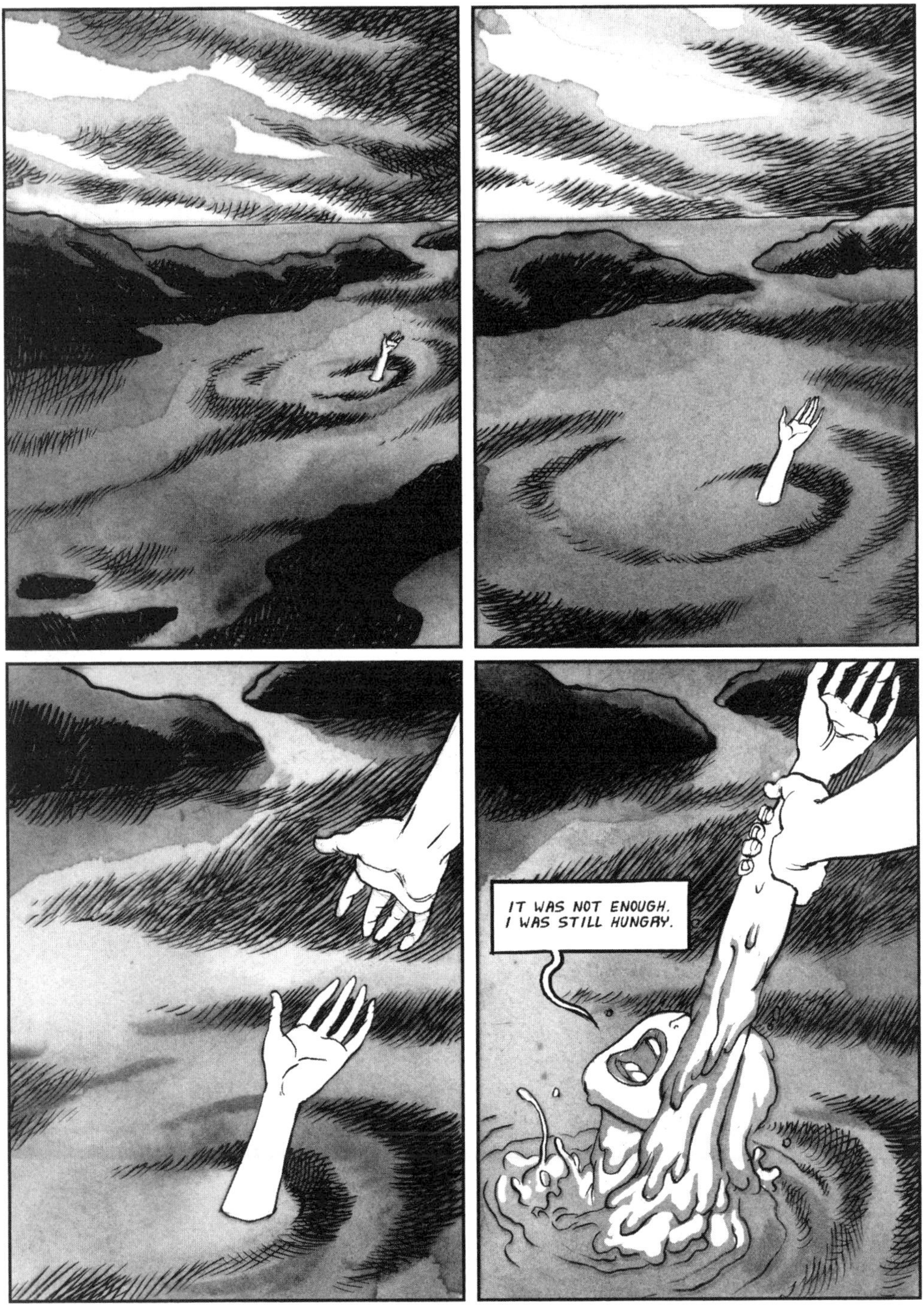
IT WAS NOT ENOUGH.
I WAS STILL HUNGRY.

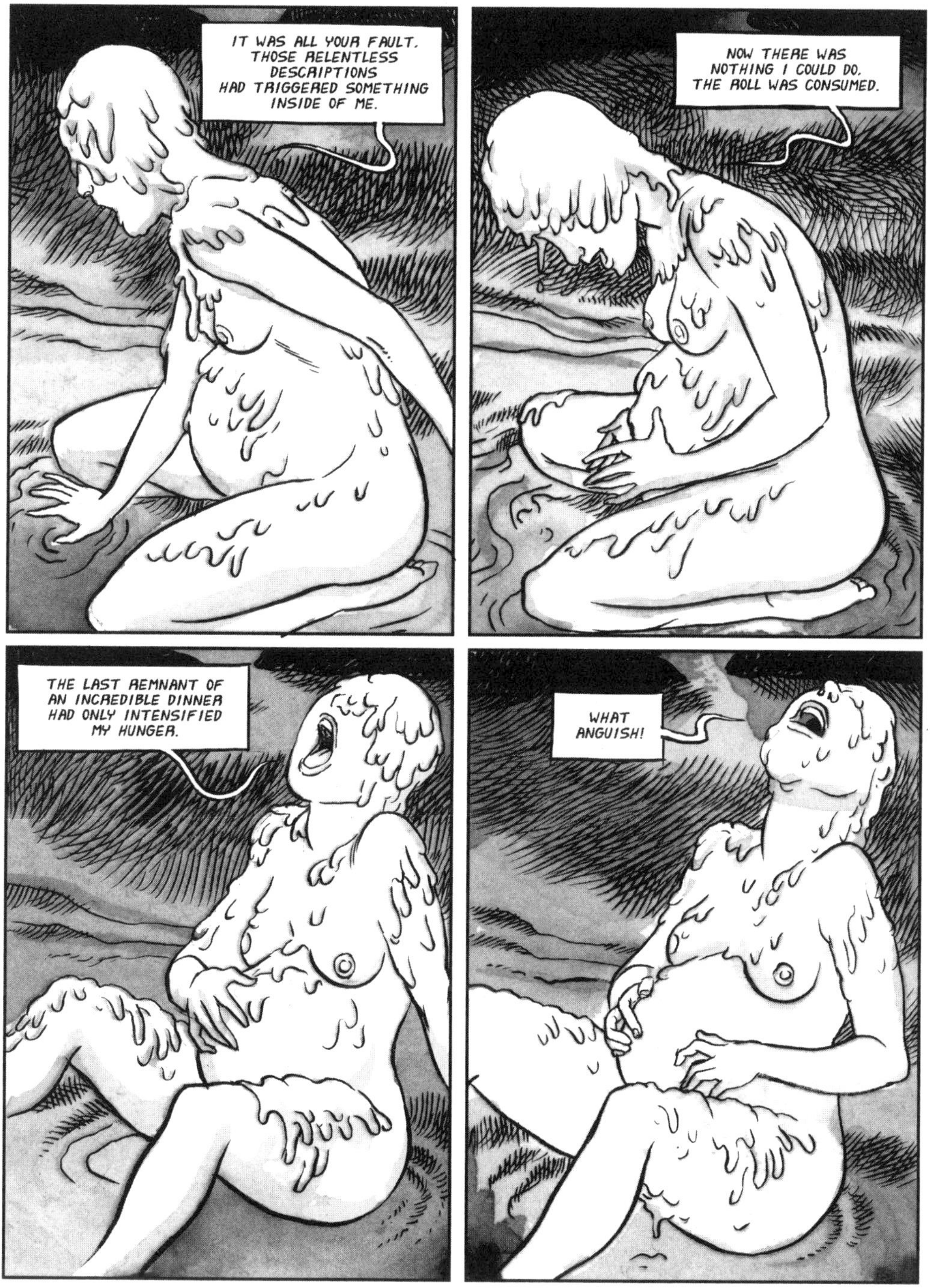
IT WAS ALL YOUR FAULT. THOSE RELENTLESS DESCRIPTIONS HAD TRIGGERED SOMETHING INSIDE OF ME.
NOW THERE WAS NOTHING I COULD DO. THE ROLL WAS CONSUMED.
THE LAST REMNANT OF AN INCREDIBLE DINNER HAD ONLY INTENSIFIED MY HUNGER.
WHAT ANGUISH!

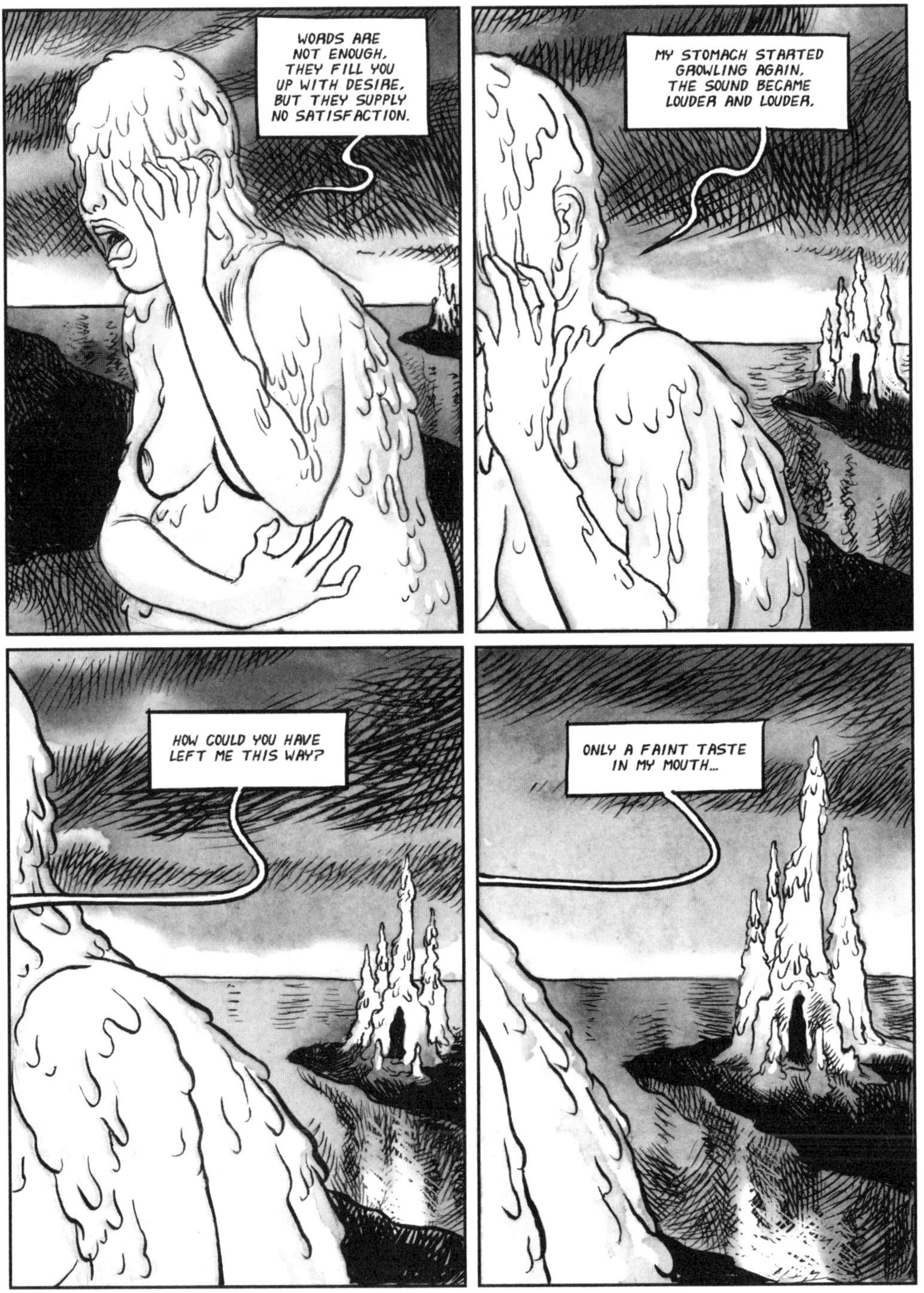
WORDS ARE NOT ENOUGH. THEY FILL YOU UP WITH DESIRE, BUT THEY SUPPLY NO SATISFACTION.
MY STOMACH STARTED GROWLING AGAIN. THE SOUND BECAME LOUDER AND LOUDER.
HOW COULD YOU HAVE LEFT ME THIS WAY?
ONLY A FAINT TASTE IN MY MOUTH...

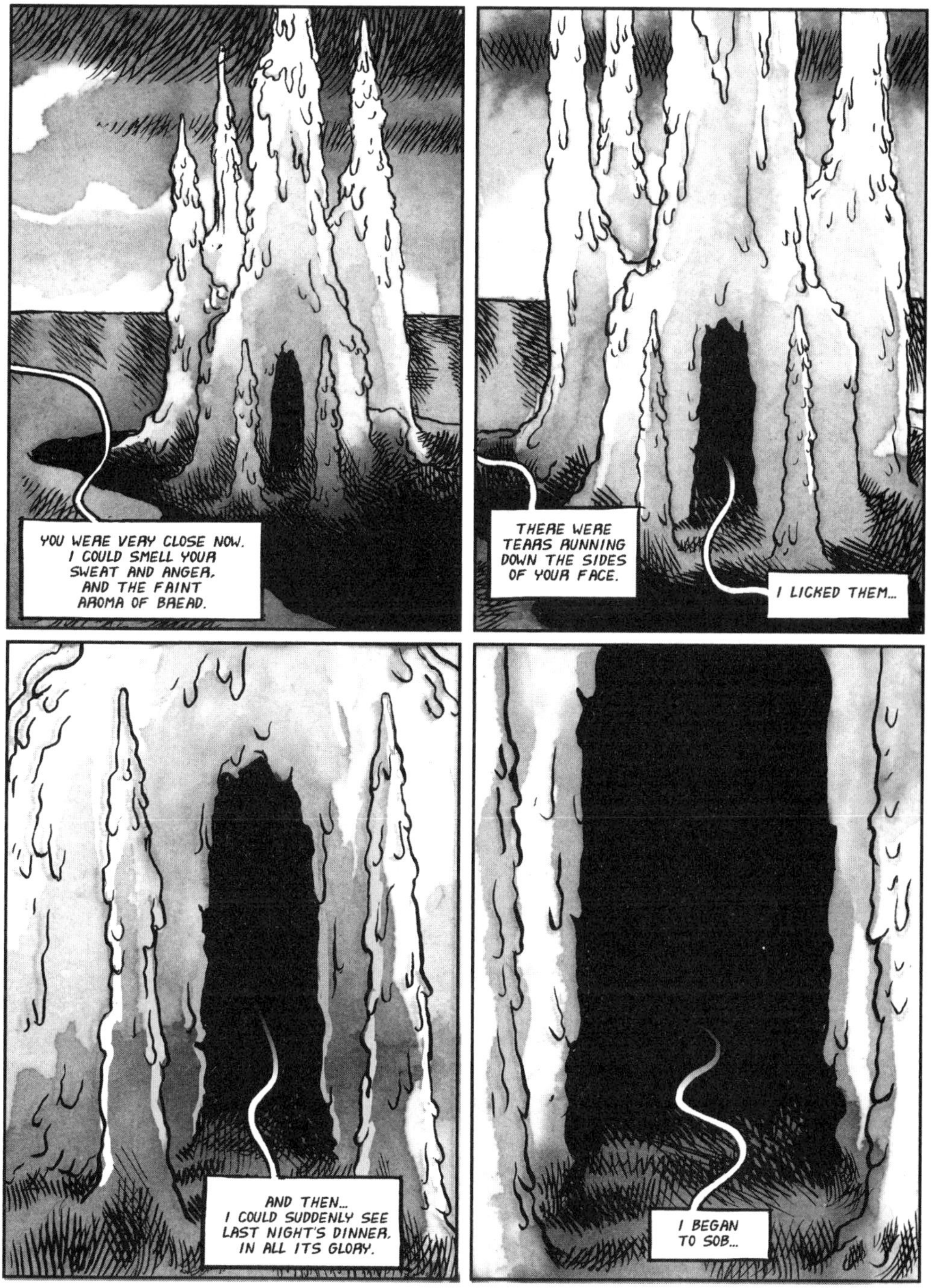
YOU WERE VERY CLOSE NOW. I COULD SMELL YOUR SWEAT AND ANGER, AND THE FAINT AROMA OF BREAD.
THERE WERE TEARS RUNNING DOWN THE SIDES OF YOUR FACE.
I LICKED THEM...
AND THEN... I COULD SUDDENLY SEE LAST NIGHT'S DINNER, IN ALL ITS GLORY.
I BEGAN TO SOB...

...AND FROM WITHIN THE
NOISE, THE GROWLING...

...THE PAIN AND HUNGER...

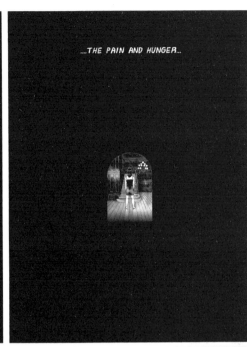

...I COULD HEAR YOUR VOICE...

YOU TURNED TO ME AND WHISPERED...

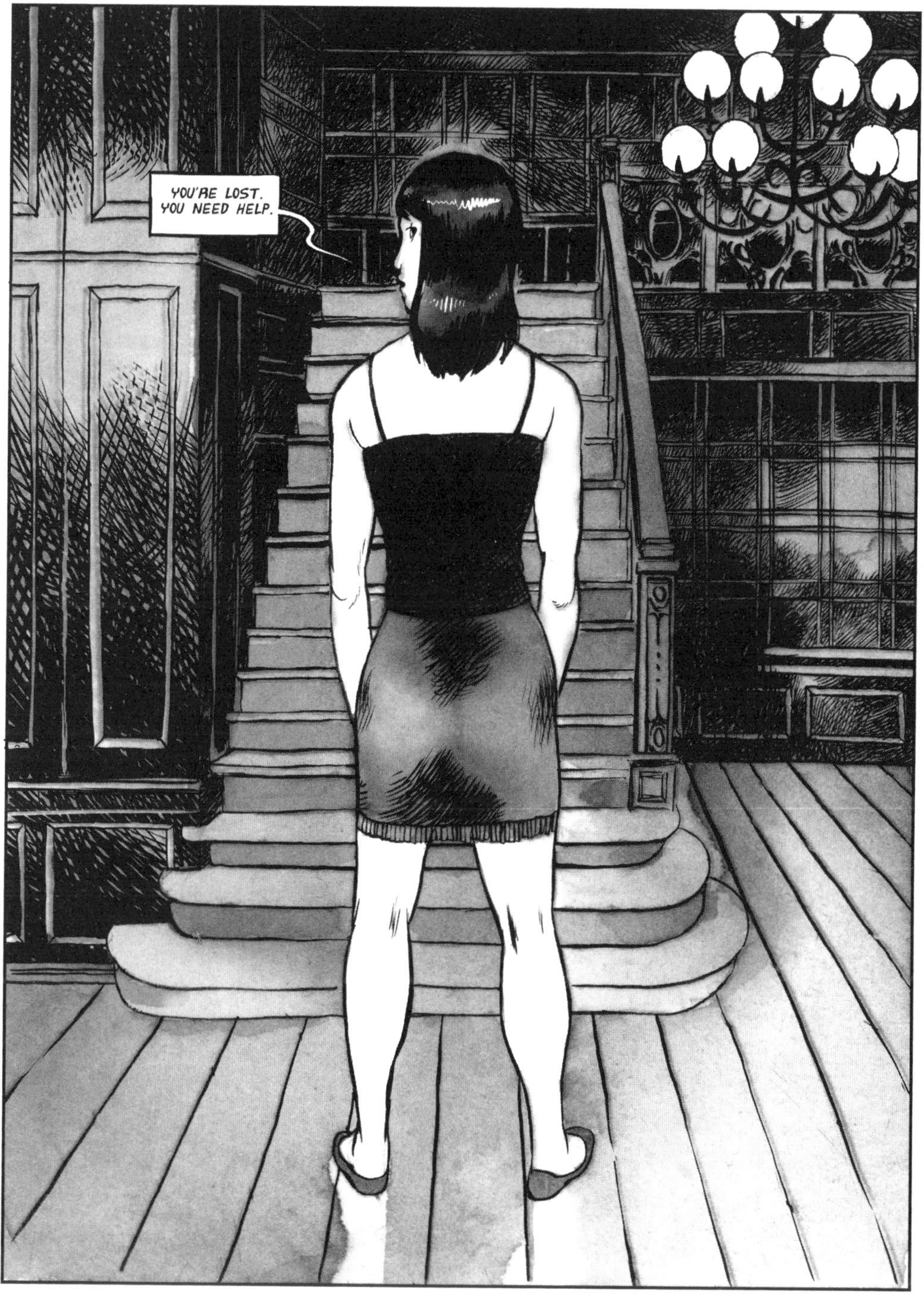
YOU'RE LOST.
YOU NEED HELP.

KOREN SHADMI was born in Israel, where he has worked since his early teens as an illustrator and cartoonist for various magazines. At seventeen, his graphic novel was published in Israel, followed by another book collecting his work from children's magazines. He then proceeded to serve as a graphic designer and illustrator in the Israel Defense Forces.

Upon completion of his service Shadmi relocated to New York to study in the School of Visual Arts, where he acquired his bachelor's degree. His graphic work has appeared in numerous international anthologies, and his books *Cours intérieures* and *Dissymétries* have recently been published in France. His illustration work has appeared in publications such as *Spin, BusinessWeek, The Village Voice, The Boston Globe, The New York Times, The Progressive, San Francisco Chronicle*, and many others.